Building Community through Hospitality

Evangelical Missiological Society Monograph Series

Anthony F. Casey, Rochelle Scheuermann, and Edward L. Smither
SERIES EDITORS

A Project of the Evangelical Missiological Society
www.emsweb.org

Building Community through Hospitality

Insights from Ethiopia for America's Loneliness Epidemic

Jessica A. Udall

◆PICKWICK *Publications* • Eugene, Oregon

BUILDING COMMUNITY THROUGH HOSPITALITY
Insights from Ethiopia for America's Loneliness Epidemic

Evangelical Missiological Society Monograph Series 21

Copyright © 2024 Jessica A. Udall. All rights reserved. Except for brief quotations in critical publications or reviews, no part of this book may be reproduced in any manner without prior written permission from the publisher. Write: Permissions, Wipf and Stock Publishers, 199 W. 8th Ave., Suite 3, Eugene, OR 97401.

Pickwick Publications
An Imprint of Wipf and Stock Publishers
199 W. 8th Ave., Suite 3
Eugene, OR 97401

www.wipfandstock.com

PAPERBACK ISBN: 978-1-6667-8255-4
HARDCOVER ISBN: 978-1-6667-8256-1
EBOOK ISBN: 978-1-6667-8257-8

Cataloguing-in-Publication data:

Names: Udall, Jessica A. [author].

Title: Building community through hospitality : insights from Ethiopia for America's loneliness epidemic / by Jessica A. Udall.

Description: Eugene, OR: Pickwick Publications, 2024 | Evangelical Missiological Society Monograph Series 21 | Includes bibliographical references.

Identifiers: ISBN 978-1-6667-8255-4 (paperback) | ISBN 978-1-6667-8256-1 (hardcover) | ISBN 978-1-6667-8257-8 (ebook)

Subjects: LCSH: Hospitality—Religious aspects | Hospitality—Biblical teaching | Christianity—Ethiopia | United States—Religion | Christianity—United States | Ethiopians—United States | United States—Emigration and immigration | Ethiopia—Emigration and immigration

Classification: BR115.C8 U33 2024 (paperback) | BR115.C8 (ebook)

VERSION NUMBER 05/30/24

Scripture quotations are from the ESV® Bible (The Holy Bible, English Standard Version®), copyright © 2001 by Crossway, a publishing ministry of Good News Publishers. Used by permission. All rights reserved. The ESV text may not be quoted in any publication made available to the public by a Creative Commons license. The ESV may not be translated in whole or in part into any other language.

Scripture quotations marked (NIV) are taken from the Holy Bible, New International Version®, NIV®. Copyright © 1973, 1978, 1984, 2011 by Biblica, Inc.® Used by permission of Zondervan. All rights reserved worldwide. www.zondervan.com The "NIV" and "New International Version" are trademarks registered in the United States Patent and Trademark Office by Biblica, Inc.®

Scripture quotations marked (KJV) are taken from The Authorized (King James) Version. Rights in the Authorized Version in the United Kingdom are vested in the Crown. Reproduced by permission of the Crown's patentee, Cambridge University Press.

Contents

Acknowledgements | vii
Abstract | ix
Glossary of Non-English Words | xi
List of Abbreviations | xii

1. Introduction | 1
2. Literature Review | 14
3. Interviews with Ethiopian Immigrants | 46
4. The Biblical Resonance of an Ethiopian Understanding and Practice of Building Community through Hospitality | 76
5. Recommendations | 120
6. Conclusion | 160

Appendices | 167
Bibliography | 177

Acknowledgements

IN KEEPING WITH THE theme of the coming pages, this book was not an individual effort. Rather, its existence would not be possible without the loving support of my far-flung but tight-knit community. Words cannot fully express my gratitude for them, but I will try:

Thank you to the professors of Columbia International University, who instilled within me what I believe will be a lifelong love of intercultural learning.

Thank you to Ed and Shawn Smither, for their faithful encouragement, consistent prayer, and true friendship over several years.

Thank you to the Billy Graham Lausanne Scholarship Program, which made what was only a dream and a prayer a reality after many years of hoping.

Thank you to my interviewees—Ethiopian and American—for their generosity to open their lives to me in order to help others, sharing with me joyful and painful experiences that have given them wise and helpful insights.

Thank you to friends all over the world who checked in on me and encouraged me in the research and writing process and bore with much patience my rambling attempts to answer the simple question, "What are you researching?"

Thank you to family members on two continents who gave their support in every way they could.

And thank you to my husband, Abeneazer G. Urga, for being my sounding board, translator, tough-love dissertation coach, and the best former research librarian that I know.

Abstract

LONELINESS PLAGUES THE WEST, and members of American Protestant churches are not immune. This book examines potential causes for the loneliness epidemic and considers biblical teaching and insights from Non-Western contexts—specifically Ethiopia—in search of antidotes and an alternative way of living that leads to a greater sense of community and belonging for the generations to come.

Ethiopia is a country known for its hospitality and has been deeply influenced by both Judaism and Christianity for many centuries, making it a fascinating example of what the ancient biblical practice of hospitality can look like in the present day. Since it is based on a presupposition of ontological interconnected interdependence of all of life, learning from the Ethiopian way of building community through hospitality has great potential to help American Christians cultivate connectedness and belonging in their congregations and wider communities.

Chapter 2 surveys existent literature on building community through hospitality, divided into three sections: works from Western perspectives, works from other African (Non-Ethiopian) perspectives, and works from Ethiopian perspectives, making clear that my book will serve to connect the dots regarding why hospitality often feels like a burden or another to-do in the USA, and articulating the importance of cultivating a more biblically-resonant interdependent identity in order to slough off the isolation of hyperindividualism and allow Americans to reconnect with one another relationally, thus beginning to heal from the loneliness epidemic.

Chapter 3 evaluates in-depth interviews with forty-three Ethiopian immigrants as well as several Americans to understand the differences between typically Ethiopian and typically American understandings and practices of hospitality and to consider how the loneliness epidemic could be addressed by hospitable Christians of all backgrounds in the United States.

ABSTRACT

Chapter 4 evaluates the biblically resonant aspects of an Ethiopian understanding and practice of hospitality—specifically placing great value on communion with God, communion with others, and the sharing of space and needs—in order to validate the benefit of contextually emulating them in the spirit of 1 Corinthians 11:1: "Follow my example as I follow the example of Christ" (NIV),[1] and also in order to show the importance of articulating the often implicitly-held value of hospitality explicitly so that it does not go extinct in the globalizing modern world.

Chapter 5 offers recommendations for Christians in the United States who desire to counteract the loneliness epidemic by offering antidotes and alternatives that are biblically resonant and culturally contextual. Learning from the modern-day example of Ethiopian Christians, Christians can recognize and eschew hyperindividualism as an isolating dead-end in favor of hospitable identities from which hospitable actions will naturally flow which go beyond highly-scheduled programs and delve deeply into daily-life proximity with others which will make possible the tangible living out of the "one another" commands in Scripture and will create spaces of care and belonging in which those plagued by loneliness can find healing within community. Chapter 6 serves as a conclusion, summarizing the foregoing research and making suggestions for further research.

---

1. Unless otherwise noted, all biblical citations are from the ESV.

Glossary of Non-English Terms

ubuntu—the Pan-African idea that emphasizes interconnected interdependence

medemer—synergy, working together interdependently toward a common goal, the Amharic equivalent of *ubuntu*

iddir, idir, eder—a community-generated organization created by Ethiopians to provide multi-faceted support to one another in the event of a death in the family

iqqub, iqub, equb—a community-generated organization created by Ethiopians in which every member pays a set amount into a common pot each month, and then the full amount is awarded to one member by lottery; enables members to make large purchases without taking out loans

qene, qiné—an Ethiopian intellectual tradition which sees everything in terms of wax and gold, that is, there is an obvious meaning on the surface, but there is also a deeper meaning that can be found through contemplation and is worth pursuing

säm—wax

wärq—gold

fissiha—joy

nätsanät—freedom in the literal sense

arnät—freedom in the sense of living the good life

däbo, dabo, debo—a community-generated organization created by Ethiopians in which farmers help each other on a rotating basis to accomplish things that one farmer could not do on his or her own

Ethiopiawinet, Ityopiawinet—the quality of being Ethiopian

List of Abbreviations

EOTC—Ethiopian Orthodox Tewahido Church

EI 1, 2, 3—Ethiopian Immigrant interviewees

A 1, 2, 3—American interviewees

EE 1, 2, 3—Interviewees who are Ethiopians living in Ethiopia

I

Introduction

IN 2018, 46 PERCENT of Americans reported frequent feelings of loneliness.[1] A year earlier, former US Surgeon General Vivek Murthy coined the idea of a "loneliness epidemic," and this idea has been increasingly accepted by medical professionals and the general public as a predictor of illness and as an urgent mental health concern in the years that have followed. Modalities of treatment have varied from pharmaceutical to psychological, but it seems well-understood by doctors and patients alike that the surest way out of loneliness is simply to create community around oneself. Judging by the ongoing problem plaguing millions of Americans, however, successful implementation of this seemingly straightforward loneliness cure is much more challenging than it appears.

American Protestant churches, unfortunately, are not immune from the plague of loneliness, at least in part because hyperindividualism has become the default orientation towards life even for those who are devout Christians. In order to address the problem of loneliness, church leaders have emphasized offering small groups (also called community groups, care groups, life groups, etc.) and have enthusiastically encouraged all members and regular attendees to get involved. While admirable as a healthy counter-cultural initiative, small groups become problematic when they are viewed as the single benchmark measuring whether a church is "doing community." If they are viewed as a starting point for the building of lasting relationships that go beyond a weekly scheduled two-hour block, they can be an excellent tool, but if they are viewed primarily as programs (which American church models can be tempted to overly focus on), these groups will remain simply that—programs.

Building a life-giving community which satisfies (in an earthly sense) and stokes (in an eternal sense) the legitimate longings of the lonely has

---

1. Cigna, "2018 U.S. Loneliness Index."

proven largely elusive for American churches, despite sincere loneliness mitigation efforts made by American church leaders. In the pages that follow, it will be proposed that inviting others into a hospitable church community—expressed corporately as well as individually by members—as a haven of belonging may be the most effective way to conduct current outreach efforts in the post-Christian West.

It could be helpful for Americans to look farther afield than their own culture in order to learn viable ways that a lifestyle of hospitality can be lived out by church members and by extension churches. A Non-Western understanding of hospitality—for the purpose of specificity and brevity, an Ethiopian understanding of building community through hospitality—will be thoughtfully examined in this research to determine its resonance with a biblical understanding of hospitality.

The biblically resonant aspects of Ethiopian perspectives on hospitality will be considered as helpful models to contextually emulate in an American context in order to broaden the typically American understanding of hospitality as a program or appointment to the more organic understanding of hospitality as an identity based upon a presupposition of ontological interconnected interdependence. Adopting a version of this understanding will enable American Christians to cultivate homes and places of worship which are characterized by welcome and can be part of addressing the loneliness epidemic by cultivating community through hospitality. Along the way, possible roadblocks—namely, the subtle Western superiority complex and the sense of "resource righteousness"—will be examined and set aside in favor of mutual learning and partnership in a globalizing world. Interviews with Americans who have intentionally made hospitality an integral part of their lives will also be incorporated, exploring what has influenced and what helps them to live hospitably even in the midst of a lonely culture which does not support this value.

Rationale and Need

The study of the biblical resonance of a Non-Western understanding of hospitality and a subsequent contextual application of this understanding within American congregations has potential to activate individuals, families, and churches as havens of belonging in an often lonely world. For the church to embody welcome and a sense of home may be one of the most important methods of reaching out to post-Christian neighbors,

INTRODUCTION

because it will show the gospel—and its outworkings with regard to human community building—to be a deeply satisfying way to address one of the modern American heart's most pressing longings. The healthy Church can be understood fundamentally as a community which simply cannot stop gathering around tables, both corporately when celebrating the Lord's Supper and in smaller groups, gathering in homes and third places.

Consequently, it is hoped that this study will benefit both the American Church and also the post-Christian society at large by activating Christians to be salt in the sense of inviting others to the table and light in the sense of setting a candle in the window to lead others home (Matt 5:13–14). This study aims to consider the Good News of Jesus Christ as not just a set of rules to obey or creeds to affirm, but as an invitation to a feast that will go on for eternity, starting now around the tables of even "two or three [who] gather together in [His] name" (Matt 18:20).

In recent years, there have been a number of American voices speaking eloquently and earnestly about the need for Christian hospitality.[2] In the pews and in American neighborhoods, however, it seems that these books produce unhelpfully burdensome feelings of guilt in readers who are overwhelmed at the prospect of planning to invite people over for dinner (the generally accepted American standard of hospitality) in the midst of their already overcrowded schedules. Many American Christian hear the message of these books and think that they are simply adding another item to their impossibly long to-do lists.

This study will propose that a possible reason why good books on hospitality written by Americans are not effecting the widespread positive change one would hope is that they do not delve deep enough epistemologically to find the real problem that needs to be fixed. Perhaps the issue is not ultimately one of calendars and potlucks but of presuppositions and identity: an insidious brand of hyperindividualism which causes Americans to over-value their own concerns over the concerns of their wider communities, ultimately causing the withering of both community and self due to its unnatural myopia.

If this is the case, then ideas from outside the American cultural context could be helpful as the American church attempts to uncover epistemological blindspots and grow in Christian orthopraxy. Millions of immigrants reside in America today, and those who come from more communal cultures often feel shocked and dismayed when they arrive and

2. Several of these authors and their books will be discussed in chapter 2.

try to settle in America because of the sudden atmosphere of loneliness and social isolation. If the dearth of Non-Western writing on hospitality is any indication, it seems that this value is an implicit one—something that is practiced rather than discussed—and is not often intentionally articulated in Non-Western communities.

The ultimate purpose of this study is to draw out this usually unspoken wisdom from the experience of Non-Western Christians and to expose American Christians to their ideas in a spirit of mutual learning and global partnership.[3] If the knowledge of a more communal, community-oriented way of life was shared with American Christians who had been divested of resource righteousness and were convinced of their relational poverty, it could be an eye-opening, balancing experience that could call hyperindividualism into question and thereby raise awareness regarding the root issue hindering the American church from being characterized by hospitality.

Research Problem, Sub-questions, Limitations, Terms

Specific Research Question

In this study, I will focus on an Ethiopian understanding of building community through hospitality, exploring what aspects of this understanding are biblically congruent, so that American churches can contextually apply these principles in their own culture in order to revitalize their own fellowship and outreach in a society plagued by loneliness.

Secondary Research Questions

How is hospitality related to the gospel? In what ways is an Ethiopian understanding of hospitality biblically congruent? In what ways is it not biblically congruent? Why is there a dearth of Non-Western voices teaching and writing on hospitality? Why is it particularly challenging to practice hospitality in an American context? What aspects of an Ethiopian

---

3. I have written elsewhere about the great potential of immigrant Christians to be true partners with the American Church: "Ethiopian Immigrants as Cross-Cultural Missionaries," 183–95. For more on how immigrants can bring about social change, see Polak, "Migrants as Agents of Social and Religious Innovation," 61–77.

understanding of hospitality could be contextually incorporated into the lifestyles of American Christians?

Limitations

I have chosen to focus on an Ethiopian understanding of hospitality, since my cross-cultural experience has been largely spent living in Ethiopia. Though I believe that many African cultures hold the value of hospitality in common, I realize that generalizing to refer to an "African" perspective is unhelpfully homogenizing hundreds of distinct cultures into one entity. Therefore, this study will be limited to an Ethiopian perspective, with the understanding that there are many distinct cultures within Ethiopia, but with confidence—corroborated by many African authors included in my literature review—that a unifying factor of the many Ethiopian cultures and even the exponentially greater number of cultures within Africa is the prioritization of building community through hospitality based on an awareness of ontological interconnected interdependence.

Likewise, the focus of contextual application in this study will be limited to examining the unique contours and challenges of the body of Christ in the United States. Contextual applications to other cultures such as Britain, which recently appointed a Minister for Loneliness,[4] would be interesting to compare and contrast with an American application, but they are beyond the scope of this study.

I will not be proposing secular solutions for the loneliness epidemic in America, though solutions should certainly be sought. Rather, this study will focus on the unique ways that a biblical understanding of cultivating community through hospitality (following the modern-day example of an often biblically resonant Ethiopian understanding of the same) can equip American congregations to create an atmosphere of welcome and belonging in their homes and corporate gatherings.

Definition of Key Terms

Loneliness epidemic: coined by former US Surgeon General Vivek Murthy, referring to the widespread feeling of loneliness experienced by increasing numbers of people, particularly in Western countries.

---

4. "PM Launches Government's First Loneliness Strategy."

Western: referring to countries including the United States, Canada, Australia, New Zealand, and countries in the European Union.

Non-Western: referring to the countries not listed in the definition of "Western." Note: There is some ambiguity in this binary categorization, with some contending that Russia or Japan should be considered Western, for example. The definitions given are accepted for the sake of utility, while acknowledging that they are far from perfect descriptors.

Hospitality: from the Greek *philoxenia* ("love of stranger"), the practice of welcoming others into one's home, heart, and life.

Biblical resonance: the degree to which a culture's mores regarding a given idea comport with Christian orthodoxy and orthopraxy regarding that idea.

Individualistic: valuing the needs and concerns of the individual over the needs and concerns of the group.

Communal: recognition that the needs of the individual must be considered as one part of the wider context of the needs of the group.

Hyperindividualism: an extreme form of individualism which, this study proposes, is a root cause of the loneliness epidemic.

Superiority complex: the belief that one is fundamentally superior to others based upon personally important criteria.

Resource righteousness: the belief that those who have more resources (money, education, books, connections, etc.) are inherently more mature and more worthy of respect, attention, or decision-making positions.

Literature Review

There are many quality resources on hospitality in an American context, most of which lament the fact that hospitality is not a natural practice for the majority of American Christians. Hospitable practices seem to go against the grain of a society focused heavily on the individual's material success. Many books and articles have been written comprehensively surveying and explaining the biblical primacy of human-to-human hospitality as an emulation of the divine hospitality God-followers have experienced themselves. I have also found diverse voices from many cultures of Africa agreeing that a high value on a lifestyle of hospitality is a characteristic that is shared in common by people across the continent. A few authors mention the unfortunate problem that those from Western cultures tend to balk at assuming a learning posture with teachers who are Non-Western.

INTRODUCTION

But I have not found a resource that takes all four categories just mentioned and blends them together to create a way forward out of the loneliness epidemic for American churches who want to become beacons of belonging in a disconnected society and who, in order to do this, are willing to question their cultural presuppositions, to admit blindspots, and to learn about hospitality from those for whom it is a cultural strength. My study will be a resource for facilitating this kind of healing.

Chapter 2 will be a literature review of resources in three categories: those written by Western authors, those written by African authors who are not Ethiopian, and those written by Ethiopian authors. These books and articles will be explored in order to show what ideas are already being discussed regarding the loneliness epidemic in the West, the emphasis placed on hospitality in both the Old and New Testaments, and the differences in the understanding and practice of hospitality between Western cultures and African cultures. In reviewing the extant literature, it will become apparent that while different resources thoroughly cover one or two of the discrete categories mentioned above, few connect the dots to look at the interconnectedness of all of these ideas and none bring together all this information in order to map a path forward for American churches to heal from the loneliness epidemic and become beacons of healthy community in an increasingly disconnected society, gleaning from and inspired by Non-Western perspectives and practices.

Research Methodology

In the field of intercultural studies, it is wise to employ an interdisciplinary approach in order to gain a well-rounded understanding of complex real-life issues. As such, I will be working in both theological and anthropological disciplines with the intention to find insight in the places where they intersect. I will also explore historical research in order to understand how theological concepts worked themselves out in people's lives in the early church, comparing the practice of hospitality in the first centuries AD with the current practice of hospitality in Ethiopia.

In this study, I will be employing a phenomenological approach. Methodologically, I will begin by gleaning what I can through bibliographic research of what has already been written by Africans on the topic of hospitality. I will explore African commentaries on hospitality-related Scripture passages, journal articles, and recordings or transcripts of teachings on hospitality. I will also consult African perspectives on *ubuntu* and its linguistic cousins in various African countries, with a particular focus on Ethiopia's *medemer* approach.

In addition to bibliographic research, I will employ a qualitative approach in order to gain insights from interviewees. I believe that a phenomenological approach will best suit this study because it seeks to "describe the common meaning for several individuals of their lived experiences of a concept or phenomenon."[5] I will be interviewing Ethiopian immigrants about their common experience of belonging mediated by hospitality in their home cultures, and their experience of loneliness and/or a new belonging mediated by hospitality in the United States. My goal, as Cresswell describes, is to "[develop] a composite description of the essence of the experience for all of the individuals."[6]

I considered a case study method but ultimately decided on a phenomenological method because my focus is not so much the actual mechanics of immigration but rather the underlying emotions it evokes—loneliness and/or belonging. My interviewees will have all gone through the life-changing experience of immigration which is often a catalyst for shifts in people's understanding of self, society, and values. Having lived life in two or more places gives people a unique insight into both cultures as insider-outsiders, so I believe that immigrants are the ideal interviewees because they will be able to speak as insider-outsiders about both their home culture and American culture.

Practically speaking, I began my research by inviting six Ethiopian immigrants who are Christians with whom I already have a relationship to join me for Zoom calls where we discussed their experiences of loneliness and belonging mediated by hospitality in their home cultures and in the United States, as well as their current practice of hospitality in the United States. I also used this opportunity to lay out my plans and ask for their feedback and advice, incorporating any guidance I received into my plans. I also asked each of them to share contact information with me regarding other Ethiopian immigrants in their network who might be willing to participate in my study.

When I got contact information for potential interviewees, I sent an initial survey via Google Forms and gave them the option to fill it out online or to set up a phone or Zoom call to discuss their answers with

---

5. Cresswell and Poth, *Qualitative Inquiry and Research Design*, 75.
6. Cresswell and Poth, *Qualitative Inquiry and Research Design*, 75.

me. I also asked each interviewee to suggest a few more people that might be interested in participating in my study, thereby expanding my network exponentially and giving me varied perspectives both from people I knew before my research began and people I have never met.

As I interviewed Ethiopian immigrants, I sought to ask questions in such a way to bring their implicit values—which are not often spoken or or written about—into the explicit realm. I believe it is important to draw out an articulation of the importance of the value of hospitality so that it will not be lost in the onslaught of globalization which threatens to spread loneliness along with the spread of technological advances and opportunities for economic advancement. I will seek to speak in particular with Ethiopian Christians who view hospitality as a key tool for expressing the beauty of the gospel in the course of their life-sharing ministry in the spirit of 1 Thessalonians 2:8: "Because we loved you so much, we were delighted to share with you not only the gospel of God but our lives as well."

After conducting forty-three interviews while following the trail of the contacts of my contacts, I compiled my data and sought to find threads of commonality in the various experiences and insights I had been privileged to hear or read. I then organized the insights into principles that could be instructive for the Church in the United States, seeking to show the incredible potential of immigrants in America to lead the way in addressing the loneliness epidemic by pursuing lifestyles of hospitality which will lead to belonging.

In order to validate my findings, I returned to the literature I had surveyed and synthesized the information coming from the interviewees in light of what I had read and continued to read. My overall goal is to serve as a conduit for American Christians to be edified and strengthened through the wisdom of their Ethiopian brothers and sisters. When compiling and synthesizing the insights from these interviews, I became aware that there was one area where most of my Ethiopian immigrant interviewees seemed to be struggling: how to live out hospitable values—which they strongly held—in a society that does not actively uphold the value of hospitality. Because one of my Ethiopian interviewees made the point that though most Americans do not live lives of hospitality, those that do seem passionate and intentional about doing so, I also will engage in secondary research via another Google Form to ask several Americans I know who have reputations for being hospitable about why and how they manage to live hospitality in the midst of a lonely culture. This addendum to my primary research will provide additional perspective and complement the wisdom from Ethiopian believers. One other addendum was added as well, surveying Ethiopians via another Google Form who had lived their whole lives in Ethiopia, seeking to provide insight into the confusion of my Ethiopian immigrant interviewees who expressed concern but lack of understanding regarding why Ethiopian culture seemed to be becoming less characterized by hospitality in recent years. This third set of interviewees filled in the gaps by sharing information on cultural change in Ethiopia which occurred in the years that the Ethiopian immigrant interviewees had been living abroad and also made clearer the imperative need to articulate the importance of building community through hospitality based on ontological interconnected interdependence such that this deeply held value will not be lost in coming generations in Ethiopia.

Chapter-by-Chapter Breakdown

This chapter has begun with a discussion of the loneliness epidemic in America which has also infiltrated the American Church. An Ethiopian understanding of hospitality has been introduced and explored for biblical resonance, that is, historical Christian orthodoxy and orthopraxy regarding hospitality will be compared with the current practice of Ethiopian hospitality, and striking similarities will be observed. Then, a contextual application of principles gleaned from this understanding has been proposed as a way forward towards a greater sense of belonging both for those born and raised in America and also for those who have immigrated there later in life. Particular attention has been given to how a Non-Western understanding of hospitality could revitalize the American Church's fellowship and outreach in a culture plagued by loneliness. Research methodology, limitations, and key definitions have also been explored.

Chapter 2 will be a literature review of resources in two categories: those written by Western authors, those written by African authors who are not Ethiopian, and those written by Ethiopian authors. These books and articles will be explored in order to show what ideas are already being discussed regarding the loneliness epidemic in the West, the emphasis placed on hospitality in both the Old and New Testaments, and the differences in the understanding and practice of hospitality between Western culture and African cultures. In reviewing the extant literature, it will become apparent that while different resources thoroughly cover one or two

INTRODUCTION

of the discrete categories mentioned, few connect the dots to look at the interconnectedness of all of these ideas and none bring together all this information in order to map a path forward for the American Church to move out of the loneliness epidemic and become a beacon of community in an increasingly disconnected society, gleaning from and inspired by Ethiopian presuppositions and practices.

Chapter 3 will explore and synthesize the experiences and insights of forty-three Ethiopians who have immigrated to the United States. As people who understand both Ethiopian culture and American culture, they will share their perspective on the differences between them with regard to the understanding of hospitality, as well as sharing their interpretation of the Bible's teaching on hospitality and suggestions for how the American Church can address the loneliness epidemic. Because these interviewees often express the fact that their implicitly (rather than explicitly) held value of hospitality has led to difficulty in living out that value when the container of a hospitable society was taken away from them, I will also include the insights gained from my secondary research among American Christians who have somehow managed to make their hospitable values explicit and are living them out even in a culture where it is not typical to do so.

Chapter 4 will expand upon the previous chapter's discussion of biblical hospitality by examining the many ways in which a Non-Western understanding of hospitality—particularly as it is expressed within the many cultures of Africa, and in the case of this specific research, in Ethiopia—is biblically congruent, balancing it with ways in which it is not resonant in order to avoid idolization of any human expression of Christian practice. After establishing the clear strengths of an Ethiopian practice of cultivating community through hospitality based on an ontology of interconnected interdependence, the chapter will go on to discuss why there is a dearth of Non-Western voices teaching and writing on hospitality and reasons why these voices should be sought out and amplified for the good of the Global Church. The current realities of global migration and the large numbers of Non-Western immigrants who have settled in the United States—most of whom have a good grasp of how to live a lifestyle of hospitality and many of whom are believers—will then be viewed through the lens of a divinely given opportunity for revitalization of the American church's fellowship and outreach if a learning posture can be assumed. An addendum will also be included addressing cultural change in Ethiopia which is creating shifts towards increasing loneliness as the country is affected by modernization, globalization, and a common destructive mentality that following Western norms is synonymous with progress. Nine Ethiopian interviewees who have lived their whole lives in Ethiopia were consulted to get their insights on if and how the loneliness epidemic is affecting Ethiopia, and how the prioritization of building community through hospitality which has historically been a defining feature of Ethiopian culture can be preserved and passed on to future generations in the midst of the changes of modern life.

Based upon insights gained through interviews with Ethiopian Christian immigrants and bibliographic research regarding Ethiopia's culture of building community through hospitality, as well as its resonance with Scriptural norms and commands, chapter 5 will delve into implications for American churches as they seek to address the loneliness epidemic. The goal will be to explore what aspects of an Ethiopian understanding of cultivating community through hospitality could be contextually incorporated into the lifestyles of American Christians for the benefit of American churches as well as for the wider society which is plagued by loneliness. Chapter six will summarize the foregoing research and will suggest topics for further research.

Conclusion

Loneliness has become a problem of epidemic proportions in America, and members of American Protestant churches are not immune. Though efforts toward cultivating community within churches through initiatives like small groups are being made, they are not sufficient to address Americans' deep and daily lack of community, because hospitality cannot be primarily programmatic if it is to be effective. Instead, addressing loneliness will require the cultivation of a lifestyle of hospitality among American believers, but this is not an easy thing to do when many Americans have not experienced this kind of hospitality, except perhaps during travel overseas or in the homes of immigrants.

This study will take the position that Non-Western immigrants are a gift to the American Church, and the goal of this study is to amplify their voices in order to inspire and activate American believers. My Ethiopian immigrant contacts will share regarding their experience of belonging mediated by hospitality in their home cultures, their immigration experience and the loss of belonging, the loss of hospitality, and the social isolation they have felt in America. They will also share their thoughts on how their Ethiopian understanding of hospitality as a lifestyle based on ontological interconnected interdependence could be contextually applied in an American setting so as to address the loneliness epidemic by activating American believers as creators of spaces of belonging in community wherever they are, whether at church or in their homes or in third places. Counter-culturally hospitable American Christians and Ethiopian Christians living in Ethiopia will also be consulted in order to shed light on how Ethiopian immigrants and even Ethiopians who still live in their rapidly shifting mother-culture, can continue to move their biblically hospitable values from the implicit realm to the explicit realm for the good of the global church and the wider global society. In a spirit of mutuality, Ethiopians and Americans can work together so that hospitable values will not become extinct due to the erosion caused by hyperindividualistic forces inherent in many globalizing and modernizing changes, but will instead be appreciated and preserved so that humanity's economic and technological progress will not be the cause of continued isolation and depletion of spiritual, mental, and emotional well-being.

2

Literature Review

In this chapter, literature on the loneliness epidemic, the importance of hospitality in the Old and New Testaments, the importance of learning from Non-Western perspectives, the struggles of American churches in practicing hospitality, the strength of African churches in understanding interconnected interdependence as normal and practicing hospitality, and details regarding various African perspectives on *ubuntu*-related ideas will be explored. This chapter is divided into three sections: resources written by Western authors, resources written by other African (Non-Ethiopian) authors, and resources written by Ethiopian authors.

This section will survey the available literature on a variety of interdisciplinary subjects, showing that they have all been eloquently discussed individually but have not been sufficiently connected to be truly helpful to the American Church in addressing the current multi-factorial loneliness epidemic in the West. In showing this, the necessity of my study will become clear, as I purpose to examine the reasons behind the loneliness epidemic, understand the biblical roots of hospitality as an essential Christian practice, and explore an African and specifically an Ethiopian perspective on building community through hospitality as a modern example that is worthy of thoughtful and contextual emulation.

Review of Literature from Western Perspectives

Robert Putnam's seminal work, *Bowling Alone: The Collapse and Revival of American Community*, reads like a prophetic prequel to the loneliness epidemic of recent years. Putnam discusses the decades-long decline in social capital due to declining participation in Americans' social involvement and provides helpful historical background for my research, and pointing toward reasons for the fraying social fabric in America, including technology and media consumption replacing in-person interaction and the trend toward suburban living. My research builds upon Putnam's work, analyzing and exploring the continued atomization of American society and the resultant loneliness epidemic, looking back to Scripture and to other cultures—specifically to Ethiopia—to consider how connection could be restored and maintained in the modern day.

In her book, *Making Room: Recovering Hospitality as a Christian Tradition*, Christine Pohl explores the practice of hospitality in Scripture and in church history and urges modern readers to return to these ancient rhythms. This study will point out that Ethiopian cultures have remained more in tune with these ancient rhythms even in modern times, contending that Ethiopians are well-suited to guide the American church in a recovery of this vital practice.

In her later book, *Living into Community: Cultivating Practices That Sustain Us*, Pohl seeks to extend upon her earlier work on the topic of hospitality in order to examine how this value is lived out in actual life in contemporary American churches, as well as how hospitality connects with other community practices. She incisively pinpoints challenges to practicing hospitality in contemporary America, including wrong definitions, viewing hospitality "as a means to another end," and a cultural tendency toward a "strong task orientation" which causes "opportunities for hospitality" to be viewed as "interruptions."[1] Pohl rightly encourages readers to return to biblical practices, but the study at hand will seek to provide some additional encouragement by showing what it looks like for hospitality to be a high value in a modern context—Ethiopia—assisting Western Christians in the reimagination of what hospitality in contemporary America could look like.

The nineteenth and twenty-first Surgeon General of the United States, Indian-American physician Vivek Murthy, recently wrote a book entitled *Together: The Healing Power of Human Connection in a Sometimes Lonely World*. In it, he explains that in his early experiences as the child of immigrant parents who tried to cultivate community and in his life's work as a physician, he has become increasingly aware that there are many who feel "a lack of belonging" which leads them to "[feel] homeless even though they [have] a roof over their head."[2] Though social isolation and its effects are increasingly recognized as a threat to public health, he admits

1. Pohl, *Living into Community*, 165.
2. Murthy, *Together*, xviii.

that he "was never trained to assess or address loneliness."[3] Echoing Pohl, Murthy also pinpoints overemphasis on efficiency[4] and task orientation or a "transactional" understanding of relationships[5] as problems which lead to loneliness. Chapter 3 of *Together* is particularly relevant to the study at hand because it explains the difference between individualistic and collective cultures and imagines the possibility of a third option that keeps the strengths of both while letting go of the weaknesses of each one. The goal of this study is to elaborate on this possibility of a third option, using a collectivist culture to shed light on the hyperindividualistic American culture in order to provide some balance and point the way toward an increased sense of belonging through hospitality.

At the end of 2021—during the writing of this book—Susan Mettes published *The Loneliness Epidemic: Why So Many of Us Feel Alone—and How Leaders Can Respond*. The research for this book occurred at a fascinating moment in history: Mettes collected preliminary data in the winter of 2020, before the COVID-19 pandemic began in the USA, and then continued her research during the first several months of lockdowns and quarantines, studying the effects these societal shifts had on loneliness, with some counterintuitive findings, such as the fact that loneliness did not increase in the first few months of the pandemic, but that the problem of loneliness became even more entrenched as time went on. This is one of the first rigorously researched books from a Christian perspective specifically looking at the loneliness epidemic and how it can be addressed by Christian leaders and communities. The publication of this book during the time of the writing of my own text confirms the need for research in this area and provides helpful quantitative information about the toll of loneliness and the need for community. My own research provides a resource in the addressing of the loneliness epidemic by bringing a different cultural perspective to bear on the subject of loneliness and building community through hospitality.

In his provocative article, "The Nuclear Family Was a Mistake," David Brooks elaborates on a thread mentioned in Murthy's work, tracing the rise and disintegration of the American ideal of a "detached nuclear family," showing how this model has crumbled in lower socio-economic brackets because of the lack of connection to wider extended family and close friend

---

3. Murthy, *Together*, 7.
4. Murthy, *Together*, 100.
5. Murthy, *Together*, 217.

kinship networks. He also asserts that the facade of the intact detached nuclear family in the upper classes is only possible through purchasing the help (nannying, elder care, tutoring, household maintenance, therapy) that extended family and close friend kinship networks would have provided in the past. Brooks also mentions in passing that he has befriended several African immigrants who have all shared with him that the most shocking thing about their new life in the USA is the loneliness that people feel. This article makes headway in diagnosing the historical reasons for the emergence of the loneliness epidemic, and also makes some helpful points about the failure of hyperindividualism. These ideas will provide an excellent foundation for my study, which will then attempt to find paradigm-shifting solutions to the problems caused by hyperindividualistic ideals and the resultant rampant loneliness plaguing American culture.

In his book, *Mission as Hospitality*, Edward L. Smither seeks to call Christians to lives characterized by hospitality because of their own experience of divine hospitality. He shows that table fellowship has been a primary, effective means of Christian witness throughout the history of the Church and suggests missional hospitality as a paradigm-shifting return to ancient ways that may be just what the modern Church needs. In my study, I seek to build on the foundation that Smither has laid, spending time examining not only individual modern examples but also a whole cohesive system which is doing missional hospitality well, that is, Ethiopian culture.

In his book, *Hospitality and the Other: Pentecost, Christians Practices, and the Other*, Amos Yong examines a biblical theology of hospitality, concluding that beyond believing doctrines, Christians are called to engage in continuing in the footsteps of Jesus, who was both needy guest and divine host in the gospel accounts and who delighted in turning conventional notions of hospitality upside down in favor of ever-more astonishing and magnificent demonstrations of God's welcome to those who did not yet know him. Yong's imaginative future orientation and his reminder that Jesus is still alive and working today through the Spirit provide hope to this study's aim to chart a way forward for American churches who want their fellowship and outreach to be characterized by hospitality.

In his book, *Saved By Faith and Hospitality*, Joshua W. Jipp roots his discussion of hospitality in God's welcome toward humans, manifested in Jesus who was frequently a guest but who was ultimately a host who shared God's blessings with the world. This divine welcome sets the path that Christians are to walk, one characterized by redemptive friendships,[6] generosity,[7] and an immigrant identity.[8] Jipp's arguments help to strengthen this study's assertion that hospitality is not merely an optional add-on to the Christian life; rather, it is integral and should shape the Christian response to current global challenges. As such, this study will propose that a typically Ethiopian practice of hospitality as a lifestyle based on ontological interconnected interdependence is therefore more biblically resonant than the current, more elective and episodic American practice of hospitality.

In his 2021 book—published during the writing of this work—Jefferson Bethke encourages American Christians to *Take Back Your Family: From the Tyrants of Burnout, Busyness, Individualism, and the Nuclear Ideal*, which is a critique of the very things I am also critiquing in this book. It is particularly interesting that this is the first book I have found that questions the nuclear family by appealing to Scripture—this is still a minority view among American Christians whose individualistic presuppositions have predisposed many to misremember history and miss the fact that in the past, family referred to a much wider network of relationships that held a community together compared to the present day. To question the nuclear family has seemed threatening to many American Christians, as if the questioner were proposing that the government replace the family. Bethke differentiates his critiques by appealing to what he observed among families in Israel—a more multi-generational, communal culture based on ideas in the Old Testament—and showing how these ideas comport with the teachings of all of Scripture such that Christians reading this book and seeking to apply their faith will likely find their mindset shifted in a way that changes their practices in a long-term way. Bethke's book is an encouraging addition to the growing body of works by American Christians seeking to address the problems that America is facing, and I appreciate that his book does not put the cart before the horse: he mostly focuses on underlying presuppositions rather than over-emphasizing particular practices. While Bethke includes several brief mentions of the influence of his time spent in Israel on developing the ideas he shares, I do think there is much more room to intentionally research, learn from, and specifically write about other, more communal cultures in seeking to rebalance the

---

6. Jipp, *Saved By Faith*, 99.
7. Jipp, *Saved By Faith*, 147.
8. Jipp, *Saved By Faith*, 123.

values of hyperindividualistic American Christians, which is what I seek to do in this book.

In his article for The Gospel Coalition, Jeremy Linneman says that "radical individualism has become the functional status for even the most devoted churchgoers," going on to show how biblically incongruent this is, since it is clear that "neuroscience supports theology" in saying humans are "wired for deep relational connection."[9] He suggests several ways that the American Church can be part of addressing the loneliness epidemic, including "refram[ing] church membership from merely a commitment to a place of belonging." Linneman concludes by asserting that "Western individualism has sparked unprecedented social isolation, so we need to work tirelessly to recover the biblical vision of human nature and community in our local churches." Without missing a beat, this study can follow on the heels of Linneman's ideas, providing an exploration of a different way of being that is not characterized by hyperindividualism in order to provide a communal counterpoint when the American Church is pondering how to heal from the loneliness epidemic and create community going forward.

In her status-quo shaking book, *The Gospel Comes with a Housekey: Practicing Radically Ordinary Hospitality in Our Post-Christian World*, American writer Rosaria Butterfield issues a clarion call to American churches to remember their identity and live out their calling to show hospitality. She contends that doing so gives Christians "street credibility" in a secular world which normally views preaching with skepticism.[10] Butterfield correctly diagnoses the creeping problem of "chronic loneliness" which is at least partially caused by and is certainly made worse through a lack of hospitality, and she casts a vision for using the home as a haven for struggling souls who can be buoyed through the difficulties of life by being rooted in an open-doored community.[11] By the example of her life and the exhortation of her writing, Butterfield encourages American Christians to view hospitality not just as something they engage in occasionally, but as a life-focus. The message of this book is remarkably aligned with the point of this study, but I believe my study will help provide a missing link which will enhance readers' application of the principles she propounds: an exposure of the epistemological gap or blindspot which many American readers suffer from, that is, hyperindividualism. Examining hyperindividualism will

---

9. Linneman, "How Your Church Can Respond to the Loneliness Epidemic."
10. Butterfield, *Gospel Comes with a Housekey*, 40.
11. Butterfield, *Gospel Comes with a Housekey*, 111.

help to explain why it quells the very desire to connect in the first place, and why many readers of this book, in my experience and conversations, have felt guilty and burdened rather than inspired by Butterfield's exhortations. The study that follows will seek to provide a helpful model—that of an Ethiopian understanding of hospitality based on presuppositions of ontological interconnected interdependence—to provide another perspective which will serve to raise awareness of this blindspot in American culture, and make it possible for the American Church to find more balance, beauty, and joy in the practice of a lifestyle of hospitality.

In their recently published book, *The Art of Hospitality: A Practical Guide for a Ministry of Radical Welcome*, Yvonne Gentile and Debi Nixon focus on how churches can be "outwardly focused,"[12] with the purpose of going "above and beyond friendliness" to create an atmosphere of "radical hospitality," which they define as "welcoming guests with a warmth, openness, and authenticity that significantly exceeds their expectations."[13] They urge churches to practice this because "our hospitality can be a bridge that draws people in and encourages them to take a next step of faith, or it can be the barrier where individuals quickly decide to disengage."[14] The book contains many helpful and practical suggestions for churches, but it does not contain any instruction on members opening their homes or living hospitable lives outside of official church gatherings. This book serves as an example of American churches seeking to be more hospitable and yet falling prey to the blindspots of a business-model, task and program-oriented mentality, rather than the more biblically resonant, holistic way of being "delighted to share with you not only the gospel of God but our lives as well" (1 Thess 2:8), which is exemplified by a an Ethiopian understanding and practice of building community through hospitality based on ontological interconnected interdependence.

Dustin Willis and Brandon Clement's book, *The Simplest Way to Change the World: Biblical Hospitality as a Way of Life* is a helpful, contextually American guide showing the why and how of practicing hospitality as Christians. These American pastors make a convincing case for why hospitality is important and also wisely diagnose some of the reasons why American Christians struggle to practice hospitality, particularly the desire to be isolated and comfortable. Readers are encouraged to just try

---

12. Gentile and Nixon, *Art of Hospitality*, 8.
13. Gentile and Nixon, *Art of Hospitality*, 27.
14. Gentile and Nixon, *Art of Hospitality*, 13.

practicing hospitality as an exercise that will hurt but will be good for them, just like starting to go to the gym after living a sedentary life. They provide themselves and some of their friends as examples of people who did not start out naturally hospitable, but who have learned to practice hospitality gradually and through trial and error. The whole message of this book is helpful, but it would be complemented by my study showing hospitality in action not just in isolated examples in the lives of a few individuals, but in a whole system which is categorically and positively different because of being shaped by the prioritization of proximity with others. Seeing another cohesively lived out way of being can sometimes uncover the blindspots in one's worldview and flaws in one's own system in ways that nothing else can. And awareness of these things is a prerequisite of change, especially when the change may prove to be at least temporarily painful. This study, therefore, adds intercultural breadth to Willis and Clements' arguments and makes them even more convincing.

In his *Three Pieces of Glass: Why We Feel Lonely in a World Mediated By Screens*, Eric O. Jacobsen contends that "a longing for belonging . . . has reached a crisis state in contemporary American culture for reasons specific to our time and place."[15] He suggests that the reasons for this crisis of belonging—which is describing the same phenomenon described elsewhere in this study as "the loneliness epidemic"—is caused by American culture's "embrace of innovations in transportation, housing design, and communication that minimize face to face interactions."[16] Because of decades of choices made over the course of several generations to deprioritize human connection, many of those continuing to make these choices today do not even know that they *are* choices, in the same way that a fish does not know water is wet. This book does some heavy lifting in order to convincingly prove that American culture is at a crisis point with regard to loneliness and belonging, as well as accurately pinpointing some of the reasons why America finds itself here. The solutions proposed in the book tend to major on "hardware" related ideas that have to do with the "physical layout of the neighborhood,"[17] which are excellent but only realistically fully possible in suburban leaning urban areas, not in the suburban leaning rural reality of the majority of Americans. The "software" suggestions Jacobs makes are more broadly applicable, as they refer to "the

---

15. Jacobsen, *Three Pieces of Glass*, 137.
16. Jacobsen, *Three Pieces of Glass*, 137.
17. Jacobsen, *Three Pieces of Glass*, 216.

patterns and practices cultivate and enacted by the residents of a particular neighborhood that actually create . . . moments of social connection."[18] These include thinking of one's neighborhood with "a parish mentality" as "a better alternative to the insular church,"[19] and also understanding one's home "in terms of parish,"[20] learning how to be a good neighbor in order to "improve the culture of a neighborhood" in terms of a sense of belonging and connection for the residents,[21] and shifting perspective to what could be called "localism" or "prioritizing the proximate," which involves eschewing modern technology's "seductive promise of eradication of distance" which may be "behind our crisis of belonging,"[22] since the belief that one can be anywhere at any given time makes being fully present in one's actual location feel foreign and even impossible. Thankfully, focusing on "belonging by placemaking"[23] in one's actual location makes it more likely that "local significance" will increase and that any community—not just those which happen to be "fortunate enough to live in the vicinity of successful public spaces"[24]—can shift the dynamics of their locale away from isolation and towards greater civic connectedness. These software suggestions are helpful due to their transferability even without the trappings of suburban leaning urban locations like the author's Tacoma, WA, context. Jacobsen is one of my major conversation partners from an American perspective in this book, and my research seeks to provide some insight from people—specifically Ethiopians—who have not been making the same arguably destructive choices that have been made in America in the last several decades, and so are in a healthier position with regard to loneliness and belonging. An Ethiopian perspective on building community through hospitality based on the reality of ontological interconnected interdependence, which has much to do with Jacobsen's topic of belonging, will be examined in order to help those who have grown up in American culture to have a point of comparison that will help create a realization that the water is, as it were, indeed quite wet.

18. Jacobsen, *Three Pieces of Glass*, 216.
19. Jacobsen, *Three Pieces of Glass*, 217.
20. Jacobsen, *Three Pieces of Glass*, 218.
21. Jacobsen, *Three Pieces of Glass*, 220.
22. Jacobsen, *Three Pieces of Glass*, 221.
23. Jacobsen, *Three Pieces of Glass*, 225.
24. Jacobsen, *Three Pieces of Glass*, 228.

While several of the authors mentioned above make brief references to welcoming immigrants, and Pohl devotes substantial time to discussing it, the resources that follow move deeper into discussing the way that migration and hospitality—or lack of it—are inextricably linked, and conversations about one naturally lead to conversations about the other. In *Religion and Migration: Negotiating Hospitality, Agency, and Vulnerability*, a diverse group of authors come together to consider how Christians can thoughtfully engage with issues of migration. Chapter 3 is particularly pertinent, suggesting that refugees are catalysts for change in the cultures where they settle, and describing the benefits of "learning from refugees."[25] This chapter provides helpful insights, but it comes from a European point of view and does not specifically talk about immigrants' ideas or practices concerning building community through hospitality. My research, therefore, will use this chapter as a springboard, building further on its ideas to suggest that immigrants can create change in order to propose that immigrants (many of whom come from Non-Western countries and have a Non-Western understanding of hospitality) can be used by God to help the American Church address the loneliness epidemic.

In "The Architecture of Loneliness in Refugee Communities," D. L. Mayfield shares from her years of experience in ministry among immigrants in the United States that "programs are well and good, but the one thing many refugees can't seem to find in America are people who have the time to visit with them."[26] Her pastor friend who is an Egyptian immigrant jokes with her that all he needs for ministry "is a couch and a pot of coffee" because his background and model for ministry is "steeped in relationship and community."[27] The study at hand will use this loneliness of immigrants living in the United States as yet another reason that demonstrates that hospitality is vital for the Church to practice. Additionally, this study will argue that the greatest partner the American Church has in welcoming immigrants is Christian immigrants themselves. These believing immigrants can be used by God to welcome other immigrants in the way God has welcomed them, but many also have the ability to encourage, challenge, and revitalize the American Church's fellowship and outreach through the way that building community through hospitality is central to the way that they live and love.

25. Polak, "Migrants as Agents of Social and Religious Innovation," 72.
26. Mayfield, "Architecture of Loneliness in Refugee Communities," para. 7.
27. Mayfield, "Architecture of Loneliness in Refugee Communities," para. 7.

In her deeply personal book, *Invited: The Power of Hospitality in an Age of Loneliness*, Leslie Verner weaves together her experiences as a stranger or guest when traveling and living in other countries with stories of learning to stay and welcome immigrants in the USA, including biblical and social insights along the way. Verner calls the Western Church beyond comfort and safety to a hospitality which is modeled in large measure after her cross-cultural experiences of being welcomed hospitably. This study is in the same spirit as Verner's book but has stylistic differences: Verner writes narratively and the book is mostly a memoir, while this study will include research which will confirm and explain experiences like hers and will be written in an academic style.

In his book *Befriend: Create Belonging in an Age of Judgment, Isolation, and Fear*, Scott Sauls challenges believers to engage in true friendship that follows the example of Jesus rather than settling for the shallow interactions common in modern society. Sauls discusses the perils of "transactional friendships"[28] from a Christian perspective, which is helpful in my comparison of transactional friendships versus relational friendships as I seek to articulate the importance of rebalancing away from hyperindividualism in order to address the loneliness epidemic. This book explores Ethiopian culture as a modern-day example of a place where relational friendships are more the norm and thus a helpful resource for American believers seeking to recover from hyperindividualism.

When American novelist Shawn Smucker had the opportunity to welcome a Syrian immigrant and his family and then write about it,[29] he hesitated because he knew that he as a Westerner was not necessarily prepared to be the kind of friend to Mohammed—the father of the family—that he should be. Nevertheless, he took the leap of getting involved in this family's life while taking a learner's posture as they taught him through their ordinary actions and lifestyle the answer to his unspoken question: "What would my life look like if I made friendship a priority?"[30] What results is a memoir that manages to be simultaneously mundane and riveting, clearly demonstrating the value of learning about hospitality from those with Non-Western perspectives. While Smucker's book is thought-provoking, he does not draw conclusions or move beyond a narrative format—he simply tells the story as a novelist would. In my study,

28. Sauls, *Befriend*, 2.
29. Smucker, *Once We Were Strangers*.
30. Smucker, *Once We Were Strangers*, 54.

I hope to build on what his personal experience has revealed, exploring a Non-Western understanding of relational hospitality in a systematic rather than a narrative way and considering a contextual application of this understanding not only to an individual's life but to the American Church's corporate and communal ethos as a whole.

In her article, "Hospitality as Spiritual Direction," Carolyn Butler considers the possibility of spiritual direction as a modality of discipleship in the African Church.[31] Along the way, she makes the point that "there are aspects of Middle Eastern culture during biblical times that were so inherent that it appears no one ever thought to write them down as rules. Hospitality is a case in point."[32] Similarly, she states that "an emphasis on hospitality has remained part of everyday life"[33] for most Africans, since "hospitality is still an everyday part of African world-views."[34] This is helpful in proving one of the presuppositions that the study at hand will lean on, that hospitality is an implicit value of both biblical and Ethiopian cultures, and that this value needs to be made explicit in modern, globalizing times so that it can be communicated to other cultures and so that it is not lost.

In his work of public theology *Christian Hospitality and Muslim Immigration in an Age of Fear*, Matthew Kaemingk ambitiously deconstructs unhelpful paradigms of interaction across religious and cultural differences and instead puts forward a viable *via media* of a Christian pluralism that eschews both extremes of "high walls" and "open doors" and instead embraces a framework of "table politics" with the aim that those with differences will be able to call each other "friend."[35] While the first three hundred pages of Kaemingk's work are necessary and helpful, he does not begin talking about table politics until the last two pages, so this study will aim to take his suggestions and keep running with them, showing table politics—by which Kaemingk means intentional hospitality across religious and cultural differences—to be a practice in which the Church urgently needs to engage in order to be effective in maintaining a witness to both those who are post-Christian as well as to those who are Muslim (and those who are from other faiths as well).

---

31. Butler, "Hospitality as Spiritual Direction," 65–75.
32. Butler, "Hospitality as Spiritual Direction," 65.
33. Butler, "Hospitality as Spiritual Direction," 66.
34. Butler, "Hospitality as Spiritual Direction," 67.
35. Kaemingk, *Christian Hospitality*, 305.

Those from Western cultures who have spent significant time interacting with or living within Non-Western cultures have much to say about learning from Non-Westerners about matters including but not limited to the practice of hospitality. In her article, "Often, Often, Often Goes the Christ in the Stranger's Guise,"[36] Cathy Ross states that "we are in a world captivated by honor and status, where the church in the West still commands unimaginable resources, prime real estate, and honorific titles and is sometimes co-opted by, or at least colludes with, secular powers."[37] She makes a powerful case that since "all theology is contextual"[38] and since part of "hospitality is paying attention,"[39] Western Christians should intentionally "create the space to listen to and learn from our brothers and sisters in the Majority World,"[40] This is an idea that this study will build upon in order to make the case that Westerners should learn from Non-Westerners in the area of hospitality, instead of viewing ministry as a one-way street. Ross additionally suggests the idea that experiences of "liminality" and "marginality" make one more keenly aware of the importance of and more eager to practice hospitality[41] which helps to prove the point that this study will make that Non-Western immigrants are uniquely suited to be leaders and guides to the Western Church as Western Christians seek to grow in their appreciation for and practice of hospitality.

In his article, "The Art of Hospitality: African Style," Del Chinchen recounts what he has learned about African hospitality from his many years of living and working in African countries in order to counsel Western Christians to open their minds to a broader understanding of what hospitality could be and how this Non-Western understanding could revolutionize their cross-cultural interactions. To date, this is the clearest explanation I have found of the differences between a Western and a Non-Western understanding of hospitality and the implications of both. This study will incorporate Chinchen's excellent articulation of a Non-Western worldview written for a Western audience, but will change the locus of application from Westerners working in Africa to Americans living in the USA.

---

36. Ross, "Often, Often, Often," 176–79.
37. Ross, "Often, Often, Often," 176.
38. Ross, "Often, Often, Often," 177.
39. Ross, "Often, Often, Often," 176.
40. Ross, "Often, Often, Often," 177.
41. Ross, "Often, Often, Often," 178.

LITERATURE REVIEW

In their book *The Art of Neighboring: Building Genuine Relationships Right Outside Your Door*, Jay Pathak and Dave Runyon tell of their experience getting their church members to identify and partner with other believers in their neighborhoods in order to love their actual neighbors, because "the solutions to the problems in our neighborhoods aren't ultimately found in the government, police, or schools or in getting more people to go to church. The solutions lie within us. It's within our power to become good neighbors, to care for people around us and to be cared for by the people around us. There really is a different way to live, and we are finding that it is actually the best way to live."[42] In fact, they assert, "By becoming good neighbors, we become who we are supposed to be. As a result, our communities become the places that God intended them to be." This book is a very helpful starting point for Christians wanting to take Jesus' command to love one's neighbor seriously, including pastoral insights for getting past resistance related to busyness, fear, mutuality and working as a team when seeking to become good neighbors. My research is complementary in the sense that it provides a perspective from a different culture to provide inspiration for what it could look like to build community through hospitality of home and heart with neighbors both literal and metaphorical.

In 2018, Leah Libresco wrote *Building the Benedict Option: A Guide to Gathering Two or Three Together in His Name* in order to make practical the ideas of Rod Dreher in his 2017 *The Benedict Option: A Strategy for Christians in a Post-Christian Nation*. While many of Dreher's philosophical assertions were controversial even in Christian circles, something that could be agreed upon in a context plagued by the loneliness epidemic is that community building should be prioritized. Since *The Benedict Option* is more philosophical treatise and less how-to guide, Libresco seeks to make practical what building community might look like in the daily life of Christians. The book is strongly contextual for an American context, likely because it is based on the real-life experiences of Libresco's growth in hospitality, and this is a strength in one sense, while in another sense, I believe my research can bring a wider perspective and thus contribute new insights to expose cultural blindspots and identify cultural barriers in the American practice of hospitality, suggesting ways to resolve and remove them in light of the example of Ethiopian culture.

In 2021, Carolyn Lacey wrote *Extraordinary Hospitality (for Ordinary People): Seven Ways to Welcome Like Jesus* in order to demonstrate

---

42. Pathak and Runyon, *Art of Neighboring*, 22.

"that hospitality doesn't have to be exhausting and overwhelming. And that is because it is not so much about *what* we do, but *why* we do it."[43] Only one thing is necessary, says Lacey: "You just need to delight in God's welcome and desire to reflect it to those around you."[44] In the pages that follow, Lacey makes connections between the way that God welcomes us and the way we have been empowered by Him to welcome others. The focus on an internal orientation toward welcoming based on an identity of having been welcomed is deeply needed and often under-emphasized in Western teaching on the topic of hospitality, so this thin volume packs an outsized punch. My research will complement its message by exploring a context in which welcoming identities and the community building through hospitality that naturally flows from such identities are more the norm than the exception: Ethiopia.

For my own MA thesis, I focused on "Preparing Ethiopians for Cross-Cultural Ministry: Maximizing Missionary Training for Great Commission Impact," which marked the beginning of cultivating what has now become a guiding presupposition of mine: skepticism of a "West to the rest" mentality and instead an intentional cultivation of mutuality in mission. In this thesis, I surveyed missiological education in Ethiopia with an eye toward enhancing existing programs and beginning new programs. My involvement in seeking to make missiological education more available and accessible to Ethiopians while frequently becoming aware of my own blindspots and learning from my students has led to an ever-increasing conviction that global mutuality in sharing the good news is the only way forward: Western Christians miss a huge opportunity if they refuse to learn from Non-Western believers because of a heretical "resource righteousness"[45] which erroneously believes that the person who holds the bigger purse also possesses the most spiritual maturity. This work seeks to provide a specific way that Western Christians can learn from Non-Western brothers and sisters in order to address the loneliness running rampant in the West: an identity-level commitment to building community through hospitality.

As a continuation of my thesis research, I wrote "Ethiopian Immigrants as Cross-Cultural Missionaries: Activating the Diaspora for Great

---

43. Lacey, *Extraordinary Hospitality*, 15.

44. Lacey, *Extraordinary Hospitality*, 15.

45. While the idea was present in this paper, I did not coin the term "resource righteousness" until my later paper, "Lives That Welcome," which is discussed below.

Commission Impact,"[46] in order to acknowledge and study the great potential of Ethiopian immigrants to become fruitful missionaries among other immigrants as well as among locals in the USA. This work continued to critique the implicitly held but still destructive idea that Western missionaries are the only ones capable of sharing the gospel cross-culturally. Instead, mutuality in mission—the idea that ideas, leadership, and mentoring can flow both ways—is crucial and will benefit all involved, including American believers. It is this presupposition that I am carrying into my own research, where I am exploring more deeply a specific way that American Christians can learn and be mentored by Ethiopian Christians.

In a 2020 conference paper at the outset of my research, I discussed "Lives That Welcome: How a Nonwestern Understanding of Hospitality Can Revitalize the American Church's Fellowship and Outreach." This paper contained the seeds of many ideas that have matured in the process of my research and writing. This paper discusses the pitfalls of a programmatic view of community building and instead proposes "non-programmatic hospitality" as "one of the church's greatest tools in effective outreach to nearly every group they are seeking to reach," whether local people in a post-Christian society, immigrants, or people in their own culture if an American is living in another country.[47] In order to cultivate non-programmatic hospitality among American Christians, I discuss the need for "learning from Non-Westerners"[48] in order to address a Western misunderstanding of what hospitality is and overly limited parameters of when and where it should occur. If such learning is to happen, then "resource righteousness" must be addressed: "believing that the culture that has more money, infrastructure, or material resources must be the culture whose members have more valuable insights to share."[49] This book is simply a continuation of the study of these topics at a deeper and more collaborative level, including the synthesis of data gathered from over sixty interviews and further bibliographic research.

---

46. Udall, "Ethiopian Immigrants as Cross-Cultural Missionaries," 183–95.
47. Udall, "Lives That Welcome," 3.
48. Udall, "Lives That Welcome," 5.
49. Udall, "Lives That Welcome," 5.

Review of Literature from Non-Ethiopian African Perspectives

In the *Africa Bible Commentary*, Emily J. Choge writes a brief article on "Hospitality in Africa," summarizing the biblical command to show hospitality as well as including several examples of hospitality in the Old and New Testaments, noting that Jesus "instructed his disciples to give a blessing wherever they were received to show that he built hospitality into his mission." Choge compares the balanced instructions on generous hospitality with built-in protections for hosts given in the Didache with the "similar guidance" shared in African proverbs, noting the challenges and suggesting ways forward to practice hospitality well in contemporary, urban Africa, where some aspects of traditional hospitality practices have already been eroded by the forces of modernization and globalization.[50] With limited space to discuss, Choge succinctly conveys the urgent need for Africans to explicitly articulate what is generally an implicitly held value in order to preserve the practice of hospitality in the midst of a changing world as well as to bless and exhort the wider global Church. My study will explore the ideas introduced by Choge in a more in-depth way, seeking to particularly focus on giving a platform for Ethiopian Christians to explicitly articulate their implicit values and exploring how these insights might instruct and inspire the American Church.

Choge's book, *An Ethic of Hospitality: The Pilgrim Motif in Hebrews and the Refugee Problem in Kenya*, focuses on the book of Hebrews as well as tracing the idea of pilgrimage throughout Scripture in order to encourage the modern-day body of Christ to interact with refugees for the purpose of caring for people in need but also to learn more about living with a pilgrim identity themselves. Choge's perspective that those who are far from home have much to teach believers about their own spiritual identity turns the typical narrative of the "poor refugee" on its head and creates a healthy spiritual expectancy and excitement about what reciprocal blessings hosts can receive from guests, reframing hospitality as a privilege rather than a duty, in the spirit of Hebrews 13:2. Choge reminds Kenyans that they are "armed with the rich resources of African hospitality" as they seek to address the challenges of caring for refugees, because "hospitality in both the biblical and the African tradition is not just about entertaining family and friends; it also reaches to the arena of one who is the 'other,' the

---

50. Choge, "Hospitality in Africa," 390.

stranger, the outsider, the foreigner." Indeed, she points out that in many African languages, "the same word is used for both stranger and guest."[51] Choge's work addresses Kenyans while acknowledging that her ideas have implications for the global Church, while my work will focus on an American context with broader implications for the global Church. The mindset of both studies is similar and synergistic, but the primary locus of application is geographically different.

In Musa Victor Mdabuleni Kunene's book, *Communal Holiness in the Gospel of John: The Vine Metaphor as a Test Case with Lessons from African Hospitality and Trinitarian Theology*, he skillfully fleshes out how "mutual abiding, which carries the giving of room and sharing of one's space with another," is related to the theme of hospitality throughout the Gospel of John.[52] Instead of the hospitality industry's hollow replica or the often shallow and transactional imitation in the modern day,[53] Kunene gives the Swazi people as an example of an alternative way to live that is characterized by *ubuntu*—a Pan-African concept which has many parallels with a Johannine or broadly biblical hospitality.[54] Indeed, *ubuntu*—with its values of openness, generosity, and mutual respect for the interconnectedness of all humanity—beautifully expresses God's hospitable vision for humanity as captured in the Prophetic books of the Old Testament in verses such as Zechariah 3:10: "every one of you will invite his neighbor to come under his vine and under his fig tree." Kunene's work provides insight into the resonance of an African understanding of *ubuntu* with a biblical understanding of hospitality, which my study will also cover before drawing implications which have potential to positively impact the loneliness epidemic's effects in the American Church.

In his article, "Social Capital and the Imperatives of the Concept and Life of Ubuntu in the South African Context," Henry Mbaya looks at the "very close parallels" between the idea of social capital in the West and the idea of *ubuntu* in Africa, discovering that both yield social cohesion but focus on different systems: social capital on "socio-economic benefits" and *ubuntu* on "hospitality and mutual support."[55] While generally promoting *ubuntu* as a concept, Mbaya also helpfully tempers his praise by

---

51. Choge, *Ethic of Hospitality*), xviii.
52. Kunene, *Communal Holiness*, 137.
53. Kunene, *Communal Holiness*, 139.
54. Kunene, *Communal Holiness*, 148.
55. Mbaya, "Social Capital," 4.

acknowledging that "the spirit of Ubuntu can be distorted for ideological purposes."[56] Mbaya's insights will be helpful in framing the comparison of a typically Western understanding of social life versus a typically African understanding of the same, with the former being more transactional and the latter more relational, purportedly pursuing the same thing but doing so in radically different ways, begging the question which will be explored further in my own study: whether there are fundamentally different understandings of the meaning of belonging at play.

In his article, "African Hospitality: Is it Compatible with the Ideal of Christ's Hospitality?" Julius M. Gathogo invites readers to consider the potential of African theologians to make an valuable contribution to the global church by articulating the value of "Ancient African hospitality as we examine its compatibility with Christ's ideal hospitality."[57] Through interactions with his own experiences growing up in Kenya, explorations of African proverbs and studies written by other Africans as well as interviews he conducted with Africans and with Westerners who spent significant time living in Africa, Gathogo gently suggests that though no culture has a corner on the market of understanding God's design for a life well-lived, African cultures do tend to practice a daily, natural form of hospitality that closely mirrors what is both commanded and commended in Scripture. Gathogo discusses how Christian ideas of hospitality have been inculturated into African church liturgies, considers how African hospitality has been abused, such as in the cases of neo-colonialism and corruption of leaders, and explains some "modern challenges to African hospitality" such as the growing "pressure of work and a task-oriented lifestyle" which is increasingly common in urban areas.[58]

Gathogo also writes an article entitled "African Philosophy as Expressed in the Concepts of Hospitality and *Ubuntu*" in which he proposes that the idea of "*ubuntu* (personhood or humanness)"[59] can be understood as a "concept that defines the individual in terms of his or her relationships with others."[60] A spirit of *ubuntu* may be useful in helping African societies heal and thrive in the post-colonial period, based on the idea that those hurt by colonialism must "reconstruct our past histories, in order

---

56. Mbaya, "Social Capital," 7.
57. Gathogo, "African Hospitality," 25.
58. Gathogo, "African Hospitality," 48.
59. Gathogo, "African Philosophy," 39.
60. Gathogo, "African Philosophy," 45.

to genuinely move forward." He makes the axiological assertion that "in Africa, an ideal person is primarily hospitable."[61] Additionally, Gathogo wisely takes "a critical approach to *Ubuntu*" which hints at the need for the term's "revitalisation (or is it reconstruction)" so as to make it ideal.[62] He acknowledges potential pitfalls of "an extremist view" of *ubuntu* with regard to de-emphasizing the individual to an unhelpful degree or prioritizing one's in-group to the detriment of others[63] (often manifested in a "balkanizing" tribalism).[64] Thus, he anticipates counterarguments and instead suggests that a true understanding of *ubuntu* would "transcend both individualism and collectivism in order to form an all-inclusive and all-encompassing community"[65] compatible with a Christian understanding of the *imago dei* of all people.

In his article entitled "Some Expressions of African Hospitality Today," Gathogo embarks on an "ambitious" and admittedly incomplete survey of "some socio-religious manifestations of African hospitality" in order to begin to rectify the fact that this crucial element in many African cultures is not much talked about in African Christian Theology.[66] Gathogo believes that despite its short-comings and despite the strength of certain aspects of "European cultural emphasis on freedom in the individual idea of choice,"[67] nevertheless, "African cultural resources are crucial" to Africa's upbuilding, and furthermore, "African hospitality has something it can bequeath to the rest of the world."[68] In the pages that follow, Gathogo shows the many parallels between various African proverbs and the ideas found in the Old and New Testaments regarding interdependence and communality between people, and also distills expressions of African hospitality into three categories: religious life, economic life, and social life. He asserts that "hospitality eradicates loneliness," citing the Zulu saying: "individuals cannot exist alone. They are because they belong."[69] Gathogo expresses *ubuntu* as the "spiritual foundation of African societies" which encompasses the

---

61. Gathogo, "African Philosophy," 39.
62. Gathogo, "African Philosophy," 50.
63. Gathogo, "African Philosophy," 47.
64. Gathogo, "African Philosophy," 49.
65. Gathogo, "African Philosophy," 52.
66. Gathogo, "Some Expressions of African Hospitality Today," 275.
67. Gathogo, "Some Expressions of African Hospitality Today," 286.
68. Gathogo, "Some Expressions of African Hospitality Today," 276.
69. Gathogo, "Some Expressions of African Hospitality Today," 283.

vertical aspect of openness to God and the horizontal aspect of openness to other people, agreeing with several other African voices who compare the African concept of ubuntu with the Old Testament concept of "spirit," which "distinguishes human life from animal life."[70]

In his book entitled *Christ's Hospitality from an African Theological Perspective: Lessons from Christ's Ideal Hospitality for Africa*, Gathogo focuses on "Christ's hospitality informing African Christian hospitality"[71] and deepening and widening that which already exists as a strength. Gathogo understands this strength to be a "natural approach" that is fundamental to life rather than based upon "pretense," as is too often the case in the West.[72] Since Christ "has many faces in African hospitality," and "is involved in our daily lives"[73] as many things, including the "healer,"[74] "the African guest,"[75] "the host/master of hospitality,"[76] and "the source of fellowship,"[77] Gathogo contends that "African Christianity, based on Christ's hospitality, can remind the world church of the importance of the concept of hospitality."[78]

Gathogo's emphases match closely with the purposes of my own study. His appreciation and skillful articulation of African perspectives on hospitality as well as his efforts to synthesize and synergize these perspectives with a biblical understanding of hospitality provide a broad and solid foundation on which to build. This study will go further to hone in on an Ethiopian perspective (not much touched on by Gathogo), discerning what is transferable from African cultures to other cultures, and then working to ideologically translate biblically resonant, African insights on hospitality into an American context in order to address the loneliness epidemic as it affects American churches and the American culture at large.

Mojalefa L. J. Koenane wrote "Ubuntu and Philoxenia: Ubuntu and Christian Worldviews as Responses to Xenophobia" in order to address "xenophobic attitudes and violence" in South Africa by appealing to the *ubuntu* ideals and the biblical teachings that the majority of South

---

70. Gathogo, "Some Expressions of African Hospitality Today," 285.
71. Gathogo, *Christ's Hospitality*, 11.
72. Gathogo, *Christ's Hospitality*, 97.
73. Gathogo, *Christ's Hospitality*, 118.
74. Gathogo, *Christ's Hospitality*, 129.
75. Gathogo, *Christ's Hospitality*, 131.
76. Gathogo, *Christ's Hospitality*, 133.
77. Gathogo, *Christ's Hospitality*, 143.
78. Gathogo, *Christ's Hospitality*, 145.

LITERATURE REVIEW

Africans claim to revere. This is an article that could be similarly written about Ethiopia, and is a helpful counterpoint to the positive image of Africa as a utopian ideal of hospitable community—the reality is far more complex. As will be discussed later in this book, I argue that Africans tend to have ideals that make the practices of hospitality come more naturally, but often these ideals need to be lived out in broader ways to include people who are different, which seems similar to the situation in the Ancient Near East when the Bible was being written, with frequent teachings and stories widening the answer to the question, "And who is my neighbor?" (Luke 10:29). Conversely, in the United States, the national conversation at least pays lip service to the idea that people from diverse backgrounds can find belonging in American society, but there is the eerie sense that these words and actions may not flow from the heart or influence daily practice. American Christians understand that they should invite people into their homes, but the underlying worldview of hyperindividualism makes living a lifestyle of openness and welcome—which includes but is not limited to scheduled dinner invitations—much more difficult, if not impossible. My book will argue that rebalancing toward more communal ideals and ontologically interdependent identities would make American efforts to address the loneliness epidemic and to thrive in its diversifying reality much deeper-rooted and more sustainable.

In her thesis for her MA in Teaching Art, "'Viens a la Maison': Moroccan Hospitality, a Contemporary View," Anita Schwartz describes her exhibit as being "an exploration of porcelain ceramics" that "feast the eyes as well as the palate."[79] In creating a context for her work, Schwartz delves into her Moroccan-Jewish heritage in which her ancestors received Moroccan hospitality and "hospitality became ingrained in our identities"[80] in order to understand and transcend a "visual anthropology" of Morocco. She displays her pieces "in a dining room setting where guests are always welcome to enter."[81]

In her doctoral dissertation, "Politeness and Offering in Libyan Arabic Hospitality," Fatheth Alsenoussi Mansor discusses how offering and receiving hospitality is inherent in Libyan Arabic linguistic practice. The author surmises that "this may be because at an ideological level there is significant

---

79. Schwartz, "'Viens a la Maison,'" iv.
80. Schwartz, "'Viens a la Maison,'" 3.
81. Schwartz, "'Viens a la Maison,'" v.

stress on hospitality as a dominant principle of daily life among Libyans."[82] Mansor shows great attention to the details of the conventions of typical Libyan small talk, showing that the very warp and woof of social life among Libyans is characterized by hospitable interchanges. Schwartz and Mansor show practical examples of hospitality being an integral part of Moroccan and Libyan culture, while my study will delve into the Ethiopian perspective and practice of hospitality with the purpose of gleaning biblically resonant ideas that can be contextually applied in the American Church in order to address the loneliness epidemic in the West.

In his article "Eucharistic Hospitality: A Bi-directional Dynamic," Levi Nkwocha writes about the simultaneously vertical and horizontal aspects of Eucharistic hospitality, commending the biblically resonant example of the Igbo people of Nigeria whose ceremonial sharing of kola nuts symbolizes and ritualizes their grasp of the interconnected nature of the divine with all of life and members of a community with each other. Nkwocha cogently critiques the inevitable ways that even this hospitable Igbo custom falls short, but he nevertheless adeptly uses it as a foil to gently expose the pitfalls of American individualism while providing "a clue to better appreciate Christian teaching."[83] The article's cultural analysis and biblical comparison provide a vivid example of the resonance between an African and a biblical understanding of both vertical and horizontal hospitality, helping to undergird the current study's suggestion that there is much to be learned from Africans when seeking to more fully live out the Bible's hospitable mandate.

In his book, *Fostering Interreligious Encounters in Pluralist Societies: Hospitality and Friendship*, SimonMary Asese A. Aihiokhai explains the hypostatic union as a prime example of the "inherent openness of God to alterity as it plays out in the divine-human relations in the incarnate Christ."[84] In light of this, Aihiokhai argues for "the necessity for religions to take seriously how their heritages affirm relationality as a means to bear witness to their religious truths in the world" and suggests that friendship and hospitality are a means of "concretizing" this affirmation.[85] With hospitality understood as a "human condition that makes friendship possible," Aihiokai contends that "hospitality and friendship are innately part of the human condition

---

82. Mansor, "Politeness and Offering," iv.
83. Nkwocha, "Eucharistic Hospitality," 189.
84. Aihiokhai, *Fostering Interreligious Encounters*, 9.
85. Aihiokhai, *Fostering Interreligious Encounters*, 1.

and that both constitute a relevant part of every religious tradition."[86] He suggests that "the conscious efforts of the religious people of Ihievbe [a town in Edo State, Nigeria] to construct healthy interreligious encounters can become a model for other societies faced with religious pluralism."[87] Aihiokhai's case study as well as his theological and cultural insights provide reasons why further study on the topic of hospitality is imperative for the global Church—and, my study would argue, particularly for the Western Church which has struggled to cultivate a full-orbed understanding and practice of hospitality—since hospitality is the means by which relationship and witness become possible in a world full of difference.

In an article entitled, "An African Ethic of Hospitality for the Global Church: A Response to the Culture of Exploitation and Violence in Africa," Aihiokhai explains that Africa has been characterized by the practice of hospitality in narratives from Judaism, Christianity, and Islam, and continues to carry the legacy of these heritages in real, if imperfect, ways. He references the loneliness epidemic in the West and observes that "existential loneliness is the end product of the false sense of self advocated by [individualism]" and that "it is not accidental that societies that have embraced this philosophy of individualism are the ones whose citizens are today suffering the psychological effects of self-alienation." In order to ameliorate this situation, Aihiokhai suggests that the Western world could learn from an African ethic of hospitality, which understands that "humans are essentially social beings and attain their full humanity in and through connectedness with others, themselves, God, and the cosmos."[88] This understanding is summed up in the word *ubuntu*, which is reminiscent of the New Testament practice of *koinonia*.[89] Aihiokhai's article is clear-sighted about the corruption, genocide, and other issues that Africa faces that seem to fly in the face of a true commitment to openness to the other, but he uses the opportunity of this acknowledgement as a clarion call to return to ideals that he believes have in some cases begun to be lost. Aihiokhai helpfully touches specifically on the very phenomenon I am trying to address in my study, and his impulse to look to an African understanding of hospitality as an antidote to chronic loneliness in the West confirms my desire to go deeper into this topic, extrapolating Aihiokhai's

---

86. Aihiokhai, *Fostering Interreligious Encounters*, 2.
87. Aihiokhai, *Fostering Interreligious Encounters*, 8.
88. Aihiokhai, "African Ethic of Hospitality," 35.
89. Aihiokhai, "African Ethic of Hospitality," 32.

suggestions in order to apply this antidote in a way that will be accessible and actionable for a Western audience.

In his doctoral dissertation, "Hospitality and Solidarity as Mediations of the Kingdom of God," Aloys Nkoua Kek writes that since (even at the time of his writing in 1989), "scientific and technological progress does not necessarily correspond with moral progress,"[90] he believes that "the practices of hospitality and solidarity constitute a timely means capable of helping both Church and world to relate significantly to the Kingdom of God."[91] Kek brings up the oft-mentioned connection in an African Christian understanding of hospitality that openness to welcome God has a direct correlation with openness to welcome strangers, since God is the Ultimate Other, suggesting that "my readiness to be hospitable . . . will therefore be proportionate to my readiness to be a disciple."[92] He then surveys history to trace threads of hospitality and solidarity from ancient times until modern times, with the understanding that God's "Kingdom is more of a relationship with, a vision of life under God's reign, and a community of life with God and neighbor, rather than a geographical place, or a political and therefore, temporal kingdom."[93] Kek asserts that "the practices of hospitality and solidarity" are "highly treasured in African tradition" and should be reclaimed by local churches[94] as a means of "emancipation."[95] Though he acknowledges that generalizing when speaking about Africa is "risky," he chooses to do so with the humble acknowledgement that "one simply cannot speak of anything in an exhaustive way," suggesting that from his experience, there are "real similarities, affinities and agreements in various areas of life throughout Africa" particularly with regard to "hospitality and solidarity." He spends time elaborating on an traditionally African worldview which sees humanity as an extended family in an interconnected yet precarious cosmos, showing that hospitality and solidarity naturally arise from this orientation toward life. Though Kek mourns the fact that in theological discourse, "hospitality and solidarity have always traveled a one-way street in the direction North-South," indicating the reticence of many in the West (which he

---

90. Kek, "Hospitality and Solidarity," iii.
91. Kek, "Hospitality and Solidarity," ii.
92. Kek, "Hospitality and Solidarity," 23.
93. Kek, "Hospitality and Solidarity," 331.
94. Kek, "Hospitality and Solidarity," 382.
95. Kek, "Hospitality and Solidarity," 220.

refers to as the North) to receive and learn from African theologians,[96] he nevertheless expresses hope that "the African experience of family offers a valuable contribution to the Christian project of building up the human family in active hospitality and solidarity."[97] The present study will seek to draw upon Kek's insights when seeking to communicate what an African understanding of hospitality looks like in theological practice.

In their article, "The African Concept of *Ubuntu/Botho* and Its Socio-Moral Significance," Mluleki Mnyaka and Mokgethi Motlhabi begin with a cautious but helpful generalization that "although there is a diversity of African cultures, there are commonalities to be found among them in areas such as value systems, beliefs, practices and others." Taken together, these areas could functionally be described as "the African world-view," with "the most abiding principle of this world-view" being "known as the notion of *ubuntu/botho* (humanism or humaneness)."[98] According to the authors and many scholars they interact with, the principle of *ubuntu/botho* is abstract and challenging to define, but this is due in large part to its expansiveness and all-encompassing nature as a "way of life"[99] which recognizes that "it is in a human community that an individual is able to realize himself or herself as a person."[100] They then explore the "attitudes of Africans in general toward strangers,"[101] asserting that while an ideal level of openness to strangers has not always been maintained in every culture, deviation from hospitality toward strangers has not generally been seen as ideal by Africans. Many factors have contributed to the eroding of a spirit of *ubuntu* in African cultures, including colonization where African hospitality was taken advantage of by white colonizers, systemic apartheid and struggles against it, and rapid urbanization of African countries. But the idea of *ubuntu*—and the "duties and rights" it assumes to be part of human life—still remain, say Mnyaka and Motlhabi, foundational to the African consciousness.[102] The thoughtful and value-specific choice by all of the African authors mentioned in this section to say that openness to strangers as guests is an essential axiological element of African cultures

---

96. Kek, "Hospitality and Solidarity," 384.
97. Kek, "Hospitality and Solidarity," 235.
98. Mnyaka and Motlhabi, "African Concept of *Ubuntu/Botho*," 215.
99. Mnyaka and Motlhabi, "African Concept of *Ubuntu/Botho*," 218.
100. Mnyaka and Motlhabi, "African Concept of *Ubuntu/Botho*," 223.
101. Mnyaka and Motlhabi, "African Concept of *Ubuntu/Botho*," 228.
102. Mnyaka and Motlhabi, "African Concept of *Ubuntu/Botho*," 236.

undergirds the present study's inclination to probe the resonance of African and biblical understandings of hospitality as openness to the other and then consider how these ideas could be learned from and contextually applied in the American Church.[103]

In an article entitled "Sex as an Expression of Hospitality: Theological Investigation amongst Some Africans," M. E. Baloyi expresses concern that misinterpretation of some biblical passages such as Judges 19 could lead to the continuance of traditional hospitality rituals in certain African cultures which involve offering young women to guests for the purpose of meeting their sexual needs. Baloyi delves into Scripture to reveal the fact that the instances where women were sexually mistreated in the Bible were not condoned by God but were rather the result of the sinful actions of men. Baloyi unfortunately attempts to tackle too many things in a brief article, trying to put the sexual "hospitality" described above in the same category as levirate marriage and polygamy, combining and then flatly denouncing them all without adequately explaining the nuanced way that the biblical narrative interacts with levirate marriage and polygamy. By widening the category too much, Baloyi ends up muddying the waters and creating confusion around more complex issues when there should be complete clarity on

---

103. There are voices who resist the comparison of African cultures with Western cultures, because of the necessary reductiveness of any such categorization. See Stuit, *Ubuntu Strategies*, whose work discusses how the somewhat fluid and ever-evolving concept of *ubuntu* is understood and applied in modern South African culture. Stuit helpfully encourages those seeking to practice *ubuntu* to live in the tension between the identities of host and guest at any given time, thus balancing power dynamics and allowing a more authentic practice of what is claimed to be an ideal. But she uses the mindset of fluidity to "repudiate" (16) any impulse to compare *ubuntu* as an essentially African cultural feature with individualism as an essentially Western cultural feature. While I appreciate this consistent desire to maintain tension rather than settling for easy dichotomies, I do also think that researchers must sometimes accept functional categories as a sort of construction site scaffolding in order to compare things which they wish to analyze as they build a more complete understanding of a subject. While of course any system of categorization is fuzzy and non-absolute, hospitality in the spirit of *ubuntu* is a widely observable phenomenon in Africa and not nearly as much in the United States. This marked cultural difference is attested by many of my interviewees in chapter 3, dozens more African immigrants to the United States that I have had conversations with over the years, as well the many African authors referenced in this section. In this study, I will take heed of Stuit's warning by acknowledging often that reductive categories are not necessarily absolute but are simply a construct to help us observe, analyze, and helpfully brainstorm—in this case—how rebalancing hyperindividualism with *ubuntu* could potentially serve to ease the loneliness epidemic which is rampant in the West but seemingly non-existent in African cultures.

the titular issue at hand: sexual hospitality as sinfully objectifying women. This article serves to inform the understanding in my study that African cultures do not always practice hospitality in ways that are resonant with a biblical understanding of the idea, and this will keep the study from casting African hospitality in a naïvely perfect light.

In her doctoral dissertation, "Integrating African Christian Refugees into the American Churches as a Strategy for Mission," Grace Kathure Gichuru explores the reasons behind the fact that African Christian refugees often have difficulty integrating successfully into American churches and looks at ways to address this difficulty. The author uncovers the fact that American church leaders consider African Christians to be successfully integrated into their churches (that is, that they have a sense of belonging) when they simply attend worship services or share a building, but African Christians themselves do not consider themselves to be integrated until they form "authentic relationships" and are "active participants in the life of the church," which they rarely feel invited to do.[104] The study concludes that "hospitality is imperative to the integration of African Christian refugees into the American churches" and that this hospitality should be long-term and ought to involve "work to build relationships" and true "partnering" in church life and mission.[105] Gichuru's work skillfully brings to light the mismatched understanding of hospitality and belonging between Americans and those from African cultures. This misunderstanding leads to clarifying questions about the true definition of hospitality: is it simply sharing physical proximity for a predetermined amount of time, or does it require mutual respect and a heart-level connection? The current study will argue that the latter definition—that typically espoused by those from African cultures—is more resonant with a biblical understanding of hospitality, and that moving from a transactional to a relational view of hospitality could help to alleviate the effects of the loneliness epidemic among both immigrants and locals in churches in the USA. Gichuru's study also implicitly brings up an idea that the study at hand will make explicit: could immigrant believers be a means God will use to revitalize the American church's fellowship and outreach through a deeper and more relational understanding and practice of hospitality?

---

104. Gichuru, "Integrating African Christian Refugees," 139.
105. Gichuru, "Integrating African Christian Refugees," 191.

Review of Literature from Ethiopian Perspectives

In his treatise exploring Ethiopian intellectual traditions entitled *Qiné Hermeneutics and Ethiopian Critical Theory*, Maimire Mennasemay gives significant attention to the Ethiopian trope of *säm ena wärq*, that is, wax and gold, which derives its imagery from the jewelry making process in which a craftsman forms a wax mold and pours gold into it to achieve the desired shape. In Ethiopian hermeneutical tradition, philosophers "struggle against the given reality (what the *qiné* tradition calls *säm* [wax]) and its criteria of intelligibility and normativity in order to produce the *wärq* [gold]—the true and the good—that is immanent in the given but transcends it."[106] Mennasemay describes "indiginous associations of mutual assistance"[107] (each of which arose as responses to struggling with challenging and changing circumstances), "as an 'ideal type'"[108] of various related traditions which have the potential to incubate "emancipatory ideas, values, practices and aspirations"[109] which have "implications . . . for our understanding of civil society."[110] These systems concretize what is put forth as a value in Ethiopian proverbs quoted by Mennasemay, such as: "humanity is the cure for humanity or each is the cure for the other's pain . . . he/she is like me/I am like her/him. . . . I also am a human being. . . . One finger does not catch a fly."[111] These proverbs, and the autopoietic systems that bring them to life, provide a significant springboard for my research because of the many insights that can be drawn from modern-day examples of living in a way that embodies the interconnected interdependence of reality, and also because of an unexpected parallel between the shortcomings of "development" in Ethiopia and so called "self-development" in America—both are short-cuts that ultimately cannot achieve what they want to accomplish in a full-orbed, sustainable way because they are based on individualistic presuppositions that do not comport with the ontological nature of interconnected interdependence.

In 2019, the prime minister of Ethiopia, Dr. Abiy Ahmed, wrote a book entitled *Medemer*, explaining the typically Ethiopian synergistic way

---

106. Mennasemay, *Qiné Hermeneutics*, 1.
107. Mennasemay, *Qiné Hermeneutics*, 379.
108. Mennasemay, *Qiné Hermeneutics*, 380.
109. Mennasemay, *Qiné Hermeneutics*, 379.
110. Mennasemay, *Qiné Hermeneutics*, 380.
111. Mennasemay, *Qiné Hermeneutics*, 387.

of seeing the world that is similar to the more commonly talked about pan-African idea of *ubuntu*—that is, an understanding of the interconnected interdependence of all that is. As will be discussed further in chapter 4, this realization of interconnected interdependence is a key difference between an Ethiopian worldview and an American mindset of Enlightenment-oriented individuality and subsequent atomization, and so the book *Medemer* provides a useful articulation of this Ethiopian idea that is deeply held by Ethiopians but not often spelled out in written resources. This book will seek to explore and contextually apply relevant aspects of the idea of *medemer* in the American milieu, suggesting that this idea points to something that is missing and in need of supplementation in American culture if the loneliness epidemic is to be sustainably addressed.

Teshager Ali and Aweke Shishigu wrote "Implications of Ubuntu/Synergy for the Education System of Ethiopia" in 2020, helpfully equating the Ethiopian idea of *medemer* with the broader African *ubuntu* philosophy, further corroborating this similarity for the purposes of my research as well as thoughtfully applying the principle to education in Ethiopia, strongly suggesting that Ethiopia should refuse to accept the notion that foreign ideas should continue to be applied in the name of education, but that thoughtful contextualization of outside ideas and, further, the articulation and propagation of local ideas, is necessary. This undergirds a presupposition of this paper that historically, the one-way flow of information and teaching has tended to be from "the West to the rest." Reading Ali and Shishigu's article made plain that this is not a healthy disposition for the receivers of the information and teaching, and I argue in this book that it is also not healthy for the sources and senders of the information and teaching either. While it would not be wise to uncritically reverse the flow and declare that now all information and teaching should flow from Non-Westerners to Westerners, a mutuality of balanced sharing and a willingness of Western cultures to learn from the admirable aspects of Non-Western cultures is preferable.

In his article, "Possessions, Greed and the Christian Community: Interrogating the Prosperity Gospel in Africa in Light of Hebrews 13:1–6," Abeneazer G. Urga seeks to address an epidemic that is plaguing Ethiopia—the prosperity gospel—by exploring the "antidotes"[112] discussed in Hebrews 13:1–6, including hospitality, explaining: "Christian hospitality's focus on others rather than on self, the emphasis on sharing with those

---

112. Urga, "Possessions, Greed, and the Christian Community," 133.

who could not repay or give back a hundredfold, and the distribution or sharing of wealth and possessions to meet the needs of others rather than the accretion of wealth help counter the practices and beliefs of the prosperity gospel."[113] The prosperity gospel is an import from outside which should be recognized as unhealthily individualistic and the traditionally Ethiopian and deeply Christian identity as interconnected and interdependent through the sacrificial sharing of resources and of life through hospitality can be used to expose what is lacking in the myopic pursuit of health and wealth. My research is an attempt to demonstrate that this Ethiopian understanding of the importance of building community through hospitality is exemplary and instructive for American Christians as they seek to address the loneliness epidemic.

The Western scholars cited above have clearly demonstrated both the existence of and perils of the loneliness epidemic as well as some of the contributing reasons for its rise. The need for Christians to practice hospitality and cultivate community has also been amply discussed. The African scholars cited next have eloquently expressed the high value of hospitality as something most African cultures share in common. Hospitality is understood by these writers to have much to do with a spirit of *ubuntu* which emphasizes that all people are interconnected and that openness to connection with other people is fundamental to what it means to be human. Chronic loneliness has been identified by several of the authors as a problem in the West, and they suggest that hyperindividualism and the resultant lack or prioritization of connection with others is to blame. Every culture has blindspots and strengths, and many of these authors identify hospitality as a blindspot of Western cultures and a strength of African cultures. Gichuru shows how mismatched Western/African understandings of hospitality and belonging can lead to problems in multi-ethnic church situations, demonstrating the urgency of studying and learning from this cultural difference. Aihiokhai and Gathogo go so far as to identify an African understanding of hospitality as a necessary and helpful antidote to the loneliness epidemic faced by the West. Gathogo and Choge also express concern that if Africans do not explicitly articulate their formerly implicit value of hospitality, they may begin to lose it due to the eroding forces of globalization and modernization. Several authors do significant legwork to demonstrate the biblical resonance of a typically African understanding of hospitality. From an Ethiopian perspective, Mennasemay explicates

---

113. Urga, "Possessions, Greed, and the Christian Community," 143.

LITERATURE REVIEW

Ethiopian intellectual traditions and practices of interdependence that will be helpful in framing the discussion of addressing the American loneliness epidemic. Ahmed demonstrates that Ethiopian culture has its own expression for *ubuntu—medemer*—and that an Ethiopian understanding of interconnected interdependence comports with the other African explanations of *ubuntu*, with Ali and Shishigu corroborating this idea. Urga emphasizes the importance of hospitality in countering one of Ethiopia's own epidemics: the prosperity gospel. My study will build upon the excellent foundation laid by these scholars, seeking more input from Ethiopians through personal interviews and approaching all findings with curiosity for what is resonant with Scripture and can be instructive and transferrable or transformable for American churches as they seek to address the loneliness epidemic in America.

3

Interviews with Ethiopian Immigrants

As I considered how to research an African understanding of building community through hospitality for a primarily American audience, I realized that the ideal research subjects would be Ethiopian immigrants living in the United States. They are people who have an in-depth understanding of both Ethiopian and American culture. By virtue of having experienced a culture different than that of their homeland (or their parents' homeland), they have developed a uniquely astute insider-outsider perspective that comes from realizing that on the one hand, they fully fit in nowhere anymore, yet on the other hand, they have developed the ability to somewhat fit in anywhere. There is grief in this experience of losing one's homeland without fully gaining a feeling of "home" in another land, but there is also wisdom. It is this grief I want to honor here and this wisdom I hope to share with the American Church in the following pages.

At the beginning of my research, I conducted in-depth interviews with a few Ethiopian immigrants who have also been my close friends for some time. They reiterated some ideas that have been part of our conversations for years—ideas that have been part of the inspiration for this book topic, and also shared insights and told stories I had never heard before.[1] After interviewing them, they gave me suggestions for who I should contact next. During each interview that followed, I asked if the interviewee knew of any other Ethiopian Protestants who might be willing to participate, and if so, I asked them to connect me for the purpose

---

1. I am particularly indebted to Dr. Mehari Korcho and Mekdes Abebe Haddis, who are both excellent researchers in their own right. Those interested in this topic and other related ones would do well to follow their writings closely.

of partnering with American Protestants to lead the way in addressing the loneliness epidemic in America.[2]

I am grateful for the help of each of my interviewees, and especially those who contacted other people in their network and explained my research topic and my personal connection to the work. Friends connecting me with their friends who in turn connected me with their friends allowed me to eventually talk with a wide range of people who together contributed a multi-faceted, nuanced understanding of loneliness and building community through hospitality from the astute, insider-outsider perspective that is unique to immigrants.

The forty-three interviewees have an Ethiopian background, and forty-one of them identify as Protestant Christians (one identifies as Orthodox and one did not specify but gave answers which indicate a Christian perspective). They live in at least twenty states (a few chose not to give their location), with two having returned to Ethiopia. They range in age from late teens to mid-fifties. The majority came to the United States as adults, but several came as teenagers, a few as children, and one was born to immigrant parents who already lived in America. They shared many stories with me, some evoking pain, some nostalgia, some hope.

The following pages will analyze their responses looking for common themes as well as identifying differing threads where note-worthy. At times I have lightly edited for clarity, but my goal is to fade into the background and to let the voices of the interviewees shine through as

---

2. In the course of promoting my research in order to find more interview subjects, I was asked by some people who belong to the Ethiopian Orthodox Tewahido Church (EOTC) why I would choose to limit my research to Ethiopian Protestants. While they made a valid and insightful point that the problem of loneliness goes beyond the Protestant Church and insights for finding solutions can also be found outside of it, I deliberately chose to limit the demographics of my study for the sake of speed and real-life application: based on my marriage to an Ethiopian Protestant, I am in the Ethiopian Protestant social network, which is quite tight-knit with very few degrees of separation, so this sped my data collection along helpfully. My sphere of influence is also mostly within Protestant denominations and institutions, and my goal for this book is to provide a readable and helpful document for the people with whom I work (in higher theological education) and worship as we seek to address the loneliness epidemic in practical, day-to-day, hands-on ways in the actual churches we attend, with their particular Protestant flavor. That said, I do hope that what I have written would also be helpful for those from any faith tradition which regards the Bible as authoritative for faith and practice. I would also welcome and cheer on similar studies done in the Ethiopian Orthodox or Ethiopian Muslim communities in the United States and hope that this study will serve as an encouragement or a springboard for further research along those lines.

much as possible, as if they are all gathered around a living room savoring tiny cups of Ethiopian coffee and talking over each other convivially while reflecting on their lived experiences.

Most interviewees have been kept anonymous for the sake of their privacy, but in quoting them I acknowledge my deep debt of gratitude for their willingness to share their life stories, their struggles, and the hard-earned insights they have gained along the way in the hopes that as Christian brothers and sisters we may find some way forward together in addressing the loneliness epidemic in America.

Experiences in Ethiopia

"The Ethiopian culture is collectivist, so loneliness is very rare," says Ethiopian immigrant interviewee (EI)[3] 18.[4] "I don't think I ever used the word 'loneliness' in Ethiopia, even post-high-school," adds EI 26.[5] For the interviewees who spent significant time growing up in Ethiopia, nearly all of them said something along the lines of: "The culture in Ethiopia is community based, everything is done together," and that they did not experience loneliness there in any significant way. The few who reported loneliness generally qualified it by saying, for example, "I can't say I have never felt lonely in my country but not as severe as I felt it here [in the United States]"[6] or saying that they remember missing their school friends during summer vacation but that they were quickly comforted by neighbors and cousins.

One interviewee asserts with hyperbolic earnestness: "Just go there [Ethiopia] and you have a million friends!"[7] Another agrees: "[In Ethiopia] I always felt like everyone was my friend."[8] In addition to this, family and

---

3. Hereafter, Ethiopian immigrant interviewees will be referred to as EI 1, 2, 3, and so on, to preserve their anonymity. Basic demographic information on each interviewee can be found in Appendix D of this book.

4. Interviewed June 16, 2021.

5. Interviewed June 30, 2021.

6. EI 20, interviewed June 22, 2021.

7. EI 33, interviewed July 6, 2021. While this statement is of course hyperbolic, I can confirm the truth of its sentiment—even as a foreigner living in Ethiopia, I feel that even the fruit seller I chat with, my neighborhood taxi driver, and my plumber are my friends, with "friendship" meaning that we have a genuine gladness to see each other and that we share an active mutual interest in each other's welfare. There is very little indifference in human interactions in Ethiopian culture.

8. EI 10, interviewed June 11, 2021.

friends were "highly socially engaged"[9] and it was common "that they take time to check on [you] every day."[10] The society is geared toward being "communal and interactive"[11] and is "all about we-ness."[12]

Being a "relative" is a relative term in Ethiopia. The idea of extended family is very broad—many people who are friends are considered to be family and are called "uncles," "aunts," and "cousins." There is the sense that one's family is very large and always has potential for growth as new people spend time in one's home and become part of one's life. These people who are considered family take their role seriously when it comes to the children among them. "My neighbors . . . [fed] and [corrected] me," says EI 16, "and my [family was] happy for it!"[13] EI 5 agrees: "[I was] truly raised by my village. Shaping my character and my overall development was not just my parents' responsibility. My teachers, neighbors, distant relatives and friends of my family all took on the responsibility seriously. They all kept an eye on me at all times and cheered me on and bragged about me when I excelled like they gave birth to me."[14] EI 18 shares that hosting relatives in one's home long-term "is very common in Ethiopia," and when she moved, EI 25 reports that she "missed neighbors as much as my own parents, because [they were] part of [my] community."[15]

"It is difficult to be lonely, actually, in that set-up," says EI 42 about the communal culture of Ethiopia.[16] Lack of privacy was jokingly acknowledged: "You're always surrounded by people, whether you like it or not!" remarks EI 33. "There is no way to feel lonely in Ethiopia," agrees EI 29. "You want people to get out of your business. You're always surrounded by friends and family. . . . [E]veryone is involved, hovering around us. You WANT to be lonely in Ethiopia."[17] EI 33 sums up the pros and cons of the two cultures comparatively: "In our culture, what I didn't like was that you

9. EI 15, interviewed June 12, 2021.
10. EI 6, interviewed June 11, 2021.
11. EI 7, interviewed June 11, 2021.
12. EI 31, interviewed July 5, 2021. Interviewees seem to use the terms "collectivist" and "communal" interchangeably when referring to the Ethiopian culture's value of cultivating a lifestyle of togetherness and sharing. These terms are understood by interviewees as being the opposite of individualism.
13. Interviewed June 12, 2021.
14. Interviewed June 11, 2021.
15. Interviewed June 30, 2021.
16. Interviewed February 1, 2021.
17. Interviewed July 3, 2021.

can't even talk on the phone without someone hearing what you're saying. You have zero privacy. Here you have your privacy, but the downside of that is that you get lonely."

Most interviewees came back to the fact that beyond the superficial annoyance they sometimes felt, they deeply appreciated and missed this way of life that they now realize is not the norm everywhere: "That social life, when I was having it, I didn't realize how important it is," says EI 33. "I [didn't] even have a moment to experience loneliness and I always have someone to talk to, run into, pray with, have coffee, laugh, cry, work . . . share my life," adds EI 12.[18] This tightly knit social fabric helps to ease mental health challenges for Ethiopians living in their home country. "[There's] no such thing as psychological burden," asserts EI 1, "for everyone is there for one another."[19] EI 39 agrees, remembering: "It is like people constantly surround me, and I don't have time to think of all the negative things a mind could process, but I am busy sharing love and care with the people surrounding me."[20] EI 37 shares: "The community back there is collective and supportive. You wouldn't go a day without meeting family and friends that you would share your feelings and thoughts with or meeting random strangers that will talk to you and make you laugh."[21] EI 8 sums up: "The social system filled all of the needs [in] sorrow[ful] and joyful times."[22]

Growing up in a rural part of Ethiopia, EI 31 remarks that though his grandma who raised him practiced hospitality as a way of life, people in his village seldom used the word "hospitality" or thought about it as an abstract concept. They simply practiced it. Conversely, EI 40, who described herself as being raised as a "global citizen" in the capital city with frequent interaction with foreigners, emphasized that

> I grew up with the understanding that Ethiopia was a hospitable country. This was communicated through media, the government communicated this, there was just this idea that Ethiopians are hospitable people, we love to welcome strangers, we are kind, we always have our arms open to outsiders. It was almost like a synonym for Ethiopia—hospitality.[23]

18. Interviewed June 11, 2021.
19. Interviewed June 10, 2021.
20. Interviewed July 8, 2021.
21. Interviewed July 7, 2021.
22. Interviewed June 11, 2021.
23. Interviewed January 22, 2021.

It seems that with increased exposure to other cultures, Ethiopians increasingly realize that hospitality is not a way of life in every culture, so they tend to articulate the value more strongly in contrast to what they see in other places and people. For many interviewees, whose backgrounds fell somewhere in the middle of the spectrum between rural/traditional and global citizen, they became thoughtful as they were asked questions about hospitality in Ethiopia, struggling to separate the two from one another. As EI 41 explained: "It's mixed! When you talk about hospitality, you talk about the culture [and vice versa]!"[24]

The ancient hospitable rituals of Ethiopia have intensely spiritual undertones and remind Christian observers of biblical stories and commands. EI 31 describes his childhood home as situated in a hub for foot travel in an area that did not have roads that could accommodate cars. Very often, a traveler would stop by their house and say the expected phrase: "I am God's guest, can you host me?" His grandma would reply warmly, "Well, this is God's house. Welcome!" She would wash their feet, feed them, give them a bed for the night, make them breakfast, and pack them a lunch for the road. "There was no wondering, 'Who are they? Where are they coming from?'" he reminisces. "My grandma just told me, 'Doing this is part of us.'"[25] EI 36 agrees: "Social life is part and parcel of who we are."[26]

Other factors were noted in the explanation of the tight-knit nature of community in Ethiopia: "People don't relocate a lot [in Ethiopia]. Therefore, it represents the people's opportunity to develop and keep a deep and strong bond with each other. The adults are very involved with their community. They are often seen visiting each other for holidays, birthdays, religious gatherings, etc."[27] In addition to this, there are cultural institutions such as *iddir* (a system in which a small group of people pay monthly to amass the money needed for when one of them experiences a death in the family, and then the group pays for the funeral expenses and is there to

---

24. Interviewed July 9, 2021.

25. Though my interviewees identified as Protestant or evangelical, the majority of them, including the interviewee quoted here, are from Ethiopian Orthodox Tewahido Church (EOTC) backgrounds, and Ethiopian Orthodoxy pervades and determines much of Ethiopian cultural belief and practice, including the biblical value of building community through hospitality. For further discussion on the influence which the EOTC on the Protestant Church in Ethiopia ideas and practices, see Eshete, *Evangelical Movement in Ethiopia*, 15, 300.

26. Interviewed July 7, 2021.

27. EI 27, interviewed July 7, 2021.

support the grieving family in receiving guests at their home and taking care of the necessary logistics of loss) and *iqqub* (a savings club system in which a small group of people pay monthly into a common purse and then a rotating member of the group gets the money to make a large purchase) which increase community connection and cohesion.[28]

Ethiopia is the birthplace of coffee, and coffee is central in the practice of hospitality and communal living throughout the country. Traditionally, coffee is made three times a day, and people gather to drink it together in each others' homes. Many interviewees fondly remember being sent to knock on neighbors' doors as children to say, "*buna fältwal*" ("The coffee is boiled/ready!"). During those communal coffee breaks, says EI 40, "that was where the news broke." People would learn "who was getting married, who was sick," and EI 41 adds that people would "discuss things with each other, [asking] 'What do you do when you face this kind of thing?'"

Hospitality as a way of life provides for the needy in Ethiopia without sacrificing their dignity. Many interviewees told stories of their family members often telling needy people in their community, "The coffee is ready!" Then when they would join those drinking coffee, the host would casually say: "Whoever wants to eat lunch, we have some, too!" EI 40 said of her grandmother: "She knew that would be their only meal for the day. But she wasn't like, 'Hey, you're poor, come and let me feed you. It was more like, you're my friend, and there's something I know that's lacking that I'm going to cover without making you feel inferior.'" In fact, Ethiopians make a point to treat even those with the least material resources with careful dignity. Mekdes Abebe Haddis[29] recalls:

> Being brought up in an economically growing country meant I was always around the needy. I regularly ran into people who asked for their daily bread when I was walking to school or driving to go meet a friend for coffee. In Ethiopia we call those individuals *yene bete*, a term that translates to "my kind" or "those like me." In fact, my parents scolded my siblings and me if we ever used the term *beggar* to describe someone in need. This term *yene bete* is used to acknowledge the *imago Dei* in others

---

28. For more on *iddir* and *iqqub*, see chapter 4 of this text.

29. Most interviewees are kept anonymous, but Mekdes Abebe Haddis writes publicly on her upbringing in Ethiopia and contributes to this chapter as EI 40 and through her recently published book, quoted below.

and remind ourselves that we are no different from those who temporarily lack material goods.[30]

In the West, one interviewee observed that in order to visit someone, "you have to call them, arrange an appointment," while in Ethiopia "you can just go, walk in, you are welcome, you will have coffee, there may be food, you can stay as long as you want."[31] Rather than focusing on a formal meal which had been planned in advance, the general sense that interviewees gave was that the hospitality practiced by their families in Ethiopia had less to do with food and drink (though if it was there, it would be shared) and more to do with "making people feel at home and comfortable around us."[32]

Ethiopia has a long history as a fiercely independent nation with isolationist tendencies. This, combined with the fact that Ethiopia was never colonized, has created the dynamics necessary for an ancient culture to be largely preserved into the modern day.[33] Only very recently has the country become more porous, with increased back-and-forth travel by Ethiopian immigrants and the abrupt advent of smartphones available in even the most rural areas when a few decades ago it was hard to find internet of any kind outside of city centers. As the country has focused intently on modernization and economic advancement, urbanization and globalization have begun to have their effects, leading to a decline in the hospitable ways of the past and also to an accompanying unease that something important is being lost, without a clear idea of what "it" is and how to recover it.

While reminiscing about the centrality of hospitality in his childhood, EI 31 concludes: "That was my experience growing up. It may not be like that now." Many others echoed this uneasy uncertainty about how modern-day Ethiopia is gradually losing the ingrained practices of hospitality. EI 27 suggests that traditionally, having less work allows more time for community involvement, saying that: "Most adults don't have very demanding jobs and, in some cases, no jobs at all; therefore, this gives people more time to socialize." Traditional hospitality also does somewhat depend on the mother of the family staying home, which is less and less possible in the modern day. In Ethiopia, says EI 41, "things are changing, with many husbands and

---

30. Haddis, *Just Mission*, 123.
31. EI 41.
32. EI 31.
33. For more information on the history of Ethiopia, start with Zewde, *History of Modern Ethiopia*; Pankhurst, *Ethiopians*.

wives both working and so they hire help to be with their kids, and they themselves are not home." There are also wider forces at play in the shift away from traditional hospitality in Ethiopia: EI 34 lists "global cultural influence, secularism, or change in the living situation by the society" as possible factors, saying that "in current times there is cultural change by the communities, and one can sense that the way strangers are treated is lacking [compared to] the traditional approach."[34]

I would argue that it is understandably challenging for Ethiopians who have never been out of Ethiopia to discern the pitfalls and shortcomings of the Western cultural norms that come to them dressed in the seductive trappings of luxury, modernity, and cosmopolitan cachet. Having not experienced significant loneliness themselves, they cannot fully foresee the dark underbelly of loneliness that accompanies an uncritical move toward materialism, hyperindividualism, and task-orientation. But there are other Ethiopians who do understand the nuances and potential pitfalls of uncritically exchanging Ethiopian culture for Western culture: Ethiopian immigrants living in the West. Listening to Ethiopian immigrants is crucial both for Westerners who are already in the grips of the loneliness epidemic, and for Ethiopians living in Ethiopia who—if trends continue in the way that they are going—run the risk of not knowing what they have until it is gone.[35]

Talking about hospitality as an abstract concept, however, is somewhat foreign even for Ethiopian immigrants, based on their background in which it was assumed and so was seldom examined or articulated: "Living in Ethiopia, I didn't mean to be hospitable, it's just how we do it, how we live life. It's more of the identity of the communal understanding of life. I don't think that there's much consciousness of really framing or naming the concept. . . . It's included in loving one another and helping one another, but it's not that much conceptualized" says EI 31 reflecting upon his family's lifestyle of hospitality.

In a sense, theorizing and conceptualizing individual ideas removed from their contexts and communities, as it were, is a decidedly Western

---

34. Interviewed July 6, 2021.

35. As an American living in Ethiopia, these trends of uncritically following Western norms of materialism, individualism, and task-orientation are painful to witness, and as such, I hope this study tangentially presents a cautionary tale to Ethiopians living in Ethiopia regarding the isolation and loneliness they may have to grapple with if they do not actively articulate and hold on to their value of building community through hospitality while pursuing economic advancement.

thing to do that sometimes frustrates Non-Westerners, who often prefer to talk about ideas in a more holistic and context-connected way. And yet, in a globalized age where more and more Ethiopians are being educated in the West or at least being exposed to Western models of thinking, it may be helpful to do some work "in a scholarly sense, theorizing and conceptualizing"[36] in order to bring something useful from the implicit into the explicit realm, for the purpose of protecting and promoting hospitality like an endangered species so that it can be appreciated rather than quietly going extinct.

Experience in America

Before immigrating to America, EI 26 described loneliness as his "blind spot," meaning that he never thought about it and did not have a category for it when living in Ethiopia, and so he was unprepared for the experience of loneliness in America. Several others acknowledged the fact that they might have had unreasonably high expectations coming from a place where hospitality is a hallmark of the culture to a place where it is not. In the initial months and even years, loneliness is a point of commonality between nearly all immigrants, since immigration necessarily means leaving all that is familiar and needing to rebuild one's network of friends and system of social support.

Several interviewees shared with some pain that one of the hardest things for them to adjust to in America was the fact that people would be friendly at first but would not progress in friendship the way to which Ethiopians are accustomed. This left them vacillating between wondering if they had done something wrong and being offended that they were not being valued in the way that they believed a person inherently should be. EI 32, who was born in America to recently arrived immigrant parents, reports that for a long while, his father thought his co-workers hated him because they would simply greet him with a nod of the head, not taking time to greet him and ask how he was doing. Then he realized that they were treating each other that way as well, not just him, and he was able to recognize that a cultural difference was at play. At first he would try to interact with people based upon his background, greeting them and asking them about themselves and their families, but then he started to give the same treatment back to others in order to fit in.[37]

36. EI 31.
37. Interviewed July 6, 2021.

EI 41 tells about a day soon after he moved into his first apartment in America. "Someone met me in the elevator and asked: 'Where are you from?' And I told him and he said, 'Don't worry, if you need anything, let me know, I can help you.'" The interviewee felt very glad to have a friend in his apartment building, but the next day, when they saw each other again and the interviewee tried to talk with him, he just walked by. "And he never talked to me again," he recounts, still astonished. "For us, this is very shocking. In Ethiopia, maybe you wouldn't have even promised help during the first meeting, but if you did, and then you just passed by the person without saying anything the next time, there would have to be some sort of issue [between you and them]."

The same interviewee says he eventually learned through this and other interactions that in American culture, the unwritten code of conduct can be summed up, "If I need something or I need to get something from you, I talk to you, but after that, that's it." What this interviewee is describing is a "transactional" view of relationships, viewed as "superficial" by many Ethiopians, which is common in America and which is displayed in several other accounts shared by interviewees. This may explain why loneliness seems to be something that has persisted among most interviewees many years after immigrating to the United States, meaning Ethiopian immigrants are not immune to the loneliness epidemic being experienced by locals but are suffering from it as well. Because of their previous experiences, many interviewees question the system in America, trying to find reasons for the unfamiliar feelings of loneliness they experience here despite physically settling and appearing to have adjusted. EI 42 laments the fact that Americans "want information" rather than to truly become friends. They ask questions "to be informed about you, not necessarily to have an ongoing relationship with you. So the information is the stage at which they say 'Ok, I know him enough.' And there is a boundary there. Ethiopians go beyond information, not only being informed about another person, but actually living with that person, having an ongoing relationship."

Instead of the Ethiopian reality of "community—people are always there," the majority of interviewees relate having to adjust to the American perspective of "you are on your own, but if you *really* need it, I can help you."[38] EI 31 describes the cultural difference between Ethiopia and America this way: "[In America] if you don't call for help, it's difficult to get help, but it was automatic in Ethiopia." This reality led to the dark question: "If you're

---

38. EI 43, interviewed July 7, 2021.

missed back home, people will come to your home (it even annoys you!), but if people die here, how long will it take for others to find them?"

A young interviewee describes the differences between the way Americans versus other international students welcomed her when she began attending American school: "For me when I first joined school, people around me were nice, meaning if I had asked for help they would help. However I haven't met any American who would approach me to offer help or make me feel hospitality. I got that more from Ethiopian and other international classmates."[39] From these accounts and more, it seems that in Ethiopia the onus is on the helper to notice the one who needs help, while in America the one who needs help must get others' attention to get the help they need.

EI 31 mentioned specifically that Americans who are struggling emotionally tend to automatically go to professional counselors to sort out their situation, potentially bypassing friends who could have lent a listening ear. While this interviewee was not suggesting that mental health counseling has no place, he muses that perhaps "hospitality is substituted by professional counseling [in America]. When you are lonely and you struggle, the thought that comes to mind is 'I need counseling' [rather than, 'I need to talk to my friends.']." He concludes: "With so many things being professionalized in this nation, whatever needs you have, there are systems for them in this country, and people can easily go for professional help rather than coming to one another, praying together and all that."

Speaking about the focus on privacy in the United States, EI 43 quips: "Minding business has become standing at a far distance." This distance feels foreign and confusing, and the loss of a sense of neighborliness in general is painful to many interviewees. "Here, nobody knocks on your door," says EI 33. "The fact that neighbors are not considered as friends (especially if living in apartments) was so strange to me," adds EI 39.

Busyness was listed by many as the reason why loneliness causes more of a problem in America than it does in Ethiopia. "People are very busy," says EI 27.[40] "Therefore loneliness creeps in when one can't find someone available to share their fear, happiness, weakness, hope, and even goof around freely without being judged." EI 12 adds: "Everyone's lives are so occupied with their own personal things and they don't seem to bother to listen to their neighbor's challenges. So while in the midst of a

---

39. EI 35, interviewed July 6, 2021.
40. Interviewed July 1, 2021.

crowd you feel loneliness." EI 26 mentions getting to know someone to the point that "I thought he/she was my friend, but the next time, he or she just passes by as if nothing had happened. I thought we would hug [and spend time greeting each other and catching up]. What did I do wrong?" EI 30 laments: "Here everyone is busy with work. Nobody has time to listen to your feelings and problems. They don't even ask you how you are doing by taking their time. Don't get me wrong, they say hi, or how are you, however, they are gone before your answer to their question as they don't have time to listen to your problem."[41]

This particular interaction: an American saying "How are you?" to an Ethiopian but moving on quickly rather than really listening to the response or asking follow-up questions (as would be typical in the extended greeting style of Ethiopian culture), was reported by many Ethiopians as a confusing and depressing aspect of their culture shock experiences. Several also added that being asked repeatedly when they were going back to their countries—even by well-meaning people—made them feel acutely unwelcome in the United States.

Being too busy for good interpersonal communication was not given as the only factor in Ethiopian immigrants' wrangle with loneliness after moving to the United States. Some interviewees feel a sense of sad empathy for those within American culture: "People here live far apart, making it hard to hang out with them with one's free time, too busy with work and personal problems, and the stress of making a living," explains EI 27. "People [in America] are good for the most part." says EI 22, "but togetherness almost doesn't exist."[42] Some interviewees were honest about the ways that they themselves have changed as they adjusted to American culture's pressure to stay busy:

> When I first moved to America, I was shocked by the fact that my host didn't know her neighbors and in general was too busy to have any meaningful deep connections with anyone. Gradually I became accustomed to what I call an individualistic lifestyle. I decided to focus on school, subsequently graduated from college and I too now am very busy. It is rare that people come over to my house to socialize. Yes, I feel lonely at times.[43]

---

41. Interviewed July 5, 2021.
42. Interviewed June 26, 2021.
43. EI 14, interviewed June 12, 2021.

Others question the supposed busyness of Americans as covering a deeper difference in cultural values: "Everyone kept saying 'I'm sorry we are just so busy.' I've never heard the word busy being overly used as it was being here. People just said they were busy even when they weren't. Then I quickly realized the value of interactions and having people around was just limited."[44] Coming from a culture where hospitality naturally happened, many interviewees experienced "culture shock [that] you need a reason to visit your friends at their home. In Ethiopia you can go anytime and you are welcome."[45]

According to EI 2, "the fear of strangers does not exist in Ethiopia." EI 36 agrees: "Ethiopians tend to open their doors for strangers and trust you very soon. Americans don't trust strangers." Indeed, EI 10 adds, "I was shocked to learn that [in America] you can be shot on sight if you trespass on the wrong house. In Ethiopia, it was common to walk through strangers' yards and even stand in their shaded porch to escape rain or sun." Security issues in America were acknowledged by several interviewees as preventing full trust of strangers, and a few also mentioned that security issues are becoming an increased concern in Ethiopia as well, particularly in urban centers, but that the issue was much more top-of-mind in America.

Many interviewees mentioned that other immigrants were the ones who primarily helped them to adjust to American culture. Those who were fortunate enough to move to places that had sizable Ethiopian populations report that their own communities have been places of support and comfort, though being in a new country did somewhat change the dynamics of their interactions with each other. "The Ethiopian community in diaspora is still an anchor to me," says EI 20. EI 30 adds: "With prayer, and being connected with Ethiopians in my area, I was able to manage the depression I had because of loneliness." Some who did not have other Ethiopians to connect with found themselves drawn to other African immigrants: "I mostly ended up with black, refugee friends," says EI 29, an interviewee who immigrated in high school. "Somalis, Sudanese—Africans stick together!"

Some interviewees have found also commonality with Asian immigrants. When EI 29 travels back to Ethiopia and her old friends tell her she's been "Americanized" she laughs and says, "No, I've actually been Asian-ified" because the majority of her close cross-cultural friendships in America have been with those from Asian backgrounds. EI 31 says that, with Asians,

---

44. EI 2, interviewed June 10, 2021.
45. EI 13, interviewed June 11, 2021.

"I also was able to relate more, because they didn't worry too much about my personal space, which for those who are raised here, not anything negative, [but] they don't want to overstep. But these Asians, they overstepped, and that's what I needed!" This interviewee posits that "for Asians and Ethiopians, it is part of their life, you cannot survive without hospitality." There is also a commonality between immigrants no matter where they come from because they understand what it means to be transplanted into new soil. Other immigrants "understood what it means to move to a new place where you don't speak the language very well," says EI 35.

Though some interviewees did not speak English when they relocated to America, some spoke it very well, and this caused different problems related to expectations. "I felt that I was adequately well-versed in American culture, so I shouldn't have a problem being accepted or welcomed," shares EI 40. "But then I'm like, 'Hey, I'm one of your guys,' and they're like, 'We have questions, why do you speak English so well?'"

Though it seems that other immigrants—those from Ethiopia and from other countries—have been the primary people responsible for helping the interviewees, there are a few born-and-raised American people who stood out to them for their welcoming attitudes and who they were careful to mention with gratitude. A few mention positive experiences attending American churches. Some joined international student ministries led by Americans who were intentional about creating space for relationships. One interviewee tells of a church who hosted his family and gave them housing for three months,[46] and another of a church that was "so generous that they gave us everything we needed, such as furniture, appliances, and clothes."[47] EI 18 says that on her first day of school, "The children and teachers were very welcoming and took extra steps to make me feel comfortable. I did not understand English, but I understood kindness." EI 42 recalls that the pastor of the American church he started attending would visit him at his student apartment each week, coming, coffee in hand, "not with any agenda, just to be a friend, to make sure I'm doing ok." EI 20 says that eventually, after years of searching, "I was able to find dear friends who are insightful and able to guide me through the culture if I ask them to."

Though a few interviewees expressed deep gratitude for the way American churches welcomed their families in practical ways, providing them with furniture and orientation to life in America over the course of

46. EI 32.
47. EI 18.

months, several others expressed pain regarding their experiences trying to find a sense of belonging in American churches, mainly related to the depth—or lack thereof—of interactions over time. EI 12 started attending church immediately after arriving and "even joined a small home group right away, [but] everything was shallow. Nothing goes beyond the meeting time." In analyzing why this might be, she mused: "Yes, they will share available resources, but they themselves weren't available."[48]

EI 20 describes that even after attending a church for a long while, few people would say hello to her, and those that did had "just a plastic smile and not paying full attention." One interviewee had completely positive things to say about the international student ministry that welcomed him,[49] while another international student (who happened to attend the same American seminary) shares that after being in America for several months, he perceived that "a lot of the [initial] welcoming was ceremonial, just for that specific time, and then when the welcome season was over, everybody was gone, and I had a lot of negative experiences."[50] He concluded that though the movie nights, game nights, and special events put on by the school were fun, they did not fill his need for deep and daily community, which he calls "natural and organic fellowship and hospitality."

Several interviewees report a shift they experienced when they began to create community in the United States rather than simply long for it. Rather than waiting to be welcomed, they began creating spaces of welcome within their spheres of influence.[51] EI 26 said that the international

---

48. For more on immigrants struggling to integrate into American churches, see Gichuru, "Integrating African Christian Refugees."

49. EI 34.

50. EI 31.

51. Urga, *Reflection on Diaspora Cross-Cultural Evangelism*, 39–40, has this counsel for African Christian immigrants—whom he calls "Diaspora Gospel workers"—who are working through their own loneliness yet trying to cultivate community through hospitality in the West: "The third obstacle a Diaspora believer faces in cross-cultural ministry is loneliness. It is an undeniable fact that the West is ultra-individualistic and explicitly postmodern. The Diaspora Gospel workers, who have come from a communal society that celebrates sharing, extended meetings, and unstructured and unlimited face-to-face conversation, has been challenged, appalled and affected by it. This environment, especially in the West, has driven many immigrants to withdrawal, bitterness, depression, flagrant sins and suicide. Recently, an old man from my neighboring country was found dead in his house and nobody knew about it until a few weeks later. If this was in his country he would have been buried on the same or the next day. Because of the me-centered, secluded life in the West, many Africans have embraced the media as a way of escape. Some watch TV 24/7. At least it helps them temporarily

student ministry at his school helped him. Then in passing a few minutes later, he mentioned that he *started* the international student ministry at his school along with a few other (mostly international) classmates. EI 42 shares: "As I continued to live in the States, I began to do hospitality, reverse hospitality. Instead of [locals] coming to me, I went to them to invite them." He was surprised to find out what nearly always happened after he broke the ice with Americans by inviting them to his home: "After I invited them over to my place, the first thing I heard was, 'Now we would like to have you over to our place.'"

EI 29 expressed longing and frustration as she and her husband struggled to live out their value of hospitality in the American context:

> We love community and we know we need people and need to support each other in this life. We know we need to live the Christian life together. Because we [immigrants from Non-Western countries] know the value [of hospitality], it's easier for us [to prioritize it in the midst of a busy life]. We tried to be creative, but no one was interested [in some of our efforts]. [A lot of] what we are trying is not working. We still try [with the perspective of] if you are opening your home and cooking, it's hard for people to say no.

Though she struggles with feeling lonely herself, EI 12 reports that "now I do all that I can do to make myself available to anyone. And it takes a lot of courage and breaking barriers." EI 25 shares: "The biggest thing I struggled with was: 'Where do I belong?' My heart has always been finding people who don't feel like they belong: they belong in Jesus, in my heart, in my home. Because of my pain and my journey, my heart is open to them. Home is where your heart is, you belong in my heart."

---

forget the piercing pain of their unmet need to socialize and be human. The fast-paced, individualistic culture that highlights individual rights, comfort and personal freedom has killed the communal, passionate Africans' zeal in preaching the Gospel to their neighbors. Individualism has not benefited the Westerners themselves, let alone the Africans. As I mentioned, it has driven many to addictions and suicide. It has created lack of accountability and disseminated the idea of selfishness and self-absorption. This dismal aspect of Western society has crippled gifted preachers, prayer warriors and evangelists from Africa, preventing them from becoming effective cross-cultural workers. In order to combat this, I believe Diaspora believers should learn how the people in the host culture meet and socialize in order to share the Gospel in a relevant way. We, as Africans, need to pick up on the cues and grasp the system people are operating in if we hope to lead many to the community of God. These days many of those who seem to glory in individualism are actually hungry for relationships, meaningful and extended face-to-face time with others. They struggle with anxiety because they lack relationships with God as well as with their neighbor."

Comparing Ethiopian versus American Understandings of Hospitality and Community

When asked whether an Ethiopian understanding of hospitality/community is different than an American understanding of the same concepts, nearly all interviewees answered affirmatively. "Hospitality is so ingrained [in Ethiopian culture] that it's almost like second nature to most people," says EI 10, whereas "in America, it seems like the concept is understood by a few as opposed to the culture as a whole." One of the only interviewees[52] who said she did not see a difference nuanced her answer historically by saying:

> I don't think so. I see a lot of similarities in an understanding of hospitality/community in undeveloped and developing countries. This leads me to believe maybe Americans forgot or let go of their hospitality and sense of community due to a cultural shift. More people now work, go to school, move to another state or country due to work/school in America, so they have gotten so busy, too self-focused they've let go of their hospitality along the way.

EI 20 observes that Ethiopian hospitality emphasizes the non-physical aspect of making others feel welcome. "They invite you home, try to chat with you and make you feel belongingness, give you a call, connect you with others, etc." By contrast, the same interviewee says that "Americans [in order to be hospitable], after they know you well try to help you with the material thing you lack," citing the example of a couple they knew who gave them a used car when the need arose. This generous sharing of resources as opposed to sharing of self is reiterated by EI 12, who observes: "In America, people will connect you with organizations that could fulfill your needs, but they themselves have very limited time or interest in getting to know you, understand you, or be there for you." EI 40 agrees: "Hospitality is not about the material stuff, it's about sharing yourself." Two people brought up an Ethiopian proverb summing these ideas up succinctly: "A welcoming face is better than a well-prepared meal."[53]

EI 25 shared earnestly that though she sees people in America coming together to support people when bad things happen (deaths in the family, for example), "People will need help after the whole commotion is over. Being part of each others' lives versus 'I will jump in when you need me, and if you don't need me, I won't.'" EI 31 sums up: "To me hospitality

---

52. EI 27.
53. EI 12 and EI 20.

doesn't have to do with just addressing my physical needs. It has to do with creating a space for me so I can be with you. Whatever comes after that is secondary, but first of all, do I have the freedom to share your personal space? That's what hospitality is for me."

Ethiopian hospitality seems to break the ice in such a way that deepening friendship occurs naturally. "In Ethiopian hospitality," says EI 3, "if we are introduced once next time we meet we have already broken the ice so there's no need to act as strangers again. But in the American culture these introductions seem to take longer and each time we meet we start from the beginning (in most cases, I know there are exceptions)."[54] Perhaps part of what allows the ice to stay broken, as it were, is the regularity of Ethiopian hospitality in contrast to the more formal, pre-planned hospitality of Americans: "In America," says EI 14, "it feels that hospitality is something you have to plan for in advance to find time and figure out what you are going to do which in my mind adds unnecessary work and complications." By contrast, "in Ethiopia it's part of life." EI 31 agrees:

> In the USA, it's more about entertaining, intentionally planning to do some things, and what that tells you is that it is not necessarily part of the culture, it doesn't happen if you just go about living your own life. This means that the culture made it an optional thing. It's still a good thing in the culture, but you can do your life without it."

There is also a difference in host/guest dynamics. On the one hand, as EI 18 posits: "The American understanding of hospitality is centered around the comfort of the host, not the guest. The host must be comfortable, know who's coming, how long they're staying, etc.," whereas in Ethiopia the focus is on the comfort of the guest. Interestingly, on the other hand, another interviewee and I had a mutually revelatory moment when we realized that in America the guest is the one who feels the most honored because they were invited, whereas in an Ethiopian mindset, the hosts are the ones who receive the honor because the guest enters their home.[55] Another interviewee reiterated this idea: "It is a privilege for me to be able to host."[56]

If these observations are accurate, then in America, the host is comfortable and the guest is honored (because he has been invited), whereas in Ethiopia the guest is comfortable and the host is honored. In this case,

---

54. Interviewed June 10, 2021.
55. EI 41.
56. EI 40.

it would make sense why Americans often say to others, "We should get together sometime! We'd love to catch up with you!" even when they do not follow through and actually arrange a meeting time due to busyness. In the American model, through saying something like this the honor of hospitality is being conveyed—the guest is being theoretically invited—while the theoretical host is maintaining her comfort by not over-scheduling herself. In an Ethiopian mindset, however, no honor or comfort are received until people are actually together under one roof.

Some interviewees expressed some qualms about the mechanics of the Ethiopian practice of hospitality. In fact, Ethiopians themselves are not always cheerful about their particular style of hospitality. According to EI 18: "If an individual is uncomfortable with a guest and their stay, they will never address the issue openly as it is considered shameful [but] people often privately complain about the toll the culture (hospitality) takes on them." EI 21 mentioned that after being the United States, he has become used to the concept of "potluck" (that is, everyone contributing something to a gathering so that no one is over-burdened) and so "whenever I go back to Ethiopia I feel 'suffocated.'"[57]

EI 31, who was born in the United States to Ethiopian parents, observed with a mixture of respect and disbelief: "They don't even let the guest move! It's like 5-star service. They go above and beyond for others." Hospitality with "no boundaries" was mentioned by a few interviewees as something that felt extreme and was difficult to practice. EI 39 reflects on boundaries: "While Ethiopians get involved in people's lives to make them feel at home, Americans give you space to decide (choose things) for yourself. Giving space could be a good thing, but I was not used to it when I first moved [to America], and so I was confused." EI 40 pushes back on those with critiques of Ethiopian hospitality by explaining that going above and beyond to care for a guest is "done to make that person feel that they are at home, whereas in the US it's kind of like 'Help yourself to whatever is available!' It's like taking leftovers rather than sharing from [the best of] what I have."

Many interviewees expressed that hospitality was simply an integral part of Ethiopian culture. They had not tried to absorb it—it was simply part of them. "[Hospitality] is all about cultural heredity in Ethiopia. People just do what grandparents have been doing," says EI 22. By contrast, "[In America], the lifestyle doesn't allow it to a certain extent. That's why we go

57. Interviewed June 23, 2021.

in an individual direction. You have to go out of your way [to practice hospitality]. That's why [Americans] struggle [to practice hospitality]. From the beginning [community] was not a value. So why would they want to go out of their way to be in that situation?"[58]

Several interviewees suggested that the differences in the understanding of hospitality between Americans and Ethiopians pointed to a deeper difference in values, that community is valued more highly by Ethiopians than by Americans. EI 29 asserts: "I don't think community really exists in the US. It's like a checkmark, go to church, check, go to Bible study, check. That's it. We are busy. Individualistic." Though churches try to start things called "community groups" and talk about "community" a lot, says this interviewee, "[Americans] don't have that value system. Community is being pushed on them."

For Ethiopians who immigrate to America, it is no wonder that it is a shock and a challenge to have to bring their value of hospitality and community from the implicit to the explicit realm. According to many interviewees, before immigrating, they did not have a category to think abstractly about the value of hospitality: it was like the air they breathed. "In Ethiopia, hospitality is more practice than concept or theory," says EI 31, "but in the USA, it's more concept and theory than it is practice. You read a lot about it, you hear a lot about it, but you don't see a lot of the practice." The same interviewee muses: "When people practice hospitality in America, they are intentional about it, but I don't think people back home are. They just think, 'I'm just living!'"

Simply put, all forty-three interviewees conveyed the idea that in Ethiopia, hospitality and community are ideas that are supported and encouraged by the culture, while in America, they are counter-cultural ideas. Hospitality and community cannot be cultivated in the United States, therefore, without intentionality. The hospitable American individuals who the Ethiopian interviewees had encountered had practiced their hospitality intentionally, many through a commitment to swim upstream in accordance with the values of their Christian faith.

---

58. EI 29.

Biblical Basis for an Ethiopian Understanding of Hospitality and Community

Forty-one of my interviewees identified as Protestant Christians (with one identifying as Orthodox and one not specifying but giving answers which indicated a Christian perspective), and their understanding of hospitality was self-reportedly linked to biblical commands which they explained to be deeply embedded in their culture due to the 4th century merging of the Ethiopian Orthodox Tewahido Church with the state to the point that religious culture and societal culture were somewhat indistinguishable for centuries.[59] The majority of my interviewees were quick to express that hospitality is part and parcel of the Christian life, with hospitality being merely the practical expression of love. One interviewee summed up: "Being hospitable is simply the way we live the word of God, and the means of showing how good our God is. Love holds everything together, and there is no good love without being hospitable." Both the interviewees' prioritization of and practice of hospitality were revealed in my interviews to be fundamentally connected to the idea of the stranger as God's guest, and all people as made in God's image.

Living an inhospitable Christian life was incomprehensible to every interviewee: "There is no meaning to Christianity without being hospitable," says EI 1, and EI 26 asserts that hospitality is "not optional but mandatory for Christians." EI 3 says: "Our hospitality is the way we make strangers feel welcomed: it is the heart of God's kingdom." The idea of being foreigners welcomed into God's kingdom was mentioned several times as well, with EI 26 noting that "the Bible is a book for strangers!"

Many interviewees expressed the idea that our hospitality toward others is an overflow of our experience of God's hospitality toward us. Regarding the Christian practice of hospitality, EI 31 asked: "Why do you do it? It's not because you will get favor. But because that's who you are! You were welcomed, and you bring nothing in return to God. As Christians, we need to reflect upon the meta-story, the grand story, for how God's

---

59. Esler, *Ethiopian Christianity*, 4, remarks that from "around 335 CE, until 1974, the Ethiopian Church [specifically the EOTC] and the Ethiopian monarchy existed continuously and in close relationship with one another." As such, "it is fair to say that the central national institutions that sustained Ethiopia for so long were the monarchy and the church, while the theological, intellectual, literary, and artistic traditions of Ethiopian Orthodoxy constituted the core of a national culture that provided a distinctive and durable identity, even when faced with major external or internal challenges."

hospitality created this space and the opportunity for us to belong to God and to one another."

EI 36 integrates the teachings of Jesus and James: "Jesus told us in the last days we will not be judged by the confession of our mouths, but by our deeds, what did you do when I was a stranger. Even if we know that it is not what saves us, but our faith should be demonstrated. It is not part of the salvation package, but it is an evidence that we are saved by grace. Treating strangers well is part and parcel of the Christian faith."

Several others emphasized that strangers should be welcomed regardless of their "race, social and economic status"[60] based upon the *imago Dei* and also upon the teaching of Hebrews 13:3: "We don't know who we are receiving or welcoming. Today they may be needy, but tomorrow we don't know who those people are going to be."[61] As will be explored further in chapter 4, ancient Ethiopian culture and other ancient African cultures are in sync with this teaching:

> In very traditional rural Ethiopia, there is this biblical concept enshrined in the culture. They might not quote the book of the Bible, Hebrews 13, but they definitely have it in their culture. What happens is, if you are a guest in the community, it doesn't matter who you are, the color of your face, whether you're old or young, if you're in a village at night, you'll be given the best place in the house. You'll be treated as the head of the household, like a king. You'll be well-fed, no matter how meager the resources in the household. The stranger is the messenger of God. We were once strangers and we might be strangers again as well, even if the system was corrupted by fighting and exploited this opening, contaminated it, but still back home if you are homeless or a stranger, you will be welcomed in the society.[62]

Suggestions for Addressing the Loneliness Epidemic in America

When asked, "What needs to change for people to be less lonely in America?" many responded immediately with some version of, "That is the million dollar question!" After pondering the question, however, each participant

---

60. EI 37.
61. EI 42.
62. EI 37.

contributed their helpful "two cents" to begin mapping a way forward in addressing the loneliness epidemic in the United States.

Church teaching was cited as a major way that people could be equipped to cultivate community through hospitality, because in addressing the loneliness epidemic, "We should pave the way for the world by starting it in the church."[63] Teaching about loneliness and the importance of building community through hospitality would "create awareness"[64] about the problem as well as beginning to address it. Small groups were seen as a helpful tool in doing this, though not as an end in themselves, because "Community is more than just meeting up once on Sunday and once on Wednesday, it's living life together."[65] Beyond teaching, the very organization of the church community itself could contribute to hospitality. According to EI 31:

> We have to organize our church community in a way that we are creating a space for people to experience hospitality, I think it has to start in the church. I call it sharing space rather than creating space. We all have personal space, so hospitality is to share that space, making people feel welcome. It's not outside of me, it has to take from my personal space in order to do it. The very idea of hospitality challenges me to really share my life, my comfort, my time, my resources, and all of that (that's what I call sharing of personal space). We all need a space where we feel freedom, nobody touches this. I don't think we should give up everything. But there are times that we have to share with other people.

EI 34 agrees: "I recommend a hospitality team in each Christian church. The strangers should be connected to the ministries and their questions answered. It's also important that the American people listen to the perspective of the newcomers." EI 40 adds that though she feels hope when observing the increased desire for community amongst Millennials and Gen-Z, she also feels concern that the church is often overly focused on simply creating programs that are task-oriented in nature, going through pre-set agendas rather than actually getting involved in each others' lives:

> [Designing these programs] comes from a really good place because the church does have a responsibility to make sure that people are in community and in the word of God, but I think

---

63. EI 34.
64. EI 30.
65. EI 29.

that limits people to think ok check, on Wed night I have been to a Bible study, so I have been "relational," so they think, and I have done my Bible study, I have a community, and that's it, and if for six days they don't see a soul except at work and taking care of their kids, and if there's no other thing that kind of muddies up their schedule, it's ok. And I feel like that's very transactional, when you only see someone for one specific thing. But when you think about relational, you think about your best friend, you call each other for whatever reason, you're having a bad day, you say "pray for me," that's a real relationship.

The same interviewee suggests that Americans learn from Non-Westerners in order to catch a vision of what building community through hospitality could look like:

The view of hospitality I have is from what I saw, it was modeled to me, therefore, it is easier for me to think about it and try to do it, not that I do it perfectly but at least I have an idea of what I'm working with, so if Western hospitality is the only thing that has been modeled to people, then that's all they know. So my advice would be, go and be a stranger somewhere else. Go and be a minority in a place that doesn't reflect your culture, your language, and you may not have to go on a mission trip to experience that. I actually am an advocate for saying, "go to the neighborhood immigrant church," There are many that are thriving and loving the Lord, just go and see what you get there. You may not understand the sermon, you may not understand the music, but you will know that you are being loved, you will know that people are going way out of their way to make you comfortable, on the spot make sure you have an interpreter or something and have you eat before you go. And I can say that with confidence, just knowing from all the immigrant friends that I have and immigrant pastors that I know. So just see how that makes you feel and then try to imitate that at your church when you see somebody standing alone that looks like they don't belong.

Growing in relationality was also a common response regarding how to address the loneliness epidemic. Instead of seeing people as "problems" to be solved, believers should "value the importance of having others welcomed in their homes and lives." This will entail "be[ing] open for interruptions" and "open[ing] our lives and our calendars" to make ourselves "available for people," moving away from merely "scheduled, hurried meetings."⁶⁶ EI 14 encourages: "Don't make it more complicated than it needs to be. Enjoy conversations."

Growing in simplicity was also suggested as a way forward to cultivate community through hospitality. The system in America is seen by many interviewees as creating loneliness, because "the need to achieve the American dream keeps people on a perpetual treadmill of working to gain more, not sharing, and further isolation."⁶⁷ EI 7 agrees: "Christians should not be carried away by an earthly lifestyle. . . . [W]herever there is less sharing in love, more loneliness arises."

From a typically Ethiopian perspective, EI 7 asserts that "Western individualistic ideology" is indicative of "selfishness," which "needs to end to build community."⁶⁸ He quotes an Ethiopian proverb which says, "He who eats alone will die lonely," concluding that "loneliness is oftentimes a form of harvesting what one plants," and that the remedy to this is "being less self-centered." EI 12 agrees, suggesting that people "avoid selfishness" and instead pursue "openness to be with your neighbor."

Shifting from valuing independence to valuing interdependence was emphasized: "Learn how to lean on each other as a community instead of always trying to 'get it together' alone," suggested EI 8. The bootstrap mentality of many Americans is described diplomatically but pointedly by EI 39 as "above-average (I didn't want to use the word extreme, but it feels extreme to me) individualistic and independent lifestyle." EI 31 points out, "[From the beginning] we wanted our freedom from the community of the Trinity, from the God who is community by His very nature. That's our Genesis understanding of this problem. Our original sin was declaring our independence" and in addressing the loneliness epidemic, "we are fighting with the idol of individualism. Satan has been using it to destroy us in the name of freedom." The same interviewee goes on to say:

> By default, church is community. And yet, individualism has affected so deeply that we are not really community when we come to church, we are just individuals gathering. Communal life where we celebrate community, when we recognize our dependency on God and each other is not there. We have to recapture what the body of Christ means. It is impossible to be Christians without the Church. The church cannot save you, but you can't

---

66. EI 2.
67. EI 4, interviewed June 10, 2021.
68. EI 26.

live being saved without the church. Discipleship is the only way to promote the Lordship of Jesus Christ. There is no lonely discipleship. We become disciples from living within community. The way we are living is almost contrary to our original message, existential identity, and mission.

EI 34 encouraged American believers to be willing to receive as well as to give, because this is what it means to be in community.

[The Bible says] when someone is sick or in need, let him call the elders to his house. But even when we are in need, we have this independence mentality that we don't want to do that. I think it's ok to be the recipient. If you're in need, acknowledge it and have someone over to help. In Ethiopia you don't think twice, it's inevitable, you're in need, you call someone over to your place and share it with that person and together you can [figure it out].

Here, people don't want to give up, they don't want to feel like they are dependent. I think asking for help doesn't show our dependence, [it just shows that] nobody is self-sufficient. For example, I know many Americans who are going and who are serving as missionaries, but they have many issues with depression and other things. But then still they want to be on the giving side not the receiving side. So I really appreciate the fact that they want to give, but I think that it's important also to be on the receiving side.

Many interviewees pushed back on extreme privacy: "The concept of 'mind your business' has gone too far," says EI 43. "People give testimonies that they were going to commit suicide, but a person said 'hi.'" This interviewee clarified that she is calling for balance, not saying that people should be "wayyyyyy in [others'] business" or "giving to get" but rather "I'm just going to show her love because that's what God created me to do and what Jesus gave to me." Practically speaking, the value of small check-ins with family and friends was emphasized by many interviewees as being indispensable to building community. "We can do little gestures of God's love, like 'Hi, how are you, how is your family?' Nobody will respond negatively to this kind of question," suggests EI 36.

Teaching children is seen as an effective way of inculcating the value of community and the practice of hospitality. "If we were created to be all about ourselves . . . then we each would have been given individual planets," says EI 5. Rather than letting children continue in their early "mine" and "my" stage, we should instead "equip our babies with 'ours' and 'us.'" EI 35 agrees: "I think we have to teach our generation/future generation how to live with people, not just be friendly but actually know how to approach people in a welcoming way to build lasting relationships. This means breaking boundaries, such as language or culture differences and going out of our way to make people feel welcomed."

EI 29 adds: "Teach children the value of community by having community at your house. If hosting is a constant for you, your kids will see it and it will become a value for them." EI 32, who grew up in America with Ethiopian parents, is evidence of this: "When a new immigrant comes over," he says, "the expectation is to help them, invite them, meet up with them, because everyone is a cousin. It's an obligation, but not in a bad way. After so many years of seeing that modeled, I have this automatic instinct to help someone, to be intentional to make that connection." EI 27 suggests: "Maintain a close relationship with family and friends. Make them a priority." EI 9 also suggested to "get to know the neighbors deeply by inviting them over for dinner, lunch, or coffee."[69] EI 25 urged those who understand the value of community through hospitality to do the work to "create community" and "to create space for us to love each other and celebrate each other."

Finally, EI 16 made suggestions that people should be warned that "digital technology" has "negative effects" on loneliness. EI 33 agreed with this idea but added a caution. When people are feeling alone, they won't just stay alone, they'll replace it with something else, often movies, internet, or social media. "When someone is an alcoholic, you don't just tell him, 'Hey, stop drinking!' You have to show him another way." In the same way, "Instead of just saying, 'Hey, stop being lonely!' we have to show people what community looks like first." But what *does* community look like in a society that does not uphold the value of hospitality? It must be intentionally cultivated such that communion with God, communion with others, and sharing space go beyond a program and become a lifestyle motivated from within even when societal structures do not support hospitable practices.[70]

69. Interviewed June 11, 2021.

70. One Ethiopian interviewee shared that he had observed that the majority of Americans did not practice hospitality or seem to care much about community, but the few who he had met who did practice hospitality seemed to him to be very intentional and committed to doing so. This made me consider that I had also observed this dynamic, and I reached out to seven American Protestant friends whose lives are characterized by the cultivation of community through hospitality, asking them why they value the practice of hospitality and how that value works itself out in their lives (though these interviewees are anonymous, some basic demographic information about them is provided in Appendix D). There were some commonalities in their responses: hospitality

Conclusion

Forty-three Ethiopian-background interviewees generously contributed to this chapter by sharing their time and experiences. Though varied in their ages and locations, they share the common bond of having lived as immigrants in the United States. From this insider-outsider perspective, they are uniquely positioned to provide wise and insightful counsel to

---

was connected to their identities at a deep level, showing that they viewed hospitality as being more about who they *were* than what they *did*. This hospitable identity was cultivated in them through hospitable families of origin, identification with traditional aspects of their own sub-cultures, and/or time spent living abroad and being exposed to a Non-Western practice of hospitality. All respondents also rooted their responses first and foremost in Scripture, explaining the importance that God places on people living in community. Referencing the parable of the great banquet in Matthew 22:1–14 and Luke 14:15–24, American 8 (A 8, American interviewees will hereafter be referred to as A 1, A 2, A 3, and so on), interviewed March 17, 2022, asks: "If God so wants sinners to dine with him, shouldn't I want to have a few fellow sinners in my home and maybe share his love with them?" A 2, interviewed March 11, 2022, adds: "The Kingdom of God seems to come in a special way around tables and hospitable spaces," referencing the way that those he lived among in North Africa for a time "concretely demonstrated these biblical values" in a way that was worthy of emulation. A 7, interviewed March 16, 2022, agrees that living in Kenya, he observed that "people always had time for people. It was perspective shifting for sure." A 3, interviewed on March 11, 2022, models her practice of hospitality on what Jesus did: "He invited people to the table. He invited people to sit and be WITH him." Likewise, when she invites someone in, "the invitation itself is a welcome to share my life." A 4, a couple interviewed together on March 13, 2022, simply share: "We value community and find that hospitality is a vehicle to form and sustain community." A 5, interviewed March 13, 2022, adds that "watching [international students] feel like they can just set aside their cares for a bit has helped us want to do this more." A 6, interviewed March 15, 2022, observes how her family's practice of hospitality is counter-cultural: "In the West, many people have the idea of their home being a showplace and/or as their private possession. We swing to the total opposite view, what is mine is yours, you are free to visit for a meal, pull up a seat in the living room or even grab a bed for the night, a week, a month or a few years!!" The same interviewee also shares that it was not until her own family made a move to a different culture that "our open house really opened [because] we could more deeply empathize with those lost in a new environment." A 7 articulates his growth away from hyperindividualism and toward valuing relationships: "When I see my possessions and time as strictly my own I find that self grows and that love grows cold bit by bit. Not only does this shrink my soul and my capacity for love, but it also leads to a less fulfilling life. To the contrary, as we obey God and follow Him on the path of love we find the things we long for—fulfillment in relationships, joy in giving, and more of His love in our hearts. Relationships are the greatest thing that this world has to offer. Ultimately our relationship with Him is primary but then also our relationships to one another. I want to be conscious of prioritizing those two in my life." Looking back on many years of hospitable living, A 8 concludes: "I don't think there's been one time I regretted the effort."

the American Church as brothers and sisters in Christ who have experienced the loneliness epidemic themselves and yet have also lived a different reality and realize there is another way. Their suggestions include reexamining the high value of privacy and the extreme emphasis on the individual, considering reducing busyness and transactional behavior in favor of simplicity, slowing down, and relationality, questioning the effects of digital technology, and committing to teaching Christians on Sunday mornings as well as on every other day and children on a daily basis at home the value of building community through hospitality. In the next chapter, we will dive deeper into the biblical resonance of an Ethiopian perspective on building community through hospitality, thereby showing the merit of looking to Ethiopian Christians to point the way forward in addressing the loneliness epidemic.

4

The Biblical Resonance of an Ethiopian Understanding and Practice of Building Community through Hospitality

THIS CHAPTER WILL BRING attention to a biblically resonant reality which most Ethiopians understand but which most Americans have forgotten: the interconnected nature of reality and the interdependence inherent to our thriving on earth. Acknowledging interconnected interdependence leads Ethiopian Christians to prioritize communion with God, communion with each other, and sharing space and needs. Three mindsets and practices stem naturally from these communal prioritizations—namely recognizing the limitations of individual humanity, building friendships that are relational rather than transactional, and enjoying and stewarding God's gifts together—and they will also be discussed along with the aim of cultivating the American Christian imagination with regard to addressing the loneliness epidemic in the United States by building community through hospitality.[1] Some Ethiopian community-generated organizations will

---

1. I do not intend to imply that Ethiopia is the only nation whose cultural emphases could be instructive to American Christians in addressing the loneliness epidemic, nor that Christian Ethiopians are the only ones who prioritize communal living in light of interconnected interdependence. For the purposes of research and based on my life experiences, I have limited myself demographically to studying Protestant Christians (the community I am most connected with) in Ethiopia (where I currently live and work) in order to have a parallel to Protestant Christians in the United States (where I am from), but I encourage further research to be done on other traditions' and religions' understanding of hospitality (for example, there is a strong emphasis on hospitality in Islam) and its relevance for the loneliness epidemic in the West, as well as further research on examples of building community through hospitality in other Non-Western countries with similar understandings of the interconnected interdependence of reality.

be explored as a practical outworking of these presuppositions and practices discussed with hopes that they can provide inspiration and ideas for Americans who are seeking to live interdependently. An addendum to the chapter explores cultural change in Ethiopia and its effects on loneliness, including insights from nine Ethiopian interviewees who have lived their whole lives in Ethiopia, shedding light on current and coming challenges to the historically Ethiopian value of building community through hospitality.

The Christian message came to Ethiopia very early on in Christian history. According to Ethiopian church historians, Queen Candace herself was converted by the Ethiopian eunuch who encountered Philip in Acts 8, thus becoming "the first Christian ruler in Ethiopia and, furthermore, in Africa."[2] In the fourth century AD, a young man named Frumentius from Tyre embarked on an expedition with his brother and uncle, but their party was attacked and Frumentius and his brother were taken as slaves to the kingdom of Axum in Ethiopia. Eventually, they were freed and tasked with educating the king's son, Ezana. Eventually, Frumentius traveled to Alexandria and was ordained by Athanasius, Patriarch of Alexandria, to be a bishop, with the goal of returning to Ethiopia to spread Christianity in about 335 AD. Ezana, who had become the king, was baptized and actively promoted Christianity in the region.[3]

From "around 335 CE, until 1974, the Ethiopian Church [specifically the EOTC] and the Ethiopian monarchy existed continuously and in close relationship with one another." As such, "it is fair to say that the central national institutions that sustained Ethiopia for so long were the monarchy and the church, while the theological, intellectual, literary, and artistic traditions of Ethiopian Orthodoxy constituted the core of a national culture that provided a distinctive and durable identity, even when faced with major external or internal challenges."[4]

In Ethiopia "writing has perdured in Christian circles ... in an unbroken line for some 1,700 years."[5] Many sacred ancient Christian texts, translated from other languages into the Ethiopian language of Ge'ez, have been preserved until the modern day in Ethiopia despite having "disappeared elsewhere in the Christian world, and a vast new corpus of literature was

---

2. An, *Ethiopian Reading of the Bible*, 87.
3. Esler, *Ethiopian Christianity*, 27–31.
4. Esler, *Ethiopian Christianity*, 4.
5. Esler, *Ethiopian Christianity*, 101.

composed in Ge'ez."[6] One such unique work is the *andemta* commentary, which, like the Mishnah tradition of Jewish interpretation, has gathered interpretive wisdom from a variety of outside historical sources as well as including interpretations from Ethiopian Christian leaders, forming a "valuable contribution to biblical literature that offers a fresh vision of many texts"[7] which "wonderfully exemplifies the dynamic relationship between tradition and context."[8]

The *andemta* commentary also exemplifies a typically Ethiopian approach to understanding the complexities of existence by emphasizing interconnection: between humans through interdependence and also between faith and practice in the lives of Christians. An notes: "The *andemta* commentary aims at helping the community of believers understand the text for their lives." He continues: "It is important to note that in the life and faith of the EOTC, it is hard to make a clear distinction between theology and the life of the believers. Theology is most properly contained and exhibited in the practices of the church, such as liturgy and the lifestyles of the faith community."[9] As such, "[Ethiopian Orthodox Christians'] daily experience is caught up in the omnipresent dynamics of sacred space, sacred time and memory, and sacred action"[10] and "in the EOTC's hermeneutical approach, there is no artificial dichotomy of meaning and significance, or meaning and application."[11]

While many sacred manuscripts—including the *andemta* commentary—which are written and preserved in Ge'ez are untranslated and therefore inaccessible and all too often unacknowledged by scholars in the rest of the world, Ge'ez continues to be the primary language of theological education and liturgy in the EOTC. Those who receive education in EOTC affiliated schools[12] are expected to undertake "memorization of huge amounts of text" taught in a predominantly oral format by an instructor who functions "as a father figure to students, promoting their

---

6. Esler, *Ethiopian Christianity*, 102.
7. Esler, *Ethiopian Christianity*, 132.
8. An, *Ethiopian Reading of the Bible*, 116.
9. An, *Ethiopian Reading of the Bible*, 137.
10. Esler, *Ethiopian Christianity*, 171.
11. An, *Ethiopian Reading of the Bible*, 227.
12. Esler, *Ethiopian Christianity*, 126, notes that "right up until the end of the nineteenth century, education in Ethiopia was the province of the church alone."

growth."[13] Those who continue on for further clerical education to become clergy or quasi-clergy in the EOTC also study liturgical music, interpretation of sacred texts, and religious poetry.[14]

This religious poetry is called *qene* (also spelled *qiné* by other authors) and is "emblematic of the potent intellectual and literary traditions that have characterized Ethiopian Orthodoxy since the foundations of Christianity in the country during the Aksumite period."[15] Esler explains that *qene* attempts to reflect upon and amidst the mystery and complexity of life, attempting to "reveal a truth that is hidden" by "say[ing] one thing while implying a different thing at the same time and in the same sentence."[16] Since this involves "key words hav[ing] double meanings," *qene* "is regarded as one of the highest forms of knowledge" by Ethiopians.[17] Esler elaborates:

> In Ethiopia these two parts, the obvious meaning and the implied meaning, are referred to as "wax" (*sem*) and "gold" (*warq*). This analogy derives from the craft of the goldsmith in making jewelry. The goldsmith first forms a copy of the desired object in wax, which is soft and easy to mold, and then covers the wax with a cast of clay or plaster and allows it to harden. When molten gold is poured into the cast, the wax melts, leaving the gold in the desired shape. Applied to *qene*, this means that the first meaning gives way to the second, richer one. It is not a perfect analogy, since in *qene* the two meanings coexist at the same time, whereas the wax and gold are consecutive, but it is a very vivid one.[18]

In the perspective of Ethiopian intellectual traditions, "all reality is 'wax and gold,'"[19] and Ethiopian Christians see "both the Bible and the natural world" as "an immense spider's web (as it were) of interconnections between the created world and divine reality."[20]

Ethiopians have a high regard for their cultural identity, calling it *Ethiopiawinet* (also spelled *Ityopyawinet*), which simply means "Ethiopian-ness" and features "the unity of humanity . . . [and] urges . . . the

---

13. Esler, *Ethiopian Christianity*, 127.
14. Esler, *Ethiopian Christianity*, 128.
15. Esler, *Ethiopian Christianity*, 125.
16. Esler, *Ethiopian Christianity*, 123.
17. Demoze and Armstrong, *Ethiopian Amharic Proverbs*, ii.
18. Esler, *Ethiopian Christianity*, 123.
19. Mennasemay, *Qiné Hermeneutics*, xx.
20. Brock quoted in An, *Ethiopian Reading of the Bible*, 144.

striking of a balance between what is good to me and what is good to my ethnic and religious neighbor."²¹ *Ethiopiawinet* rests on the idea that "interdependence is constitutive of human life, and that interdependence is not a one-sided dependence on the other but an active form of trans and inter-individual relations."²²

While some in the EOTC have historically viewed Ethiopian Protestantism as a foreign import, it is notable that in my interviews with a total of fifty-two Ethiopian Protestants (forty-three immigrants and nine who have lived in Ethiopia for their whole lives), it was quite apparent that they were deeply influenced by Ethiopian Orthodox heritage and ideas (whether directly, through having grow up in an Orthodox family, or indirectly through the general culture-shaping influence of the EOTC), to the point that I would argue that *Ethiopiawinet* regarding interconnection, interdependence, and valuing building community through hospitality remains similar regardless of whether a person is a member of the EOTC or an Ethiopian Protestant church. "Though Protestant missionaries introduced evangelical Christianity to Ethiopia from the West," Ethiopian evangelical historian Tibebe Eshete acknowledges, "its growth and expansion result mainly from contributions of native agencies, given the legal and cultural restrictions under which the Western Protestant missionaries operated and granted that the remarkable expansion of the movement occurred during the times of the Ethiopian Revolution in the conspicuous absence of the external agencies." Because of this local leadership since the very early stages of the Ethiopian Protestant Church's development, Eshete continues,

> the Ethiopian situation did not allow Western agents to engage in efforts of "civilizing missions" and to impose Western culture in their pursuit of evangelization. This was basically because of the existence of countervailing forces and institutions and embedded nationalistic sentiments that were widely shared by most Ethiopians, including evangelical Christians, particularly those who came from the Orthodox background.²³

Far from breaking entirely from their Orthodox heritage, most Protestant interviewees with whom I interacted respected and were grateful to the EOTC for "laying the foundations of Christianity in Ethiopia and the rich fund of experience upon which the evangelical Christian faith

21. Mohammed quoted in Esler, *Ethiopian Christianity*, 242.
22. Mennasemay, *Qiné Hermeneutics*, 411.
23. Eshete, *Evangelical Movement in Ethiopia*, 314.

advanced."[24] Indeed, "viewed from a historical and analytical perspective, the evangelical faith as embraced by Ethiopians does not signify desertion or denial. Rather, it is an expression of the latent dimension of an already existing faith. Significantly, for those who tuned into the faith from the Orthodox background, Christianity simply took renewed emphasis and meaning.... As viewed by the converts, the process was essentially one of reinforcement, rather than abandoning."[25]

Numerous Ethiopian proverbs illustrate, emphasize, and inculcate the *Ethiopiawinet* orientation toward interconnected interdependence, often referring to the power of community.[26] One can observe the nuanced, clear-eyed wisdom birthed from experience (and divested from naivete) in the multifaceted shading of their descriptions of how to live well with other people:[27] Some find direct parallel in Scripture (in this case, specifically Prov 27:10b): "It is better to have a neighbor (close) than a relative who lives far away."[28] Another related proverb expresses the negative side effects of neighbors not living up to their interdependent potential: "A bad neighbor makes one self-sufficient."[29] Interdependence—expressed aptly in the proverb "Fifty lemons are a load for one person, but for fifty people they are 'perfume'"[30]—is talked about often as the balance between too much dependence and too much independence. On the one hand, "If one does not call for help, a neighbor will not come to the rescue,"[31] and "When one lends to a person in need (trouble), it is considered as though he had given it to him. *That is, there is a virtue in lending to one in real need.*"[32] On the other hand, "Charity that exceeds what is normal will leave you empty"[33] and "Thinking that I would be righteous, I put her on my

---

24. Eshete, *Evangelical Movement in Ethiopia*, 15.

25. Eshete, *Evangelical Movement in Ethiopia*, 314.

26. Demoze and Armstrong, *Ethiopian Amharic Proverbs*, iii, observes that "Culture and proverbs ... are intertwined, and to learn about one is to clarify the other."

27. In this book, due to linguistic constraints, only proverbs in Amharic will be referenced, but it should be acknowledged that Ethiopia is the home of scores of languages which also are replete with proverbs.

28. Demoze and Armstrong, *Ethiopian Amharic Proverbs*, 93.

29. Demoze and Armstrong, *Ethiopian Amharic Proverbs*, 82.

30. Demoze and Armstrong, *Ethiopian Amharic Proverbs*, 43.

31. Demoze and Armstrong, *Ethiopian Amharic Proverbs*, 79.

32. Demoze and Armstrong, *Ethiopian Amharic Proverbs*, 59.

33. Demoze and Armstrong, *Ethiopian Amharic Proverbs*, 2.

back, but she remained hanging there (or she refused to come down)."[34] Guests are warned in a proverb directed at them: "A guest is at first like gold, then later like silver, still later like common metal."[35] The contradictions involved in an attempt at this balance are not ignored: Demoze and Armstrong comment that "At times the proverbs appear to contradict themselves. One says that pride is no substitute for a dinner (proverb number 214), which is used of one who is too proud to accept things from others. But another says self-respect is as good as a dinner (proverb number 215).... The proverbs make clear that life in Ethiopia is no less paradoxical than in any other part of the world."[36] When an interdependent balance is found, people find that they can do far more together than they could ever do alone: "When spider webs unite, they can tie up a lion."[37]

Ethiopians tend to have a sense of reverence for their roots and a strong identification with their cultural *Ethiopiawinet*[38] and its accompanying proverbs and practices, making it possible for ancient practices such as building community through hospitality[39] to persist up until the modern day. These proverbs and practices are undergirded by powerful presuppositions—namely the understanding of reality as interconnected and interdependent— that lead to a prioritization of certain things, namely communion with God, communion with others, and the sharing of space and needs.

Communion with God

In the Christian creation story, before anything else was, God existed. Instead of being alone, God's very essence was and is loving community. The

---

34. Demoze and Armstrong, *Ethiopian Amharic Proverbs*, 9.
35. Demoze and Armstrong, *Ethiopian Amharic Proverbs*, 28–29.
36. Demoze and Armstrong, *Ethiopian Amharic Proverbs*, iii–iv.
37. Demoze and Armstrong, *Ethiopian Amharic Proverbs*, 76.
38. I realize that there are many distinct cultures in Ethiopia, but I also see commonalities between them especially when it comes to the value of hospitality. They also form an affinity group in which the cultures included are more similar than dissimilar, so for the purposes of this book, I will refer to "Ethiopian culture" in the singular, with the understanding that there is much diversity within this group.
39. One of the first things that Holland, *Culture Smart!*, 50, mentions about *Ityopyawinet* (the "quality of being Ethiopian"), is that Ethiopians "are hospitable to guests and strangers" and she later, 92, adds that "Ethiopians have a long established culture of care of guests."

act of creating the world was not done from a place of existential lack but as a joyful invitation for humankind to participate in that already-existing community.[40] Thus, God's first interaction with humans was characterized by hospitality, as the "host of creation."[41] Not only were Adam and Eve invited into fellowship with God Himself,[42] receiving visits and spending time walking with God in Eden, but they were given a place to live and provided for in every way. Even after they broke fellowship with God and had to leave the place he had prepared for them,[43] God's loving care continued through the promise that through the hospitality of the womb of a descendent of Eve, Immanuel would come to dwell among humans once more.[44]

God's identity is multi-faceted and cannot be pinned down with one descriptor, but one of the most common ways the Bible describes God is as

---

40. Boff, *Holy Trinity, Perfect Community*, xii, suggests that the "Western framework, which is strongly marked by the concentration of power in a few hands" has influenced the development of modern Christianity to resemble a functional "'a-trinitarian' or 'pre-trinitarian' monotheism," suggesting that re-introducing a "radically trinitarian understanding of God" could be helpfully balancing. Boff, 2, continues, "If God means three divine Persons in eternal communion among themselves, then we must conclude that we also, sons and daughters, are called to communion. We are the image and likeness of the Trinity. Hence, we are community beings. Solitude is hell. No one is an island. We are surrounded by persons, things, and beings on all sides. Because of the Blessed Trinity, we are called to maintain relationships of communion with all, giving and receiving, and together building a rich and open shared life, one that respects differences and does good to all."

41. Hall, "Hidden Conversion," 30.

42. Assohoto and Ngewa, "Genesis," 13, clearly labels Genesis 2:4–25 as "Creation of the Human Community," commenting: "the biblical writer . . . establishes the second vital element in human identity: not only are we made in the image of God, but we are also made to live in community. It is in community that we manifest the image of God. That is why God created the first human relationship, establishing a community as an example for us to follow."

43. Assohoto and Ngewa, "Genesis," 15, refer to Genesis 3:1–6 with the sub-heading "*A flaw in the community*" and frame the fall of mankind in terms of community: "Satan's first step was to interfere in the communion between the man and the woman. . . . Making a major decision alone led [Eve] to enter into a relationship with the evil one (a new community), thus abandoning her relationship with God (the primary community) and distancing herself from her relationship with her husband (the secondary community). . . . [Adam joined Eve in sinning and] the first couple were thus united in their sin and created a sinful community apart from God."

44. Assohoto and Ngewa, "Genesis," 16, explain: "In uttering this promise, God is already hinting at the coming of his new community and the deliverance of human beings and the world from the power of Satan."

a host.[45] Despite their near-constant complaints, God provides food and water for his people in the wilderness (Exod 16–17). He is "a refuge" for his people (Ps 18:2; 61:3). He "prepare[s] a table" for David, "anoint[ing]" David's head and satisfying his thirst until his "cup overflows" (Ps 23:5). Christine Pohl also points out that "Israel's covenant identity includes being a stranger, an alien, a tenant in God's land—both dependent on God for welcome and provision and answerable to God for its own treatment of aliens and strangers."[46]

Throughout the Old Testament, God is seen consistently pursuing communion with his people and facilitating times (such as the sacrifices, feasts and festivals of Israel) and spaces (such as the Tabernacle or the Temple) for the divine and human to commune despite the continued presence of sin. Yet the Tabernacle became defunct after God's people moved beyond their wilderness days, and the Temple was destroyed when the people went into exile. Moreover, "it is impossible for the blood of bulls and goats to take away sins" (Heb 10:4) and they were only ever meant to be a temporary measure to make possible the continued fellowship between God and mankind. The ultimate invitation of the Divine Host was yet to come.

"When the fullness of time had come" (Gal 4:4) and Mary's womb had stretched to the fullest expression of bodily hospitality, Jesus "made his dwelling among us" (John 1:14).[47] And the reaction of humans to his coming is framed in terms of hospitality or lack of it: "He came to that which was his own, but his own did not receive him. Yet to all who did receive him, to those who believed in his name, he gave the right to become children of God" (John 1:11–12). And Jesus is still seen in the book of Revelation seeking to commune with humans through hospitality: "Behold, I stand at the door and knock. If anyone hears my voice and opens the door, I will come in to him and eat with him, and he with me" (Rev 3:20). Jesus came and still comes—welcoming and being welcomed by those who recognize him—because God and humans belong in communion with each other.

As someone who had "nowhere to lay [his] head" (Luke 9:58), Jesus' earthly ministry depended upon the hospitality of others. And yet Jesus showed hospitality toward those who followed him, providing the

---

45. For a more in-depth analysis of God as the host and the hosted and its implications for human practices in the biblical text, see Jipp, *Saved By Faith and Hospitality*; Pohl, *Making Room*; Smither, *Mission as Hospitality*; Yong, *Hospitality and the Other*.

46. Pohl, *Making Room*, 16.

47. Quenum, "Hospitality of God," 6, says: "God through the Logos is the guest of honor of the human family."

multitudes listening to his teaching with food, caring for their bodies and not just their souls (Luke 9:10–17). Emily J. Choge comments that Jesus "instructed his disciples to give a blessing wherever they were received to show that he built hospitality into his mission."[48]

Jesus' teaching also framed the kingdom of heaven in terms of hospitality as well: he tells the story of a king giving a wedding feast to which the poor and marginalized are invited (Matt 22:1–14). When Jesus speaks of his impending death, resurrection, and ascension, he speaks in hospitable terms of preparing a place for his beloved ones to be together with him: "In my Father's house are many rooms. If it were not so, would I have told you that I go to prepare a place for you? And if I go and prepare a place for you, I will come again and will take you to myself, that where I am you may be also" (John 14:2–3).[49] Both Old and New Testament writers dream of the day that is coming when they will dwell in God's house forever (Pss 23:6; 27:4; 61:4; 2 Cor 5:1).

The book of Revelation proclaims:

> "Hallelujah!
> For the Lord our God
> the Almighty reigns.
> Let us rejoice and exult
> and give him the glory,
> for the marriage of the Lamb has come,
> and his Bride has made herself ready;
> it was granted her to clothe herself
> with fine linen, bright and pure"—
> for the fine linen is the righteous deeds of the saints. (Rev 19:6b–8a)

Soon after, an angel tells John: "Blessed are those who are invited to the marriage supper of the Lamb. . . . These are the true words of God" (Rev 19:9). The end of the New Testament reads like an audible sigh of relief as God's people are welcomed to "know fully, even as [they] have been fully known" (1 Cor 13:12), experiencing the face-to-face consummation of full communion with God:

---

48. Choge, "Hospitality in Africa," 390.

49. For an in-depth look at how communion or "mutual abiding" is related to the theme of hospitality throughout the gospel of John, see Kunene, *Communal Holiness*.

> Then I saw a new heaven and a new earth, for the first heaven and the first earth had passed away, and the sea was no more. And I saw the holy city, new Jerusalem, coming down out of heaven from God, prepared as a bride adorned for her husband. And I heard a loud voice from the throne saying, "Behold, the dwelling place of God is with man. He will dwell with them, and they will be his people, and God himself will be with them as their God. He will wipe away every tear from their eyes, and death shall be no more, neither shall there be mourning, nor crying, nor pain anymore, for the former things have passed away. (Rev 21:1–4)

Having a sense of being created for communion with God deeply influences the great implicit value Ethiopians place on cultivating community through hospitality. Rather than viewing the world in a dichotomistic way, with the Divine far away in heaven and the natural world simply governed by impersonal scientific laws, Ethiopians embody the idea that "in him we live and move and have our being" (Acts 17:28)—that spiritual forces are near and actively involved in everyday life, never far from people's thoughts.[50]

On an observational level, it seems that deeply religious societies and deeply hospitable societies are quite frequently one and the same,[51] and Ethiopia is no exception. As seen in the previous chapter, there is consensus among the Ethiopian interviewees that hospitality is integrally connected with God's love and is in fact an outflow of that love. Having been welcomed by God, Ethiopian Christians naturally imitate his welcoming character toward those around them, for hospitality toward strangers in their understanding is simply part of the Christian faith.

It also seems common that in deeply religious societies, particularly in Africa, "the stranger is the messenger of God."[52] People are therefore eager

---

50. Quenum, "Hospitality of God," 4, explains: "Through their interactions in community with other forces of the universe (animals and inanimate objects) human beings as vital forces participate in a dynamic human world based on relationships." For more on a Non-Western view of spiritual forces being involved in everyday life versus the more dichotomistic Western view of God as separate from the natural world (which creates excluded and unaddressed "middle" which has been a blindspot and a stumbling block for Western missionaries and those who are discipled by them for centuries), see Hiebert, "Flaw of the Excluded Middle."

51. Conversely, it would seem that the more secular a society is, the less value is placed on community through hospitality. These observations were first articulated to me in a personal conversation with Abeneazer G. Urga.

52. See chapter 3, "Interviews with Ethiopian Immigrants"

to open themselves up to strangers, because to do so is to experience divine blessings in mysterious but real ways. Hebrews 13:2 is thus parallel with an accepted ancient African orientation toward generous welcome: "Do not neglect to show hospitality to strangers, for thereby some have entertained angels unawares" (Heb 13:2).[53] This expectancy to encounter the divine leads naturally to the idea that to host is an honor, not a burden.

The general consensus in Ethiopian culture, regardless of which religion any person follows, is that to participate in communion with God is life's highest goal. Interestingly, the central Christian ritual of eating the bread of Christ's body and drinking the wine of his blood affirms this longing and is appropriately called communion. In Scripture, the word "communion" is κοινωνία (*koinōnia*), as in "the cup of blessing that we bless, is it not the communion in the blood of Christ? The bread that we break, is it not the communion of the body of Christ?" (1 Cor 10:16 KJV).

Communion with Each Other

In Scripture, the "body of Christ" is understood to be made up of believers around the world. The idea of existing primarily as an individual in a vacuum of autonomous desires and actions is a relatively modern idea that is discordant with the teaching of the New Testament. This does not mean that God has no concern for the individual, however. Paul says clearly: "Now you are the body of Christ and individually members of it" speaking of different spiritual giftings (1 Cor 12:27). But this statement is made after an earlier verse sets the tone and limits of individuality: "To each is given the manifestation of the Spirit *for the common good*" (1 Cor 12:7, emphasis mine). Each individual, then, is intricately connected to every other individual within the body, such that "the eye cannot say to the hand, 'I have no need of you,' nor again the head to the feet, 'I have no need of you'" (1 Cor 12:21). Instead, as "many parts, yet one body" (1 Cor 12:20), Christians are to "care for one another. If one member suffers, all suffer together; if one member is honored, all rejoice together" (1 Cor 12:25b-26).

The idea of *koinonia* is both assumed and practiced throughout the New Testament, enabled by the Holy Spirit at work within each member of Christ's body (2 Cor 13:14; Phil 2:1). Acts 2:42–46 describes the earliest

---

53. Even in a book on political science and economics, Fobanjong, *State of the Continent*, 13, mentions off-handedly that "Africans have always lived by the biblical teaching in Hebrews 13:2" whether they claim the biblical text as their motivation or not.

church as being "devoted . . . to the apostles' teaching and the fellowship [*koinonia*], to the breaking of bread and the prayers" (Acts 2:42). Paul sees his relationship with other believers as being a "partnership [*koinonia*] in the gospel from the first day until now" (Phil 1:5).

In the New Testament, the ideal person is characterized by generous hospitality. In giving qualifications for elders in the church, Paul emphasizes that they should be "hospitable" (1 Tim 3:2; Titus 1:8). The richness of this description is a bit flattened in modern English translations: the King James Version gives a better sense of the Greek φιλόξενος, saying that the elder should be "given to hospitality" (1 Tim 3:2) and a "lover of hospitality" (Titus 1:8).[54] A study of φιλόξενος also adds another shade of meaning, with Strong's Concordance indicating that to be hospitable is to be "fond of guests."[55] These renderings indicate a focus first and foremost on an internal disposition that influences behavior, rather than the behavior itself.[56] The Ethiopians in my interviews certainly shared the New Testament assumption that the ideal person is known for their generous hospitality.[57] One shared:

> I grew up with the understanding that Ethiopia was a hospitable country. This was communicated through media, the government communicated this, there was just this idea that Ethiopians are hospitable people, we love to welcome strangers, we are kind, we always have our arms open to outsiders. It was almost like a synonym for Ethiopia— hospitality.[58]

---

54. Interestingly, Andria, "Titus," 1510, omits the mention of hospitality as a qualification in his summary and discussion of Titus 1:8, while mentioning most of the other words used in the verse: "upright and self-controlled, and not guilty of pride, anger, or greed." This could suggest that hospitality is assumed by Africans to be a natural part of being an upright person.

55. *Strong's Exhaustive Concordance of the Bible*, s.v. "5382 philoxenos," https://biblehub.com/greek/5382.htm.

56. The behavior or practical practice of showing hospitality is certainly not denigrated in Scripture, however. In 1 Timothy 5:10, for example, Paul indicates that godly widows who will be supported by the church should have gained a reputation for having "shown hospitality" (again, the language of the KJV is more vivid and closer to the Greek ξενοδοχέω: "lodged strangers").

57. Kunene, *Communal Holiness*, 145, also comments that in other African and even in other marginalized, impoverished communities worldwide, people tend to "perceive generosity as the hallmark of achievement and the primary virtue."

58. See chapter 3, "Interviews with Ethiopian Immigrants"

To claim to have a personal, loving relationship with God and yet live in such a way that is not deeply involved in loving and generous fellowship with other humans is incomprehensible to most Africans (including Ethiopians)[59] and to the Apostle John, whose first epistle focuses heavily on "fellowship" with God and with "one another" that is characterized by sacrificial love:

> Beloved, let us love one another, for love is from God, and whoever loves has been born of God and knows God. Anyone who does not love does not know God, because God is love. In this the love of God was made manifest among us, that God sent his only Son into the world, so that we might live through him. In this is love, not that we have loved God but that he loved us and sent his Son to be the propitiation for our sins. Beloved, if God so loved us, we also ought to love one another. No one has ever seen God; if we love one another, God abides in us and his love is perfected in us.
>
> We love because he first loved us. If anyone says, "I love God," and hates his brother, he is a liar; for he who does not love his brother whom he has seen cannot love God whom he has not seen. And this commandment we have from him: whoever loves God must also love his brother. (1 John 3:7–11, 19–21)

Based on the above passage, Ethiopian theologian Eshetu Abate comments: "One of the marks of true disciples of Jesus Christ is love. Love cannot be love if it is not translated into action. [As] the Apostle John writes, ... Love requires interaction. It cannot take place in seclusion or isolation.

---

59. It should be noted that I am certainly not implying that Ethiopians are without room for improvement in their practice of *ubuntu/koinonia* principles. Indeed, I recently had a conversation with Ethiopian researcher Tizita Seifu about what she sees as the disconnect between Ethiopians believing that people are made in the image of God and yet letting ethnic divisions trump their humaneness toward those from different tribal backgrounds and being lackluster in their response to internally displaced people and refugees entering Ethiopia. Gathogo, "African Philosophy," agrees, speaking of the pitfall of a misunderstanding of *ubuntu/medemer/koinonia* that must be addressed so that it does not lead to tribalism and in-group, exclusionary thinking and actions. However, I do think that Ethiopian culture can be a biblically resonant example (insofar as any human culture can be) of a foundational mentality of interconnectedness and interdependence with others, which is a perspective that those from Western cultures typically lack. Every culture has room to improve in imitating the hospitable God, so it is my hope that Ethiopian believers can build upon their God-honoring relationally focused foundation by expanding their answer to the perennial question: "And who is my neighbor?" (Luke 10:29).

The present seclusion and individualism seen in some cultures should be weighed carefully on the basis and concept of love."[60]

A common Ethiopian story illustrates the connection between loving God and loving others in order to encourage Christians to show patient compassion for guests in the same way God does:

> There was a man who is well known for his entertaining guests in his house. When a guest came to his house, he washed his feet, prepared a meal for him, and gave him a Bible to read. One day, a sixty-year-old man came to his house. After washing his feet, he invited the old man to read the Bible, but he became angry and refused to read the Bible, saying, "I do not know God." Soon the owner ousted the guest from his house in the middle of the night. Then he asked God, "God, what kind of man did you bring in my house?" God answered him back, "How old was the man you had expelled tonight?" He replied, "Sixty years old." Then God said to him, "How could you not spare him for one night, while I have carried him for sixty years?" Christians, God is the God of mercy who carries us to the end of our ages.[61]

Generosity of spirit is seen in Scripture as integrally related to *koinonia*, naturally arising as part of the virtuous cycle of participating in a community headed by a sacrificial Savior (Rom 15:26; 2 Cor 8:4; 9:13) with whom we participate in "the fellowship of his sufferings" (Phil 3:10). John has more to say on this topic: "By this we know love, that he laid down his life for us, and we ought to lay down our lives for the brothers. But if anyone has the world's goods and sees his brother in need, yet closes his heart against him, how does God's love abide in him? Little children, let us not love in word or talk but in deed and in truth" (1 John 3:16–18). While "whoever does not love abides in death" (1 John 3:14b), believers are given the ability to "lay down our lives for the brothers" because Christ "laid down his life for us," (1 John 3:16), knowing that "we have passed out of death into life, because we love the brothers" (1 John 3:14a). Believers are called to follow Jesus "outside the camp" as sojourners who "have no lasting city" (Heb 13:13–14), and they are instructed to sacrifice in ways that are an outflow of the sacrifice of Christ on the cross: first, "a sacrifice of praise to God" (Heb 13:15), and second, "do good and share [*koinonia*] what you have, for such sacrifices are pleasing to God" (Heb 13:16).

---

60. Deressa, *Christian Theology in African Context*, 106.
61. An, *Ethiopian Reading of the Bible*, 185.

Far from being a burden, the divine blessing is seen as primarily being received by the generous givers,[62] with the Macedonian believers "begging [Paul and his colleagues] for the favor of taking part in the relief of the saints" (2 Cor 8:4). Additionally, in this passage generosity is seen as a way that love is proved to be "genuine" (2 Cor 8:8), that their "abundance at the present time should supply [others'] need" and "so that their abundance may supply your need" (2 Cor 8:14a). Generosity is not one-way, but is understood in the context of a mutually supportive community which flexes and bends with fluctuations of need, with daily bread shared according to stewardship of God's daily provision, not amassed in order to pursue independence from the rest of the body.

Interdependence is a reality that is mainly assumed in Scripture and in Ethiopian culture. Life "under the sun" (Eccl 1:3) is full of toil and uncertainty, and human mortality means that we are beginning to fade away just as soon as we arrive. Feeling that it is necessary and even a point of pride to face life alone with a sense of rugged independence is a tragic misperception of the truly interconnected nature of reality. Such an unnaturally individualistic mentality results in severe side-effects such as loneliness, anxiety, and societal disconnection. This quintessentially American orientation toward life will be examined further in the next chapter, but is mentioned here to show its novelty and contrast with a more ancient acknowledgement of the interconnectedness of humanity and the resultant necessity of interdependence which is shared by the biblical writers and most Africans, including Ethiopians.[63] As Mercy Oduyoye comments, to be hospitable—that is, to participate actively in interdependent life—is "inherent in being African, as well as in adhering to a religion that derives from the Bible."[64] Ethiopian theologian Megersa Guta reflects on fellow Ethiopian Reverend Gudina Tumsa's approach to interdependence when he adds, "The Book of Ecclesiastes 4:9–10 states the interdependence of human beings during the time of need. It reads: 'Two are better than one, because they have good return for their work. If one falls down, his friend can help him up. But pity the man who has no one to help

---

62. In the context of generous hospitality specifically, Mbiti, "Forest Has Ears," 23, explains the blessings the hosts receive through hosting: "when a visitor comes to someone's home, family quarrels stop, the sick cheer-up, peace is restored and the home is restored to new strength. Visitors are, therefore, social healers—they are family doctors in a sense."

63. Mbaya, "Social Capital," 372, explains simply yet profoundly that "Africans are engaged in networks of human relationships."

64. Oduyoye, *Introducing African Women's Theology*, 94.

him up.' The question put to Cain: 'Where is your brother Abel?' (Gen 4:9) indicates that a person is responsible for the well-being of another person (interdependency). In the Ethiopian context, neighbors are interdependent. Social interdependence is a fact of life."[65]

In explaining a value of interdependence which seems to be held in common by the majority of African cultures, many African leaders have made use of the term *ubuntu* (a Nguni Bantu word meaning "humanity" which has corresponding words in many other African languages)[66] to describe an idea that they propose as a quintessentially African "philosophical orientation"—which forms "the basis of African metaphysics, axiology, and epistemology"[67]—and which I propose is also thoroughly resonant with the biblical idea[68] of loving one another through *koinonia* and thus worthy of emulation by those in other cultures.

Desmond Tutu attempts to translate the word's meaning for an English-speaking audience by saying:

> Africans believe in something that is difficult to render in English. We call it *ubuntu*, *botho*. It means the essence of being human. You know when it is there and when it is absent. It speaks about humaneness, gentleness, and hospitality, putting yourself on behalf of others, being vulnerable. It embraces compassion and toughness. It recognizes that my humanity is bound up in yours, for we can only be human together.[69]

Tutu goes on to say:

> In our African language we say, "a person is a person through other persons." I would not know how to be a human being at all except (that) I learned this from other human beings. We are made for a delicate network of relationships, of interdependence. We are meant to complement each other. All kinds of things go horribly wrong when we break that fundamental Law of our being. Not even the most powerful nation can be completely self-sufficient.[70]

---

65. Guta, "Between 'Dependence' and 'Self-Reliance,'" 129.

66. Kamwangamalu, "Ubuntu in South Africa," 25, for linguistic equivalents in several other languages.

67. Ali and Shishigu, "Implications of Ubuntu/Synergy," 3.

68. Kunene, *Communal Holiness*, 138, affirms that "the philosophy of ubuntu" has "similarities to ancient Jewish culture" which make it "particularly helpful."

69. Tutu, *Words of Desmond Tutu*, 69.

70. Tutu, *Words of Desmond Tutu*, 71.

Nelson Mandela explains the idea of *ubuntu* narratively and connects it directly with practical hospitality:

> A traveler through a country would stop at a village and he didn't have to ask for food or for water. Once he stops, the people give him food, entertain him. That is one aspect of Ubuntu but it will have various aspects. Ubuntu does not mean that people should not address themselves. The question therefore is: Are you going to do so in order to enable the community around you, and enable it to improve?[71]

Kenyan scholar Julius Gathogo writes extensively about the idea of *ubuntu* as compatible with a biblical worldview and as helpful both for Africans and for the wider world. While taking a cautious approach to the idea—acknowledging, for example, that an extreme or overly narrow application of this idea could actually lead to anti-*ubuntu* "animal like behaviors"[72] such as tribalism[73]—he argues that as "an aspect of African hospitality," *ubuntu* is "very critical in the socio-reconstruction of postcolonial Africa,"[74] in that it is a recovery of ancient wisdom and identity, some of which has been lost in the introduction of foreign ideas, whether through colonization, globalization, or both.[75] Though the articulation of this value in these terms has been relatively recent[76]—perhaps in response to increased exposure to other ways of living through globalization— a recognition of the interconnected reality of existence, the necessity of interdependence and thus a tendency to live hospitably in community has historically been the implicit *modus operandi* in Africa in general, and in Ethiopia's Christian community specifically.

---

71. Bartolo, "Concept of 'Ubuntu.'"
72. Gathogo, "African Philosophy," 46–47.
73. Gathogo, "African Philosophy," 47.
74. Gathogo, "African Philosophy," 52.
75. Ali and Shishigu, "Implications of Ubuntu/Synergy," 3, agree with Gathogo from an educational perspective: "Ubuntu has the potential to rescue people from their loss of identity and let them regain their cultural and social values [as opposed to unconsciously absorbing Euro-centric values]. Thus the epistemological, axiological, and ontological underpinnings of the African education system should base their foundation on such indigenous philosophy that caters to the values and wisdom inherent in society." For more on the biblical resonance of the idea of *ubuntu*, see Koenane, "Ubuntu and Philoxenia," 1–8.
76. Banda, "Ubuntu as Human Flourishing?," 203–4.

In Ethiopia, Prime Minister Dr. Abiy Ahmed has put forth the idea of *Medemer* in his so-titled 2019 book. *Medemer* comes from the root word *demer*, which means "to accumulate, to gather, to store, to wrap, to unify, making it stand in unison, to bring it together and make it one." In use, the word gives the sense of synergistically working together. This book has not yet been translated into English, so I have relied primarily upon a summary and translation of key terms and passages by Dr. Abeneazer Urga and an in-depth book review written by Dr. Alemayehu Mariam. Dr. Urga translates Ahmed's explanation of where this philosophy came from as follows: "*Medemer* is our idea [as opposed to being imported from outside] . . . [it is sourced and developed by] the values that have resided in the centuries past of our history and still reside with us today. These values were and are born out of national cultural traditions, and the society's heartbeat is tuned by them." Dr. Mariam agrees that the idea of *medemer* is "a worldview rooted in Ethiopian traditions, cultures, history, politics and economics" which "resonates [with] an old Ethiopian saying. 'If the silk in spiders' web could be made into twine, it could tie up a lion.'"[77] Mariam also adds that he "regard[s] 'Medemer' not so much as a 'book' but as the 'philosophical' equivalent of an open source 'software' such as Ubuntu for use or modification as users/practitioners or other 'developers' see fit."[78] Esler comments that "Medemer is a concept that appeals to the moral outlooks of Christianity, Islam, and indigenous African religions while not being so freighted with the distinctive beliefs or identity of any one of them as to alienate the others or, indeed, people of goodwill with no faith at all. Like Ethiopiawinet, medemer is a highly astute superordinate moral outlook with room for all Ethiopians in its embrace."[79]

Indeed, Ahmed focuses on the same fundamental idea of interconnected interdependence that is espoused not only by people of various faiths within Ethiopia but by the many other African thinkers quoted above who spoke about *ubuntu*, also touching on how the idea of *medemer* addresses loneliness:

> There is nothing that is whole by itself. Everything transitions from nothing to existence, from not happening to happening, in striving for wholeness. Things go through the process of change, the ups and downs, in order to bring wholeness. So, in order to bring

---

77. Mariam, "Interpretive Book Review."
78. Mariam, "Interpretive Book Review."
79. Esler, *Ethiopian Christianity*, 242.

this wholeness, they have to make a connection with their environment, and in making this connection, they gather what is necessary for their wholeness. When they have difficulty making this connection that is necessary for their journey of wholeness, loneliness happens. Loneliness has a big place in the social life of humanity. When humans strive to make themselves whole, that striving created different societal structures. Wholeness is not something you can tangibly grasp, but in their striving to grasp it or concretize it, they make connection with their environment, and that makes them look for something to fill their lack.

The process of trying to fill the loneliness void brings holistic growth in humans. More than any creature, humans seek support and collaboration to maintain their existence. Alone, a human cannot feed himself, protect himself sustainably from danger, and remain alive. Therefore, collaboration is one of nature's laws. Humans, without collaboration, cannot maintain their existence. Even if humans fulfill their basic survival needs, we are still social creatures that cannot live by ourselves.[80]

When loneliness is present, says Ahmed, disconnection from others is the culprit: "Because of various reasons, they disconnect from or decrease their connection with their environment and this leads to loneliness. But the main source of loneliness is the imbalance that is found between competition and collaboration,"[81] which could perhaps also be explained as an imbalance between independence and interdependence.

Dr. Mariam summarizes and explains Ahmed's thoughts on unbridled individualistic competition as follows: "For an organization or society to be successful, the functional elements cannot consist of merely individuals working independently and exclusively in their own self-interest. They must be part of a larger community that shares a common purpose, goals and objectives and apply social, political and economic synergy to create a public good."[82] Echoing Mandela, Ahmed proposes a healthy synthesis of competition and cooperation. Mariam notes that in a *medemer*-influenced society: "competition is more of an exception than a rule. Competition often ends up being a zero-sum game in which the winner takes all. It has a high tendency to lead to cyclical conflict in nature. Therefore, organisms as a rule maximize their survival by engaging in cooperative, not

---

80. Ahmed, *Medemer*, 36–37.
81. Ahmed, *Medemer*, 38.
82. Mariam, "'Medemer' by Abiy Ahmed, Ph.D., An Interpretive Book Review."

competitive, behavior. Their own needs and desires force them to cooperate to ensure their long-term survival." Mariam concludes by summing up Ahmed's arguments on the balance of cooperation and competition that acknowledge humanity's interconnected independence: "Ultimately, survival and success are achieved not on the basis of individual effort but as a result of the collective efforts of many individuals."[83]

As is the case with many world leaders, Ahmed is a controversial character, beloved by some and detested by others. It is not within the scope of this paper to take a political stance on the prime minister or his policies. Rather, my aim in citing this book is simply to point out that Ahmed's stated ideas are self-admittedly not new but are a call-back to traditional ideas already embedded within Ethiopian culture.

In summing up Ahmed's book, Dr. Mariam concludes: "Medemer aims to harness the aspirations of individuals and unleash their energies for the collective good. In contrast, the singular pursuit of individual self-interest is ultimately self-defeating. We are involved with each other as individuals. Our destinies are intertwined."[84] Thus, *medemer* is an ancient-made-modern Ethiopian equivalent to *ubuntu*, and its acknowledgement of interconnected interdependence comports well with the biblical idea of *koinonia*.

Sharing Space and Sharing Needs

Interconnected interdependence as an ontological idea[85] is worked out in daily life through the sharing of space and needs. While independence is ultimately a costly illusion, interdependence is an acceptance of a reality that no one person has what it takes to weather life alone. When a person admits this, his or her life is opened to connection with others. If people truly believe—whether implicitly or explicitly—that humanity is interconnected, then they will inevitably move *toward* others in pursuit of interdependence, since people naturally move toward what is necessary for their survival and instrumental in their flourishing.

In addition to the somewhat primal truth that it is not good to be alone, proximity is necessary in order to carry out the fullness of the dozens

---

83. Mariam, "'Medemer' by Abiy Ahmed, Ph.D., An Interpretive Book Review."
84. Mariam, "'Medemer' by Abiy Ahmed, Ph.D., An Interpretive Book Review."
85. I first encountered the phrase "interdependence is ontological" in Mennasemay, *Qiné Hermeneutics*, 383.

of "one another" commands in the Bible.[86] Believers simply cannot "love" (Rom 12:10; John 13:34; 1 John 3:11; etc.), "welcome" (Rom 15:7), "be kind" (Eph 4:32), "encourage" (1 Thess 5:11), "serve" (Gal 5:13), "live in harmony with" (Rom 12:16), "comfort" (2 Cor 13:11), "pray for" (Jas 5:16), "walk in the light with" (1 John 1:7), or "stir up one another to love and good works" (Heb 10:24) if they are not in close contact with one another. And God-glorifying, loving interaction with those who do not yet follow God also requires proximity: one cannot gently and respectfully explain "the reason for the hope that is in you" (1 Pet 3:15) if there is no relational space for the question to be asked. Gentiles ought not to need binoculars to "see your good deeds and glorify God on the day of visitation" (1 Pet 2:12; see also Matt 5:16). Likewise, when Paul instructs the Colossians to "walk in wisdom toward outsiders, making the best use of the time," he assumes that their lives have space for regular conversation with these outsiders: "Let your speech always be gracious, seasoned with salt, so that you may know how you ought to answer each person" (Col 4:6).

Open-heartedness is a quality integrally related to hospitality in the Bible, and it leads to the opening of one's hands. Indeed, the opening of one's home must also be accompanied by the opening of one's heart in love and one's hands in generosity if true hospitality is to be practiced. Paul commands the Romans: "Contribute to the needs of the saints and seek to show hospitality" (Rom 12:13), and after being instructed to show hospitality in 13:2, the Hebrews are soon after reminded: "Do not neglect to do good and to share what you have, for such sacrifices are pleasing to God" (Heb 13:16). The Old Testament context for these New Testament commands is the idea that "the foreigner [someone in need of welcome] residing among you must be treated as your native-born" and that God-followers are to "*love* [foreigners] as yourself" (Lev 19:32, emphasis mine). 1 John 3:17 perhaps most punchily conveys the intensely practical nature of proximate love expressed through hospitality through a haunting question: "If anyone has the world's goods and sees his brother in need, yet closes his heart against him, how does God's love abide in him?" Opening one's heart requires *seeing* the needs of others, which requires getting close to others. Practically speaking, closeness is made possible through hospitality.

---

86. During the global pandemic beginning in 2020, it has been a topic of conversation that believers can indeed love one another even while not being in physical proximity with each other. But it has also become clear that something is missing from these loving but distant interactions. The actual sharing of physical space is the arena where practical love works itself out most powerfully for non-omnipresent humans.

In Ethiopia and in the biblical text, proximity is assumed. In most of history and even in modern-day Ethiopia, privacy was or is a privilege that most cannot even imagine, due to factors such as multi-generational households, small living quarters, farming land or running small businesses together, or making use of public transportation. In the Ancient Near East and in Ethiopia still, pedestrian traffic was and is also the norm,[87] meaning that even when one is not intentionally connecting with a specific another person, there are people all around (this could perhaps be called "ambient community") with whom one can experience what Eric O. Jacobson calls "public belonging"[88] and "civic friendship,"[89] which turns out to be good for the well-being of everyone involved.[90]

Proximity includes with it the sense of habitual rather than occasional nearness. And regularly being in one another's presence leads to a different level of intimacy and a shared day-by-day history that means not having to orient another to the general topography of one's life but being able to zoom in further and dig deeper in conversation and friendship.[91] In Ethiopia, it is typical to either regularly see (or regularly call, in an accommodation to modern life) one's friends and to have a sense of what is

---

87. Haddis, *Just Mission*, 115, describes her shock about the lack of pedestrian traffic in the USA as compared to her native Ethiopia as follows: "The first memory I have of coming to America is the loneliness I felt after being picked up from the airport by a family member. I was driven to their beautiful home in the suburbs of Dallas, Texas. The loneliness didn't initially come from being homesick, since I had just landed and was excited about exploring all the amazing things awaiting me in America. It came from feeling like I was on another planet as we drove for almost an hour on highways and entered suburban neighborhoods where there was no foot traffic. It was an experience of isolation that seeped into my heart and left me wondering, *Where are all the people?* It was mind-boggling to see no sign of life. It was otherworldly and felt unnatural."

88. Jacobsen, *Three Pieces of Glass*, 11.

89. Jacobsen, *Three Pieces of Glass*, 14.

90. Jacobsen, *Three Pieces of Glass*, 15.

91. I have noticed this dynamic in my life and believe it may be a universal phenomenon: with certain friends with whom I have proximity (whether through regular physical nearness or through intentional and frequent keeping in touch), I am able to share in a much more detailed way (such as a specific story from this very afternoon, an update on a complicated situation at work, or a deeper dive on something I had been thinking about last week) which would feel strange to share with the friends with whom I only catch up a few times a year. With the more "occasional" friends, the questions have to be more general, simply getting a handle on the broad contours of each others' lives by asking general questions such as "How's life? How's work? What are the kids up to lately?" and giving answers ("We're good! Busy!") that conceal or leave out as much or more than they convey.

going on with one another at any given time. When seeing one another or talking with one another even after a slightly longer than average period of separation, it is common for one or the other of the friends to exclaim, "*Tafa(s)h!*" (literally meaning "You are lost!") to dramatically indicate that the person has disappeared from the speaker's social orbit and was missed. To go long periods without seeing or contacting friends is seen as abnormal and deeply concerning.

In Ethiopia, it is not typical to go away to be by oneself when one is feeling sad or sick. Instead, one's friends are expected to come close to bring comfort particularly in these times, the times of one's need. So Ethiopians are naturally on the lookout for when they are needed by their friends, and they tend to have wide networks of people who they consider to be their friends. As far as I have seen and heard, this disposition of empathetic awareness for a large number of people and desire to be close to them in good times and bad is not explicitly taught to children as much as it is modeled through the circumstances of daily life. Perhaps it could be said that by connecting with others physically through shared space or emotionally through empathetic awareness, Ethiopians are simply living out a reflection of their understanding of reality as fundamentally interconnected and interdependent.

When there is a high level of proximity, needs do not go unnoticed. Being physically near and/or closely connected with others helps Ethiopians to be highly empathetic and aware of what may be missing in another's life (whether physical or emotional) that they could provide for through the open heart and open hands of generosity of spirit and of resources.[92]

---

92. As a privacy-oriented but proximity-curious American living for years in Ethiopia, I have often been initially made uncomfortable by the uncanny awareness of Ethiopians about my physical and mental state, and have then become grateful for it. It is typical to have people in my home every day on an informal basis, coming and going, and they often can take one look at me and say, "I see you're feeling sad. What's wrong?" or "Are you tired today? How can I help you?" I generally cannot hide what is going on with me from them, and I wonder if this may be because they have generally been trained in empathy through daily proximity with others in a country where privacy is nearly non-existent. For cultural contrast, see Uhls et al., "Five Days," 391, which found that American "children who were away from screens for five days with many opportunities for in-person interaction improved significantly in reading facial emotion . . . compared to those in a control group." It should be noted that smartphones can be extrapolated from this study to be a contributor to the erosion of empathy in American young people, and it remains to be seen (or perhaps it is already starting to be seen) how skyrocketing smartphone ownership in Ethiopia will affect the value of empathy and other communally oriented ways of living in the Ethiopian culture in the generations to come.

Indeed, empathetic proximity is largely what allows for provision for so many impoverished citizens in Ethiopia who are cared for by regular, almost casual generous almsgiving and the subtle inclusion of the proximate (neighbors, beggars nearby, etc.) into mealtime and coffee rituals. Because they are near,[93] the poor are seen, and because they are seen, they are compassionately provided for through the habit of hospitality.[94]

When considering proximity, the question is raised: what of personal space? Every culture—even a communally minded one—has a sense of physical personal space, but the size of that space varies from culture to culture.[95] Predictably, an Ethiopian sense of personal space is smaller than an American one, with physical touch and closeness (whether handholding, arms around each other's shoulders, sitting close to each other, etc.) forming a fundamental aspect of any friendship. Though cheek kisses between Ethiopians are generally reserved only for a greeting between two females nowadays, Paul's command to "greet one another with a holy kiss" (Rom 16:16–18; 2 Cor 13:12) does not seem as wholly out of place in spirit in Ethiopia as it does in the West.[96]

Apart from physical personal space, there is a deeper aspect of personal space that may be even more challenging to share if one is privacy-oriented, but will be natural to share if one is proximity-oriented: hospitality of the heart. "To me hospitality doesn't have to do with just addressing my

---

93. There are many reasons for this nearness, including the high level of pedestrian traffic in Ethiopia and the mixed-income nature of Ethiopian communities, about which Holland, *Culture Smart!*, 64, comments: "In Ethiopian cities, rich and poor live in the same neighborhoods, and the incongruity of having slums nestling next to opulent hotels elicits little comment from Ethiopians."

94. This combination of interdependency as a value and proximity as a practical catalyst renders the prioritism versus holism debate moot in Ethiopia, according to Urga, *Reflection*, 31: "There is a huge tendency in the West to dichotomize or compartmentalize. This tendency has affected our current topic in tremendous ways. In the West, Christian workers often pigeonhole themselves as Prioritists (preaching first/alone) or Holists (social work and then preaching/social work alone). But for an African, even for the early Church fathers, this dichotomy is surely an absurdity. How can one choose one over the other? They are inseparable! You always preach the Gospel—it is your obligation in light of the Great Commission—but at the same time you do not forget if your neighbor is in need. Putting one of these things above the other does not fit the African worldview, for Africans have a communal lifestyle."

95. For more on how personal space varies from culture to culture, see Sorokowska et al., "Preferred Interpersonal Distances."

96. For more on both the importance of and lack of platonic touch in the lives of Americans—particularly American men—see Reiner, "Power of Touch."

physical needs," says one interviewee. "It has to do with creating a space for me so I can be with you. Whatever comes after that is secondary, but first of all, do I have the freedom to share your personal space? That's what hospitality is for me." The idea that this interviewee speaks of—creating space—is almost entirely opposite than the concept common in America of "giving space." The notion that when one's friend is having a hard time, the thing to do is to "give them space" is entirely foreign and even shocking to Ethiopians because it seems unnatural.

Perhaps "sharing space" is an even better way to explain the idea of heart hospitality, since "creating space" envisages conjuring up the space out of nothing, whereas "sharing space" brings to mind the giving of oneself and the gaining of a friend. According to the same interviewee:

> We all have personal space, so hospitality is to share that space, making people feel welcome. It's not outside of me, it has to take from my personal space in order to do it. The very idea of hospitality challenges me to really share my life, my comfort, my time, my resources, and all of that (that's what I call sharing of personal space). We all need a space where we feel freedom, nobody touches this. I don't think we should give up everything. But there are times that we have to share with other people.

Sharing of space physically and emotionally is natural only when one holds the value of relationships being more important than tasks, as is the case in Ethiopian culture. If relationality is highly valued, visitors of any kind (whether they arrive at one's office door or one's home for dinner or one's caller ID) will be regarded with joyful anticipation as the most important work of the day—the work of building relationships.[97] If, on the other hand, tasks are more important than relationships, then the arrival of visitors is a bothersome interruption which hinders the accomplishment of the more important, task-based work.[98]

---

97. Nnamunga, "Theological Anthropology," 224, lists six aspects of East African hospitality which are corroborated by my interviewees: "welcoming, interaction, identification, sharing, integration, and mutual dialogue."

98. Pohl, *Living into Community*, 165, explains that part of growing in hospitality is allowing for and even welcoming interruptions. For more on time/task orientation versus event/relational orientation, see Lingenfelter and Mayers, "Tensions about Time."

Outworkings of Communal Interdependence

Valuing communion with God and communion with others and living those values out through the sharing of space and needs leads Ethiopians to several God-honoring, biblically resonant beliefs and practices, including recognizing the limitations of individual humanity, building friendships that are relational rather than transactional, and enjoying God's gifts together, sometimes through community-generated groups which manage to simultaneously benefit each individual member of the group while also benefiting the group as a whole.

Recognizing the Limitations of Individual Humanity

When one acknowledges that one is intrinsically connected with God—in whom humans live and move and have their being—and with others, without whom one can never be whole, then one necessarily recognizes one's own limitations. To be human is to be small, only one part of a larger whole. In general, Ethiopians have a healthy grasp of their own smallness and limitations, leading them to open-handedness regarding the control of circumstances and to focus instead on cooperation with others for mutual benefit: the "many members" which are part of "one body" (1 Cor 12:12) using each one's "manifestation of the Spirit for the common good" (1 Cor 12:8).

Building Relational Friendships

When one recognizes the limitations of one's individual humanity, one is naturally pulled toward connection with others through friendship. At first blush, the phrase "relational friendships" seems redundant, but when contrasted with "transactional friendships,"[99] the adjective is clarifying. In Ethiopia, friendships tend to be relationally focused, with friends focusing on friends as whole people rather than viewing them as means to an end, objects, or projects, which can too often be the case in the transactional

---

99. Sauls, *Befriend*, 2–3, explains that "transactional friendship treats other people as means to an end. When we relate this way, we come to view people more as resources than as human beings. Instead of loving and serving them as we would in a real friendship, we *use* them to advance our careers, build our platforms, gain access to their social circles, increase our self-esteem . . . impress others . . . and so on."

friendships which are more common in the West (with friends focusing on how their friends can help them reach their goals or achieve higher status, even as a do-gooder). Scripture favors the former kind of friendship when Paul urges the Philippians to have the mind of Christ and to "do nothing from selfish ambition or conceit, but in humility count others more significant than yourselves. Let each of you look not only to his own interests, but also to the interests of others" (Phil 2:3–4).

Enjoying and Stewarding God's Gifts Together

When friendships are relational rather than transactional, they are focused on enjoying God's gifts together, because "what do we have that we did not receive?" (1 Cor 4:7). Ethiopians prioritize expressing thankfulness toward God together as one of life's most important practices. Joyfully receiving God's gifts naturally leads to an open-handed posture, which facilitates generosity. Generosity of spirit leads to celebration, which is best done in community with others, naturally leading to hospitality in which everyone can simply enjoy and steward God's gifts, accomplishing more together than they could ever do alone.

Forming Community-Generated, Community-Building Groups

The extremely poor are not the only ones provided for in a culture that values communion with God and others, understands that all of reality is interconnected and interdependent, shares needs and shares space. Ethiopians also voluntarily join together for the express purpose of sharing needs and sharing space in a way that will benefit all involved, enriching their lives and allowing them to accomplish more together than they ever could alone.

Rural farmers in Ethiopia, called "peasants" by Mennasemay, have long used a rotating system called *däbo* (also spelled *dabo* or *debo*) to help each other with farm projects that entail more than one farmer can do alone.[100] In doing so, "The participants act together as a group to achieve

---

100. For more on *däbo*, see Bartels, "Dabo."

a goal that enhances both the welfare of the individual member[101] and of the group."[102]

At first glance, this system seems like the utilitarian trading of manpower to get jobs done, but

> To grasp the emancipatory ideas that gestate in *däbo*, it is important to go beyond the instrumentalist conceptualization of *däbo* in terms of "exchange" of labor. Given the dominance of capitalist market values in "development" theory and practice, the term "exchange" is preloaded, as it were, with social atomism and utility maximization. It thus blinds us to the fact that *däbo* involves a different mode of thought, practice, and social relatedness that spurn individualistic ontology, competition, and the commodification of labour.... *Däbo* is more like a "gift of labor" than an "exchange of labor." It involves a mutual commitment to the wellbeing of the members of *däbo* and of *däbo* itself as an association.[103]

An example of what this gift of labor looks like in practice is the fact that when there is a sick or disabled farmer who is unable to contribute his own labor to the labor pool, the other farmers will still work his land,[104] because of the understanding—held in common with all African cultures that subscribe to an *ubuntu*-adjacent worldview—that "*yäne bite*"—meaning "he/she is like me, I am like her/him."[105] Based on their

---

101. In communally generated groups like *däbo* and others which will be mentioned later, an individual's existence and needs are not subsumed or negated by the existence and needs of the community. Rather, the individual is seen as an important part of the group which simply does not make sense on its own, like an individual part of a body—despite the fact that it is very important and valuable in and of itself—does not make sense without the rest of the body. Interdependence is assumed as ontological and, as such, is seen as the proper context for individual flourishing. For more on ontological interdependence versus ontological individualism, see Mennasemay, *Qiné Hermeneutics*, 383, 455; Ali and Shishigu, "Implications of Ubuntu/Synergy," 3. Seen from this perspective, Mennasemay, *Qiné Hermeneutics*, 384, remarks that "unlike the capitalist development paradigm, which sees human needs from an individualistic standpoint, *däbo* produces surplus meanings that conceive human needs as socially created, enabled, and fulfilled, hence its informal philosophy of *säw läsäw mädhanitu* (humanity is the cure for humanity)."

102. Mennasemay, *Qiné Hermeneutics*, 382.

103. Mennasemay, *Qiné Hermeneutics*, 384.

104. Mennasemay, *Qiné Hermeneutics*, 384.

105. Mennasemay, *Qiné Hermeneutics*, 383. This proverb encapsulates an Ethiopian understanding of *ubuntu* or *medemer*.

assumption that "interdependence is ontological"[106] and that "the other is immanent in me; that his/her need is mine, as mine is his/hers,"[107] Ethiopian peasants transcend the difficult circumstances of their existence and instead "create and own a social time and space that allows them to pursue that which the hegemonic structures and beliefs put out of their reach [as poor, disenfranchised people]: self-determination, rationality, the pursuit of the common good, and nobility of soul."[108]

The power of *däbo* lies in the fact that the community it builds and nurtures is not based primarily upon identity—whether national or tribal—by birth, nor is it simply a gaggle of individuals who happen to engage in transactions with each other in order to further their personal goals: rather, it is a fundamental choice[109] to live out the proverb, "When spider webs unite, they can tie up a lion."[110] According to Mennasemay, "*Däbo* is neither an 'aggregate we' of atomic individuals nor a 'communal we' rooted in primordial relations." Rather, "the 'we' of *däbo* is rooted in shared needs, shared intentions, and shared commitments to pursue a commonly shared goal through commonly shared decisions and actions." In this sense, *däbo* is "an active collectivity."[111]

Interestingly, the strategy of those who exploit Ethiopian peasants is the atomization of individuals: "Those who exploit the peasantry . . . do so through a process that fragments the peasantry such that the Ethiopian peasant finds himself alone facing powerful forces that he cannot cope with. It is this forced individualization that prevents peasants from acting together in defense of their dignity and commonly shared needs and interests."[112] Thus, when peasants organize themselves in grassroots associations such as *däbo*, they are engaging in "'silent' rebellion, because

---

106. Mennasemay, *Qiné Hermeneutics*, 383.

107. Mennasemay, *Qiné Hermeneutics*, 383.

108. Mennasemay, *Qiné Hermeneutics*, 385.

109. Jacobsen, *Three Pieces of Glass*, 176, talks about the difference between ad hoc choices and fundamental choices regarding potential lifestyle changes in the socially disconnected United States. Ad hoc choices are one-off decisions that are unlikely to affect the rest of one's life or change one's lifestyle, whereas fundamental choices are choices, though made once (such as, in this case, to join a *däbo* in one's farming community), but that one decision alters one's existence in fundamental ways and helps to create an ongoing difference in one's lifestyle going forward.

110. Demoze and Armstrong, *Ethiopian Amharic Proverbs*, 76.

111. Mennasemay, *Qiné Hermeneutics*, 382.

112. Mennasemay, *Qiné Hermeneutics*, 386.

they go against exploitative and oppressive relations, not by challenging them politically but by creating a space and time they own. The organizational principles and functioning of *däbo* [and other similar groups which will be discussed later] and their surplus meanings express a kind of 'opting out' from the ambient socio-economic space and time of powerlessness."[113] The practice of "*däbo* projects the idea of the common good as the 'unity' of joy[114] and substantive rationality, of responsibility and freedom, of equality and solidarity, of individuality and sociality, and of labouring and universality. The surplus meanings of *däbo* affirm that a life of the common good is possible and preferable. In sum, *däbo* expresses ... utopianism without utopia."[115]

As Ethiopia began to urbanize and modernization led to a greater variety of jobs, *däbo* was no longer a practical system for an ever-increasing number of Ethiopians. Instead of cultivating the land, many people now had to manage the novel challenges of living in the city away from their home villages and extended family networks. With the principles of *däbo* imprinted in their memories, Ethiopians in these new circumstances created the *iddir* (also spelled *idir* and *eder*) system as "a creative response to the inadequacies of the old society and of the new society to respond to the challenges, desires, and threats that the new conditions created."[116] Over time, *iddir* "eventually grew and became a wide-spread mutual aid association,"[117] made up of small groups all over the country whose members number thirty-nine million.[118] These groups are "not connected with any kind of official organization or government initiative";[119] rather, they are the grassroots efforts "of Ethiopians to create a space of meaningful social relations in the new context of living that seems to pay scant attention ... to the welfare of those who do not have adequate resources to cope with the precarities [of life or] to their desires and efforts to create a decent habitable context of life."[120] It is a "constructive response" to the problem of previ-

---

113. Mennasemay, *Qiné Hermeneutics*, 437.

114. For more on the connection of joy (*fissiha*) and the common good experienced in community, see the introduction of chapter 5.

115. Mennasemay, *Qiné Hermeneutics*, 389.

116. Mennasemay, *Qiné Hermeneutics*, 392.

117. Mennasemay, *Qiné Hermeneutics*, 392.

118. Mennasemay, *Qiné Hermeneutics*, 427.

119. Mennasemay, *Qiné Hermeneutics*, 390.

120. Mennasemay, *Qiné Hermeneutics*, 392.

ous ways of living not being adequate to deal with rapid social change and its associated challenges. Through engaging in healthy, creative, collective adaptation in liminal spaces, members gain a "secondary identification" which includes a sense of belonging that goes beyond family, tribe, region, or religion.[121] In this sense, "One could say that [like its older sister *däbo*][122] *iddir* signals a utopianism without utopia."[123]

Technically, the stated purpose of an *iddir* is to "[provide] primarily moral and financial support to members in case of death [of any family member in what are generally large extended families]," but functionally speaking,

> its social role is much wider. It helps members who have other urgent needs; it serves as a social space for members to air and share their opinions on various issues of common concern; it is a milieu that makes possible the hatching and cultivation of friendships. An iddir could engage in various social interactions that enhance mutual understanding, respect, and solidarity; it could also involve itself in projects such as building roads, health centers, and schools or in a small scale productive activities and home industries.[124]

Another system which has been developed through decentralized grassroots efforts by Ethiopians and is now a cultural feature whose members number twenty-one million[125] is called *iqqub* (also spelled *iqub* or *equb*). At its most fundamental level, *iqqub* is an association of people who all agree to pay a certain amount of money into a common pot each month (or another stated interval of time), and then to award the total amount to one of the members by lottery. Thus, its purpose is "to make available to its members financial resources that are out of reach in terms of each

---

121. Mennasemay, *Qiné Hermeneutics*, 393.

122. One can see the similarity between *däbo* and *iddir* in Mennasemay's, *Qiné Hermeneutics*, 393, description of the *wärq* (that is, surplus meanings) of *iddir* that is quite similar to a previous description of the *wärq* of *däbo* quoted above: "In iddir gestates a non-tradition [meaning it is not a tradition nor is it anti-tradition]: the idea of individuality without individualism, an idea about active and free interdependence that is expressive of neither primordial relations nor of mere aggregation of individuals."

123. Mennasemay, *Qiné Hermeneutics*, 392.

124. Mennasemay, *Qiné Hermeneutics*, 390. For more on *iddir*, see Aredo, "Iddir"; Stuer et al., "From Burial Societies to Mutual Aid Organizations"; Haile Mariam, "Ethiopia."

125. Mennasemay, *Qiné Hermeneutics*, 427.

individual's capacity."[126] Though the lottery is by its very nature random, the members of the group have the power to override the results and give the gathered monthly sum to a particular group member if that member expresses an urgent need which will cause suffering in their lives if they do not have sufficient funds to deal with it immediately. Needs like this are not something to hide and try to deal with oneself in Ethiopia. Because of the precarity of the majority of people's financial situations and the mentality that the concern of one is the concern of all, Ethiopian culture encourages the sharing of needs and the importance of bearing each others' burdens. Several proverbs inculcate and reinforce the cultural feature of sharing needs, including: "One who hides his illness has no medicine,"[127] "If one does not call for help, a neighbor will not come to the rescue,"[128] and "Fifty lemons are a load for one person, but for fifty people they are 'perfume.'"[129] In this sense, *iqqub* shines as primarily a human institution rather than a financial one,[130] showing, like *iddir*, the creative potential for the "modernization of *däbo*" with its concern for "the common good"[131] in the midst of the challenging liminal circumstances of cultural change. "*Iqqub* stands at the juncture of the old conception of money (*gänzäb*) that sees it in terms of personal relations and the new conception of money (*bir*) that sees it as a neutral abstract commodity that has impersonal powers of its own to which human needs are secondary."[132] *Iqqub* attempts to understand money as both/and rather than either/or, and so to navigate modern life well while also holding on to the members' intrinsic humanity.[133]

126. Mennasemay, *Qiné Hermeneutics*, 397. Haddis, *Just Mission*, 125, adds that *iqqub*-like groups are not limited to Ethiopia: "This tradition is practiced in other African countries as well. In Nigeria they call it *sousou*; in Somalia it is *hagbad* or *ayuuto*; in Jamaica it is known as a 'partner.' In Guyana it is a 'box hand,' in Haiti *min*, and in South African *stokvel*."

127. Demoze and Armstrong, *Ethiopian Amharic Proverbs*, 42.

128. Demoze and Armstrong, *Ethiopian Amharic Proverbs*, 79.

129. Demoze and Armstrong, *Ethiopian Amharic Proverbs*, 43.

130. Haddis, *Just Mission*, 126, says that in *iqqub*, "Not only are financial needs attended to but also emotional and communal needs. It is about caring for the whole person, as money alone cannot buy happiness." She also draws a parallel between this practice and the early church practice of caring for one another in Acts 2:44–45, saying, "This approach also reflects the beautiful horizontal philanthropy the early church practiced."

131. Mennasemay, *Qiné Hermeneutics*, 389.

132. Mennasemay, *Qiné Hermeneutics*, 396.

133. For more on the practice of *iqqub*, see Aredo, "Rotating Savings and Credit

BIBLICAL RESONANCE

Official institutions in the governmental, financial, and non-profit sectors have taken careful note of indigenous systems of mutual aid such as *iddir* and *iqqub* and have tried to interest members in making their organizations official in various capacities, such as getting insurance coverage together,[134] and have also tried to interest Ethiopians in loans for their financial needs instead of being part of an *iqqub*, but so far, such efforts have largely been unsuccessful. Ethiopians are attached to their self-generated systems precisely because they have been self-generated, and as such, embody creative, contextual solutions to problems by coming together collectively for the common good. By stark contrast,

> the practices of the formal financial sector project a social imaginary of discrete individuals who calculate their interests, are in competition with each other, and self-regulate themselves through the capitalist market to increase their utilities. The social imaginary that subtends the financial market is that of an aggregate of *homo oeconomicus*. The values and norms of *homo oeconomicus*, which articulate the emerging Ethiopian capitalist sector [of which the banking system is a part], personalize the causes of the social sufferings that members of *iqqub* encounter in their lives and consider such social sufferings as individual problems that are to be self-managed. Such an imaginary devoid of the ideas of shared needs, social bonds, and co-obligation is antithetical to the social imaginary that informs *iqqub*.

Thus, there is a fundamental incompatibility between the presuppositions of *iqqub* and those of banks, because "the primacy of need and co-obligation in the operation of *iqqub* goes against the primacy of profit and of individualistic interest in the formal financial sector."[135]

Däbo and its more modern counterparts, *iddir* and *iqqub*, shine in their flexibility based upon friendships which grow through self-generated organization and commitment to pursue the flourishing of each member and of the group as a whole. All three have general principles by which they operate which can be overridden by the group's unanimous decision to counter the powerlessness of a particular suffering member with the full weight of the group's support, be it through man-power or money. This is done not out of

---

Associations"; Aredo, "Iqqub"; Bisrat et al., "Are There Financial Benefits?"; Teshome, "Role and Potential of 'Iqqub.'"

134. Mennasemay, *Qiné Hermeneutics*, 428.

135. Mennasemay, *Qiné Hermeneutics*, 399.

outsized pity or charity,[136] but because the members realize as fundamental truth the ideas contained in proverbs such as *yäne bite* ("He is like me, I am like him"), *eném inko säw näñ* ("I also am a human being"), and *säw le säw mädhanitu* ("Humanity is the cure for humanity").

Just as there are similarities between *däbo* and *iqqub* in form, there are similarities in their detractors and distractors. Both the exploiters of peasants and the large for-profit and non-profit sector institutions attempt—whether from good intentions or bad—to atomize people into individuals who must deal with their problems individually, without support from the wider community. The reasons for the unpopularity of the formal insurance system, for example, become obvious when one compares the "culturally appropriate, flexible, easily accessible, and cost-effective *iddir* system which is based upon "solidarity, friendship, and mutual assistance among members," to the alternative, which is "limited to high income households" and whose terms and conditions are fixed, inflexible, and impersonal regardless of the unexpected twists and turns life takes.[137] The potential of both *iddir* and *iqqub* also greatly exceeds that of more formal institutions in terms of the common good since "the payoff of the openness that characterizes the operations of these associations is the growth of mutual trust and respect that allows members to discuss and tackle new issues or engage in ad hoc activities that may not be covered by the tasks assigned to the association but are beneficial to the community."[138]

Addendum: Cultural Change in Ethiopia

Staunch isolationist policies throughout much of her history have made it possible for Ethiopia to maintain a unique, ancient culture even while much of the rest of the world was being shaped by modernizing forces. While increased travel both to and from Ethiopia in the last few decades had begun to open the door to globalization, the advent of the smartphone and readily available internet access has—nearly overnight—flung wide the metaphorical borders of Ethiopia such that ideas from other

---

136. Mennasemay, *Qiné Hermeneutics*, 436, is clear that true community "rejects the degradation of solidarity into charity." Charity as understood in the modern day is individualistic, one-way, and momentary, whereas solidarity involves collectivity, mutuality, and ongoing relationship.

137. Aredo quoted in Mennasemay, *Qiné Hermeneutics*, 428.

138. Mennasemay, *Qiné Hermeneutics*, 389.

cultures are suddenly changing the dynamics of Ethiopians' lives at a pace that feels out of control and is thus alarming to many of the interviewees profiled in chapter three.

While there have certainly been some positive aspects of these changes, several interviewees profiled in chapter three expressed the concern that modernization (with its pull toward not only economic success but also increased materialism) as well as globalization, spearheaded by the Western-sourced gospel of individualism, are forces which are insidiously and often unconsciously eroding the value of hospitality in Ethiopians. Though these interviewees were disturbed by many Ethiopians' gradual move away from what had historically been the culturally central value of hospitality, as immigrants who had been away for some time, they were somewhat uncertain what should be done to regain what may be gradually being lost in Ethiopia. In other words, if the structure[139] upholding the value shifts or crumbles, how can the value be preserved?

Because my family and I relocated to Addis Ababa, Ethiopia, during the writing of this book,[140] I initiated another round of interviews in order

---

139. Mbaya, "Social Capital," 370, remarks: "In African communities, collaborative activity becomes possible precisely because of the existence of the traditional participatory structures that promote consensus" and compares this to Putnam's observations in the seminal book *Bowling Alone*, about the key role that "voluntary organisations" used to play in maintaining social cohesion in the USA, concluding simply: "the social cohesion of African communities thus depends very much on such structures."

140. Re-settling back in Addis Ababa after four years away was somewhat shocking for me in terms of the cultural change that had occurred during the relatively brief interval in which we were away. One specific change—the prevalence and affordability of mobile phones and high-speed internet—has truly managed to change the cultural landscape in ways I am still being surprised by as we get reacquainted with life here in Addis Ababa. One example can represent a hundred stories: in our neighborhood, there is a communal grassy area where children and teens spend every spare minute they can, and my children are no exception. Because I have a three year old who is not ready to be sent out independently, I am one of the few parents who is outside for significant amounts of time per day, so I have become a friend and confidante of several pre-teen Ethiopians whose schools have ensured that they are fluent or at least highly conversant in English, and who sometimes want a break from playing soccer and climbing trees. In a conversation with a particularly chatty and astute eleven year old and his nine year old cousin visiting from across town, the eleven year old asked, "Can I ask you a question? Can money buy happiness?" I laughed and remarked what a very grown-up question it was, then asked him what he thought. He said he was unsure, but "when I watch YouTube from Dubai, they seem to be telling me that money *can* buy happiness." We talked about the difference between being rich and being spoiled—a topic with which he seemed to be personally wrestling—and his cousin remarked that he thought there were a lot of spoiled kids in America. "Well, you're probably right," I began, but he was

to answer my previous interviewees' gnawing questions, this time with nine Ethiopian Protestants in their twenties and thirties who had lived their whole lives in Ethiopia. Unlike my previous interviewees, they did not have any chronological gaps in their understanding of the shifts of the social and cultural landscape in recent decades in Ethiopia, so I enlisted their help to understand the current situation in Ethiopia, to assess the possibility of a global spread of the loneliness epidemic, and to consider what can be done in Ethiopia to preserve and pass on the Ethiopian cultural value of building community through hospitality to the next generation even in the globalizing modern world.

I asked the nine interviewees, "Do you feel that the Ethiopian value of building community through hospitality has been less expressed in recent years? If so, why? If not, why not?" and the related question, "Do you think the loneliness epidemic that is currently affecting the West is beginning to affect Ethiopia? If so, in what way? If not, why not?" My interviewees thoughtfully nuanced their answers, expressing the complexity of a nation simultaneously still deeply influenced by its roots and also being increasingly affected by global winds of change.

All interviewees acknowledged that the value of hospitality has been somewhat less expressed in recent years.[141] Six went on to say that they be-

---

not finished and interrupted, exclaiming, "TikTok tells me America is full of racists and *Karens*!" He then watched carefully for my response. Partially because of his accent but mostly because I was not expecting a nine year old Ethiopian to be familiar with the term "Karen," I asked him to repeat himself twice. Finally, he literally spelled it out: "K-A-R-E-N-S—Karens!" After I recovered from my laughter, we ended up having a good conversation. My unofficial park research is helping me to extrapolate how culture change will in all likelihood continue rapidly in Ethiopia as the new generation grows up with an attraction to and knowledge of (at least through media) the whole world rather than just their corner of it. While there are positives in this global connectivity, it concerns me greatly that important and biblically resonant aspects of Ethiopian culture could be lost to the global (primarily Western-culture influenced) internet culture that the pre-teens in my neighborhood—and, it could be extrapolated, many of the children of the educated elite in Ethiopia—seem to primarily live in, despite standing with me on the ground in a park in Addis Ababa.

141. For two weeks in May 2022, I was asked to teach a Sunday School class at International Evangelical Church in Addis Ababa, Ethiopia, on my research topic, and enjoyed lively discussions with believers from Ethiopia, Kenya, and Zimbabwe about loneliness and hospitality in global perspective. These conversations convinced me more than ever before that the topic of loneliness and hospitality is a particularly crucial one for our times, not just in the West but around the world. Participants from the other African countries mentioned described a similar dynamic as the one I have observed in urban Ethiopia, with the advent of widespread internet and global social

lieve the loneliness epidemic is already beginning to affect Ethiopia, while three said that it is not, or at least not yet. In other words, there was consensus among interviewees that the practice of building community through hospitality is lessening, at least in the urban areas (where I and all nine of the interviewees live and work), but there is a difference of opinion regarding whether underlying values are shifting or remaining constant.

EE (that is, Ethiopian living in Ethiopia; these interviewees will be hereafter referred to as EE 1, EE 2, EE 3, and so on) mentions that in his lifetime (all interviewees are under forty years old), there has been a sharp change in communal values being expressed: "Growing up, I remember a lot of good values in the society I was raised in. Every part of the community knows that the community is more important than the individual. This is true regardless of gender, race, and/or religion."[142]

Over the course of the past few decades, however, political changes seem to have drawn harsher dividing lines even between countrymen. "The political narrative" is cited by EE 5 as contributing to the breakdown of the "communal fabric" of Ethiopia, since "ethnic violence everywhere has affected how households look at their neighbor. The suspicion of each other and the othering of people"[143] is changing the long-standing tradition of building community through hospitality as an expression of ontological interconnected interdependence.

EE 8 broadens this idea to include recent history as well: "Especially after the military leadership came to power in 1974, . . . [they] introduced atheism which is new to our culture and they tried to eradicate the role of the Ethiopian Orthodox *Tewahido* Church in the Ethiopian leadership and culture. They also persecuted Christians. In this process, the community loosened with the principles of Christian values, one of which is hospitality."[144] Into this void created by years of enforced atheism, this interviewee continues, globalization rushed in after the fall of the military leadership and was able to shift Ethiopian culture because of its weakened root system.

---

media exposure bringing with it an increase in an individualistic mindset that has correlated with a weakening of community and an increase in loneliness compared to even relatively recent years past, so while loneliness is not yet at what they considered "epidemic" levels, they expressed a high level of concern in general regarding waning community in modern day life in their respective countries and as newcomers to Ethiopia's bustling capital city as well.

142. Interviewed May 16, 2022.
143. Interviewed May 17, 2022.
144. Interviewed May 27, 2022.

Several interviewees agreed that globalization has played a role in changing the culture in Ethiopia in many ways, including in the expression of hospitality in Ethiopia. Globalization may be at least partially responsible for "suppressing [the value of building community through hospitality] due to its incompatibility with the concept."[145] Technology is a de facto tool of globalization, and EE 8 expressed concern that "social media seems to replace an actual friendship or community." EE 1 describes the modern Ethiopian society in such a way that—if read without context—could be describing the West:

> Nowadays people are always on their phone instead of talking to each other. You can even see this in the church service where people are interacting during prayer, sermon, and singing time. Or you can see people taking pictures in case of an accident or something like that instead of offering help. Another example would be lack of social circles among the young generation. Previously, people used to have friends, classmates, and cultural social groups they are part of. But now, many young folks do not have those groups. All they have is many friends on Facebook.

Urbanization has also been a factor in decreasing the expression of hospitality—Addis Ababa has become a megacity as more and more people relocate there for work and the city expands rapidly and somewhat haphazardly outward like the rings of a tree. Housing demands have necessitated the building of new, multistory apartment buildings which are cited by some interviewees as well as in casual conversations as being places devoid of tight-knit community where neighbors do not know each other in the way that was more common when single (often multigenerational) homes were the norm. EE 8 questions the idea that this loss of community is inevitable in newer housing options, however: "It is true in Ethiopia that modern life is making more people live alone in the urban areas. But loneliness and aloneness are not the same."

By contrast to the above descriptions of modern, urban life in Ethiopia, several interviewees reported that there is much less cultural shift regarding the expression of hospitable values in rural areas. EE 8 explains: "Yes, [the value] has been less expressed in recent years. . . . However, the magnitude of the change [in the expression of hospitable values] is different in rural and urban areas. In urban and semi-urban areas, the magnitude is quite high."

---

145. EE 6, interviewed May 17, 2022.

Concern for finances—exacerbated by the mindset that "the modern life is preferable"[146]—is another reason that hospitality is less expressed than before, according to interviewees. "Life has become busy," says EE 9,[147] and EE 5 exclaims: "Everyone runs and labors to have bread! When it is due, the sunset comes. There will not be time for living together."[148] EE 1 adds that "the struggle to provide for family decreases the amount of time one has for a community." EE 9 explains further that "since everything is getting more expensive people are trying to get extra income doing more than one job which takes away the time to socialize. Even so the essence is still there." Conversely, EE 8 sees financial lack as actually inhibiting the spread of the loneliness epidemic, because people without a financially secure position are forced to rely on each other and live in interdependence both person-to-person and through participation in social groups: "Our economic situation makes us socialize on different levels and platforms to overcome the economic challenges, like [for example] 'eder.'"

There were three interviewees who maintain that the loneliness epidemic is not affecting Ethiopia. EE 7 says: "We are still a community based society. People still have one way or another to build community that is sustained with the fuel of their social need."[149] EE 9 agrees and hits upon an explanation for the in-between place where Ethiopians find themselves: the value of building community through hospitality is still there, but there are increasing time pressures that may make the expression more cramped than before.

> There are [so] many people checking on you. Or you're having coffee or lunch with someone or someone is coming to your house. In my life and the ones around me it's actually hard to get an alone moment. Especially if you've commitment at church. There's always a prayer or a meeting or someone to visit. There's not enough time. That's how I see it.

The six interviewees who do believe the loneliness epidemic is beginning to affect Ethiopia are especially concerned about young people. EE 1 mentions that the loneliness epidemic is particularly beginning to affect "the young and educated part of the society . . . [which is] influenced by Western philosophy about the meaning of life, religion, success, etc. Not only that,

---

146. EE 8.
147. Interviewed May 28, 2022.
148. Interviewed May 28, 2022.
149. Interviewed May 25, 2022.

[this segment of the population] uses social media as a communication, entertainment, and educational platform. I think these two reasons are the primary ones that are promoting individualism." Regarding individualism, EE 2 concludes that among Ethiopia's youth "there are a volume of signs that people are more focused on their personal engagements than being concerned for others."[150] The same interviewee goes on to say:

> I agree that loneliness has its shadows [in Ethiopia], though it is difficult to call it an "epidemic." Because there is an overlap between the generations, a generation who have preserved hospitality even within the urban setting whereas there is part of society that is in loneliness situations. However, there are data explaining the loneliness epidemic is going to emerge in the near future due to changing lifestyles of families and their ways of raising children.

In analyzing and synthesizing the thoughts of my interviewees in this section of interviews, I see that the identity-level *value* of building community through hospitality seems to be alive and well in the hearts of Ethiopians who are in their late twenties and above. However, the *expression* of that value is being hampered and cramped by the various factors discussed above. There is an inconsistency (openly acknowledged by several interviewees) between how many Ethiopians want to live in 2022 and how they are in fact living. While entirely understandable, this gap between value and practice does corroborate concerns for the value of building community through hospitality being lost within a generation, since children imitate what they see parents do rather than what they hear parents say (or—possibly more to the point—what their parents implicitly value without articulating it). As EE 6 puts it, parents "are supposed to take the lion's share in teaching their children and letting them see what they do."

Interviewees suggested several helpful ways forward for Ethiopians to preserve the ancient value of building community through hospitality, focusing primarily on appreciation and articulation to the next generation, since "safeguarding" this value "is about transferring of knowledge, skills, and meaning of the use of hospitality in our community development."[151] EE 7 says: "by acknowledging our valuable culture of building a community through hospitality, we can sustain this value of our nation. Second, creating awareness on how losing that cultural value will affect a society at large might be used as a preventive method of the loneliness epidemic." Ideas

---

150. Interviewed May 17, 2022.
151. EE 8.

focused on guiding children toward forming strong relationships with family and friends instead of over-relying on technology. More broadly, EE 2 suggests "creating awareness and teaching the coming generation about the significance of hospitality culture. This can be done by presenting spiritual/biblical, social, and psychological benefits of preserving the value of building community through hospitality in a modern, globalizing world."

EE 3 shows how appreciation and articulation of this value could work out in practical daily life in Ethiopia:

> I recommend preserving and passing on the Ethiopian cultural value of building community through hospitality. By acknowledging and teaching in social and religious institutions the benefits of the cultural value of hospitality. Besides, by strengthening the social associations: such as "Idir," "Equb," and "Maheber" [an Orthodox tradition of gathering in homes to celebrate saints' days].[152] Explicitly these associations have the cultural values of building community through hospitality. Thus, strengthening these associations helps people to be hospitable to one another.[153]

Several interviewees suggested that the Ethiopian government, educational institutions, and other organizations could use the cultural value of hospitality as a rallying point of commonality between tribes:

> Educational institutes (theological and secular), the government, and NGOs have to study the idea of hospitality in different ethnic groups and tribes. Then, they should also promote these ideas. This would create harmony among the many ethnicities and tribes within Ethiopia.[154]

Several also emphasized the role that churches can play in appreciating and articulating this value. EE 1 begins, "this sounds cliché, but establishing what the Bible teaches about fellowship and community is fundamental." The beginning of the quote poignantly demonstrates the clash between the traditional culture and the new globalized culture. While talking about hospitality in church truly might have been

---

152. For more information on the Ethiopian tradition of *maheber* (also spelled *mahbär*), see Flemmen and Zenebe, "Religious Mahbär in Ethiopia."

153. Interviewed May 17, 2022. These types of voluntary associations are the very thing talked about in Putnam, *Bowling Alone*, and Jacobsen, *Three Pieces of Glass*, etc., the fading of which has arguably led to a significant weakening of the social fabric in the United States.

154. EE 1.

somewhat cliché at one time since people were already living out this value, nowadays perhaps talking about hospitality in church is not just not cliché but vital if the value is to be preserved.

I propose that this value is alive in Ethiopia but in danger of being eroded because up until now it has been assumed—upheld by the container of a society which was itself set up to foster hospitality—rather than actively articulated and purposely cultivated.[155] This is not a criticism of this generation or any generation before it, but simply an acknowledgement that in the past, it was not as necessary to intentionally cultivate the value of building community through hospitality in Ethiopia as it is now. In the modern, globalizing world, it is incumbent upon Ethiopian Christians to bring the value of hospitality from the realm of the implicit into the realm of the explicit, so that this beautiful and biblically resonant aspect of Ethiopian culture will not fade away but can be intentionally embraced even if doing so becomes increasingly counter-cultural and practices need to be contextualized to allow for modern, globalized realities.[156] In articulating this value, Ethiopian Christians can also be increasingly and sustainably activated to be a blessing to the wider global community, particularly to those in the West who are in need of a model to see how biblical ideas regarding hospitality can be worked out in our times.

Flowing from an understanding of their connection with God and others through the sharing of space and needs, Ethiopians' lives have tended to be characterized by recognizing the limits of their individual humanity, building relational friendships, and enjoying and stewarding God's gifts together so as to promote the flourishing of both individuals and the communities of which they are part. Together, these elements make up a recipe that is a nourishing and powerful antidote to loneliness, but there are valid concerns that this recipe could be lost to history if it is not

---

155. The interview quote that most brings this idea home (though it was reiterated by several other interviewees as well) is from EI 31: "Living in Ethiopia, I didn't mean to be hospitable, it's just how we do it, how we live life. It's more of the identity of the communal understanding of life. I don't think that there's much consciousness of really framing or naming the concept. . . . It's included in loving one another and helping one another, but it's not that much conceptualized."

156. In Wrogemann, *Intercultural Theology*, 1:221–22, it is mentioned that in the "Glocalization" view of Robertson: "Increasing globalization also elicits counterreactions of increasing localization" which wrestle with "the question of what defines truly 'African' Christian theology and praxis." Wrogemann notes that wrestling does not "constitute a return to the 'pure' traditions of yesteryear; rather, they reformulate certain aspects of the tradition within the framework of an ongoing globalization."

intentionally preserved and habitually prepared. The next chapter will explore how this recipe can be made contextually and in bulk to address the loneliness epidemic in America, with possible preventative application to the rapidly globalizing cultural landscape in Ethiopia.

5
Recommendations

EVEN BEFORE THE CORONAVIRUS, Western societies were plagued with loneliness and a sense of social isolation, and those in Protestant churches were not immune. While technology continues to connect the world in ways that have been unprecedented in the rest of human history, mental health issues such as depression and anxiety are rising at alarming rates in the USA, often stemming from feelings of being disconnected. This seeming paradox was clarified by the pandemic because most agreed that though Zoom and other digital means of maintaining relationships were helpful (and preferable to no connection at all), there was still something missing in these disembodied, screen-mediated meet-ups. Real people encountering real people in person and truly connecting with one another is necessary for well-being, but this is something that is becoming more and more rare in the West, and loneliness has reached epidemic levels.

In this book, I have suggested that what is needed to address the loneliness epidemic is not the band-aid of adding a few dinner parties to the already filled up calendar. The solution is not found in a quintessentially American fix-it mentality or task-based thinking. Instead, what is needed is an ontological identity shift and acknowledgment of what has already been true—that we are mortals and as mortals need each other. This shift will enable a return to a more ancient psychology of the naturalness and necessity of togetherness. This togetherness is assumed in Scripture, and it is the context of the many "one another" commands in the New Testament and the reason for the many exhortations to live hospitably. In a society which has lost the value of community, it can seem overwhelming and even impossible for Christian leaders to encourage American congregations toward hospitable living. It is much easier to focus on numbers who are attending a weekly "community group" than to facilitate and midwife the gradual process of heart-change toward truly valuing the common good over individual comfort and success.

RECOMMENDATIONS

While the Bible should certainly be primary in guiding believers to value hospitality, it is enormously helpful to have supplemental modern-day examples when seeking to inculcate this value in one's own life or the life of a congregation. In this book, I have proposed that Ethiopian culture is a good choice for such an example. While certainly not a utopia, Ethiopia is known for its hospitality and my dozens of Ethiopian interviewees confirmed to me that loneliness was very rare when they were living there. Synthesizing their insights regarding cultural differences between the United States and Ethiopia with further bibliographic research led me to conclude that these low levels of loneliness can be attributed to the community's focus on communion with God, communion with others, and sharing space.

As a deeply religious people, Muslim, Orthodox, and Protestant Ethiopians all highly prioritize being in connection with God in the midst of daily life. Ethiopians of all religions also highly value connection with others, since they—as is typical in Non-Western cultures—recognize that an individual's humanity is fully realized only through connection with other humans. This *ubuntu* spirit naturally leads to the sharing of space by intentionally prioritizing hospitality and time spent enjoying life together. In chapter 4, I delved into Scripture and found that the aspects of Ethiopian culture mentioned above are deeply resonant with biblical teaching and thus worthy of emulation, and my Christian interviewees self-report that it is Scripture which informs their prioritization of an expansive view of hospitality and regular practice of it, stretching back generations.

But how is it possible to imitate the example of hospitable Ethiopians in Ethiopia—inasmuch as it is biblically congruent to do so—while living in America? This is not an easy question to answer, and the Ethiopian immigrants I interviewed are actively grappling with what this looks like in their own lives and are also concerned about cultural shifts in urban centers in Ethiopia, where ancient cultural values seem to be eroding in the face of modernization and globalization. In order to complement my original research with Ethiopian immigrants, I also interviewed several Americans who are known for being radically hospitable even in the midst of a culture where social isolation is the norm. My goal in doing this was not to supersede the insights that the Ethiopian interviewees had, but to complement their ideas from the perspective of people who have somehow managed to hold the value of hospitality counter-culturally (instead of being upheld by a culture whose structures are set up for hospitality). Together, these interviews have shed light on what it might look like to contextually emulate biblically resonant aspects of an Ethiopian understanding and practice of hospitality in American society—and specifically among American Christians—in order to live out in the modern day the God-given mandate to live hospitably and to address the loneliness epidemic in the West.

Before delving into recommendations for how American Christians can learn from the example of Ethiopian Christians in seeking to build community through hospitality, it is necessary to address a concerning unconscious mental block which is common among Americans related to learning from other cultures: resource righteousness. I have coined this term to refer to the mentality that the one who has more resources—often someone from the West—is inherently more righteous, more spiritually mature, and should be the one with the most power in a relationship with someone from a materially less wealthy background.[1] This bias poisons the well, so to speak, so that a healthier mutuality and two-way learning are impossible and the only way the relationship can continue is through "the conscious practice [of the one with less material resources] of epistemic self-repression through the uncritical adoption of" Western ideas "as if all these were finished products embodying unquestionable rationality and universality."[2] This arrangement is demeaning and stifling for the person with less material resources and isolates and reinforces the blindspots of the person with more material resources in his myopic bubble of resource righteousness. There is a better way which is healthier for all parties: the way of mutuality.

It should be noted that if the person with more material resources awakens to the problem of resource righteousness and humbles herself to pursue the equality and mutual learning inherent in true friendship across cultural barriers, this is a kind of miracle, since the current world system is set up to reinforce resource righteousness. There is a "tendency of the social sciences to universalize Western ideas, values and practices,"[3] but it should be immediately noted that this tendency "is in many cases a *reflection of Becoming Western*—of the political, economic, epistemic, and cultural power that the West has exercised and still exercises over Non-Western societies—rather than an expression of the *intrinsic rationality*

---

1. Haddis, *Just Mission*, 58–59, observes: "It seems to me that Western theology has intertwined financial poverty with spiritual poverty and is producing disciples of the religion of capitalism."

2. Mennasemay, *Qiné Hermeneutics*, 448.

3. Mennasemay, *Qiné Hermeneutics*, 455–56, emphasis mine.

and universality of Western social sciences, practices, and values." While Western ideas certainly have some merit—it is not my intention to argue that any culture's ideas are wholly bad or wholly good—it is well-attested that a Western worldview "champions . . . 'atomism,' i.e. an understanding of society as an aggregate of freestanding and unattached individuals, and an understanding of social relations in terms of utility and instrumental rationality."[4] As has been discussed in the foregoing chapters, atomism is at odds with the ontological reality—seen in the Bible, in the understanding of most ancient cultures, and in the Non-Western world today—of the ontologically interconnected interdependence of all of life. It is not difficult to deduce that this Western atomism—which could be called "ontological individualism"[5]—has not been helpful in addressing the loneliness epidemic in Western societies. Rather, atomism is arguably artificial, unnatural, and damaging; it is one of the factors exacerbating or even causing the problem of rising loneliness in the first place.

Because of the tendency of Westerners, including Americans, toward resource righteousness, "There are two general dispositions the Diaspora Christians fall into when it comes to their attitude in engaging the Western culture: *the West is the best* or *the West is the worst*. Both are dangerous dispositions."[6] A remedy to the polarity of these reactions and a healthier way forward can be found—among other places—rooted in a historically Ethiopian worldview: "Ethiopian critical theory refuses to be a hostage to the false dichotomy. . . . Inspired by Ethiopia's intellectual traditions, particularly *qiné* hermeneutics, Ethiopian critical theory rejects dualism"[7] of the either-or choice and also rejects the "monism"[8] that would lead to attempts at hegemony of cultural domination from any direction. Instead, an environment of mutual curiosity and learning is preferred in which the reality of what is finds acceptance while being subjected to critical evaluation and purification (called *zäräfä* in Amharic) in order to bring forth even more beautiful insights for future growth: Mennasemay explains the never-ending *qiné* hermeneutical "*säm ena wärq*" ("wax and gold") approach as follows:

---

4. Charles Taylor, quoted in Mennasemay, *Qiné Hermeneutics*, 455.
5. Mennasemay, *Qiné Hermeneutics*, 455.
6. Urga, *Reflection on Diaspora Cross-Cultural Evangelism*, 45.
7. Mennasemay, *Qiné Hermeneutics*, 45.
8. Mennasemay, *Qiné Hermeneutics*, 461.

> Recall the *qiné* hermeneutical idea that reality . . . *wärq* . . . and emancipation (*arnät*) are always incomplete, and therefore are open-ended processes. This openness suggests that utopian thinking is not only possible but is also necessary, so as not to close artificially the incompleteness of *wärq* . . . and *arnät*. In the incompleteness of these incubate new historical possibilities and utopian impulses that we could bring forth and use for distancing ourselves from the given, and for critically reflecting on it and on its possible transformations.[9]

The utopian thinking that Mennasemay references does not refer to retreating into fantasy but rather to accepting the current reality while believing with hope that things could be different, and that human action could create positive change in the world that points toward eternal goodness, beauty and truth. Mennasemay is fond of referring to "utopianism without utopia"[10] in order to emphasize the real-world application of this mode of thinking. To bring this expression into American Protestant parlance, it might be said that thinking this way is pondering how to live in the already-but-not-yet state between the incarnation and the *parousia* in such a way that—in seemingly small and surprisingly significant ways—God's kingdom of *shalom* would come and his will would be done on earth as it is in heaven, even now, today.[11] For the specific purposes of this research, "participation [in utopian/kingdom-minded/*shalom* pursuing living] can begin to shift our imagination toward a world where community and belonging are more highly valued."[12] While the fullest expression of belonging

---

9. Mennasemay, *Qiné Hermeneutics*, 389.

10. Mennasemay, *Qiné Hermeneutics*, 389. Mennasemay further describes this kind of thinking, 399, as a "social imaginary, a social ontology one could even say, that provides both descriptive and prescriptive criteria of what a 'good' person is, what a 'good' society is, and what 'good' social relations are," and as such, "Utopian desires, impulses, and the emancipatory aspirations they incubate awaken us from our self-forgetfulness" (453).

11. Urga, *Lord's Prayer*, 43, comments: "'Your Kingdom come' places the eternal before our eyes without overlooking the temporal."

12. In this particular quote, Jacobsen, *Three Pieces of Glass*, 193, interacting with Smith, *Desiring the Kingdom*, is assuming the idea that it is difficult to change through a Cartesian model of thinking alone because there are "limitations of cognitive solutions to problems" (190); rather, action, particularly the force of habit developed through everyday "liturgies" of life, is necessary, since "Descartes doesn't account nearly enough for the way our bodies and our habits influence our behavior and even shape our thinking." I agree with his idea but would nuance and add to it using his related ideas of malformation and formation by suggesting that the rational mind, the affective aspect

in community will only be experienced in the divine hospitality of the marriage supper of the Lamb (Rev 19:6–9), the hospitable liturgies Christians engage in as they live in the world can serve as a "sign," "instrument," and "foretaste" of the divine feast to come.[13]

Unfortunately, utopian thinking is short-circuited when Western ideas about the good life—whether articulated through theology, philosophy, social science, or in habitual lifestyle "liturgies"[14]—are accepted as the final word which cannot be questioned, critiqued, or even *seen* with clarity, because, if only Westerners are considered qualified to speak on these matters, they are unaware of their cultural blindspots just like a fish is unaware that water is wet. Because of lack of mutual learning and the adaptive preferences[15] that result when one lives in a particular unhealthy manner over the

---

of the heart (which Jacobsen does not emphasize but which I think should also be considered), and the habitual actions carried out in life interact with one another to create a positive or negative synthesis, moving us in the direction of growth or atrophy. Just as one aspect necessary for growth, such as sunlight, should not be emphasized to the exclusion of water or clean air or undisturbed nutrient-rich soil in the growth of a tree, so various aspects of formation and malformation should not be pitted against each other but should be seen as multifaceted and complementary aspects of the same process when speaking of human growth.

13. Jacobsen, *Three Pieces of Glass*, 18.

14. Jacobsen, *Three Pieces of Glass*, 192, observes, still interacting with Smith, *Desiring the Kingdom*, that we are shaped by habit more than conscious thinking, and he calls these habitual lifestyle choices "liturgies": "Secular liturgies influence us through our bodies; therefore, teaching our minds is of limited use. The best way to oppose the false teaching of secular liturgies, Smith maintains, is not just to teach truth to minds but also to employ Christian liturgies. . . . Christian liturgies are based on a picture of the good life (shalom) as portrayed in Scripture. Insofar as Christian liturgies shape our behavior and convictions, they will draw us toward this picture."

15. Adaptive preferences are a change in what a person wants based upon not getting what they really want. They shift their expectations to avoid being disappointed, and it begins to appear that they like their circumstances which they previously tried to change, like a dog adapting to its chain or a zoo animal to its cage. Mennasemay, *Qiné Hermeneutics*, 425, explains that "the idea of 'adaptive preferences' refers to the fact that people living in conditions of powerlessness 'adjust their preferences to what they think they can achieve, and also to what their society tells them a suitable achievement is for someone like them,' and consequently they 'often learn not to want things that convention and political reality have placed out of their reach.' Adaptive preferences contribute to the naturalization of the existing . . . systems' mechanisms of oppression and exploitation as one's own values, thus subverting resistance to a system whose very political and economic structures produce unfreedoms and inequalities." In reference to development in Ethiopia, Mennasemay comments: "In the language of *qiné* hermeneutics, adaptive preferences consider the Ethiopian subject as not having the capacity to go beyond his/her *säm* existence," that is, not having the ability to be anything more than she already is,

course of generations, "we are far too easily pleased,"[16] and there can be only limited ideation or imagination among Americans regarding the crucially healing question: *What if the good life is something somewhat different—and enormously better—than we could have imagined alone?*[17]

Relevant to the specific research at hand, Mennasemay argues: "The West has not exhausted human possibility; or, as the *qiné* tradition would put it, since reality and the knowledge of reality are always incomplete, it is impossible to claim that [Ethiopians] cannot create new realities and new knowledge that are unknown to the West." After significant experience teaching in Ethiopia and elsewhere in the Non-Western world, An observes the existence of a "theological monopoly [which] is prevalent in many different places in the world" which assumes that those with Western worldviews should do the teaching, while the rest of the world should listen quietly, thereby skewing the power dynamic and killing any potential for mutuality, since "genuine interdependence is possible only when the entities in a relationship are independent. A healthy relationship is not one-sided—the 'give' of one side and the 'take' of the other side—but

---

that is, not having the ability to grow or improve her life. Adaptive preferences can also cause Americans to look at their existence with a shrug and a sigh, saying that they like being introverts and that nightly Netflix alone while scrolling Instagram after a day of frazzled individual productivity is their definition of the good life, and privately accepting that gnawing loneliness is just a part of life and wanting more is too complicated or simply futile. Many Americans are stuck in the adaptive behavior of habitual isolation.

16. In writing this section, I was reminded of the quote from Lewis, *Weight of Glory*, 26, talking about being satisfied with material things when intangible things are far more satisfying: "It would seem that Our Lord finds our desires not too strong, but too weak. We are half-hearted creatures, fooling about with drink and sex and ambition when infinite joy is offered us, like an ignorant child who wants to go on making mud pies in a slum because he cannot imagine what is meant by the offer of a holiday at the sea. We are far too easily pleased." Mennasemay, *Qiné Hermeneutics*, 388–89, also mentions that, in Amharic, while *dästa* "means pleasure or happiness in the utilitarian sense" that implies "an individualistic experience," *fissiha*, by contrast, means "joy . . . [which necessarily involves] the community," since "only humans who pursue a commonly shared aim and act transindividually [that is, they are 'actively interdependent'], freely, rationally, responsibly, and in solidarity with each other could experience *fissiha*."

17. Mennasemay *Qiné Hermeneutics*, 458, helpfully distinguishes that this kind of question is one of possibility that enables growth rather than assuming the current circumstances define a person's identity: "[Applying Ethiopian critical theory] changes our self-interrogation as Ethiopians from the current inert question of 'who are we?' that cultivates identity fetishism to the dynamic, present-rooted, and future-oriented questions of 'what are we becoming?' and 'what should we become?'"

reciprocal—the 'give and take' of both sides."[18] Specifically regarding global mutuality in interpretation and application of Scripture, An adds: "A local reading of the Bible reveals certain aspects of God's truth. The biblical interpretations of local faith communities throughout the world contribute together to enrich our understanding of God's truth in the Bible. Hermeneutical communities in various contexts can teach and learn from each other through their interpretations of the Bible."[19] Both Mennasemay and An demonstrate that "Ethiopia . . . has space for questioning the path of development that Becoming Western embodies—a space that is absent in the West . . . a 'space' for critique that the process of Becoming Western seems to have erased in the West."[20] Mennasemay cogently asks: "Would not then the specific context of life that 'development' has created in Ethiopia give Ethiopians the opportunity to conduct [critical] readings of their conditions and that of the West, explore the unnoticed emancipatory possibilities that Ethiopia's specific internal and external conditions gestate, and lay down the foundations for an emancipation or *arnät*[21]-centered modernity as an alternative to the market-centered modernity of the West?"[22] In my 2020 conference paper for the Evangelical Missiological Society on the same topic as this book, I observed:

> It is very difficult to change a centuries-long cultural bias and an unconscious sense of resource righteousness, but desperate times do indeed call for desperate measures, and the loneliness epidemic in America is indeed becoming more desperate by the day. Perhaps there will be a tipping point when Americans decide that our skyrocketing mental health issues and plummeting quality of life assessments have got to change, and then they will be open looking for answers. This paper proposes that life-giving answers can be found in observing and adopting the

18. An, *Ethiopian Reading of the Bible*, 2.
19. An, *Ethiopian Reading of the Bible*, 232.
20. Mennasemay, *Qiné Hermeneutics*, 460.
21. Interestingly, Mennasemay, *Qiné Hermeneutics*, xxi–xxii, explains that he makes the point of using *arnät* instead of *nätsänet* when referring to the idea of emancipation as a utopian goal. Though both mean "freedom" in Amharic, *nätsänet* has a simpler and more individualistic connotation of "self-determination" and being "independent," while "*arnät* has a more comprehensive horizon" of being free from both external and "internal oppression," and "covers the whole sphere of becoming human" and the common-good flourishing and empowerment of individuals and of the communities of which they are a part such that "good living" is possible.
22. Mennasemay, *Qiné Hermeneutics*, 460–61.

ancient rhythms of hospitality still kept alive and practiced in many Non-Western cultures.[23]

Studying and applying insights from Ethiopia—particularly those related to the interconnected interdependence of reality and the spiritually motivated prioritization of building community through hospitality—can be valuable for those who can reject resource righteousness and pursue mutual learning in the spirit of "säw le säw medhanet näw" (humanity is the cure for humanity).

In making recommendations, it should be reiterated that in no way do I desire to remake the USA in the image of Ethiopia. Aside from being impossible, that would be overly simplistic, heavy-handed, and would miss the point of learning from one another. When gleaning from another's example, the goal is not to literally become that person—losing oneself—but to thoughtfully incorporate the exemplary aspects of that person's character into one's own personality and context.[24] So it is with learning between cultures. While America will not and should not seek to simply become Ethiopia, learning from the biblically resonant aspects of Ethiopian culture will be profoundly healthy for the American Church, which for too long has thought that giving and mission and expertise and discipleship only go one way—from the West to the rest—and so has

---

23. Udall, "Lives That Welcome," 5.

24. Mennasemay, *Qiné Hermeneutics*, 447, differentiates unhealthy and healthy learning from others by describing the former (specifically in terms of Ethiopia learning from the West) as "Gibbonism," that is, "the outsourcing of thinking [from outside] on Ethiopia and the uncritical borrowing of ideas," and the latter as zäräfä, that is, "an activity that involves . . . transforming what we borrow in light of the emancipatory needs, interests, and aspirations that are immanent in our social practices, past and present. What emerges from such a transformative process is a product of our *eje* (hand)" (8). This idea of adopting aspects of Ethiopian culture for use in American culture may bring up the concern of appropriation, but I propose that appropriation is a type of shallow reverse Gibbonism, which takes the outward form of a thing (the *säm* or "wax" in the parlance of *qiné* hermeneutics) from Ethiopia and assumes it to be the sum total of the thing, likely, in the case of America, reducing the thing to its lowest common denominator and commodifying it for profit, like a Cinco de Mayo themed margarita mix supposedly celebrating "Mexican culture." What I am proposing is entirely different than appropriation, because I am suggesting zäräfä in order to dig down into the deeper meaning underneath Ethiopian cultural forms (the *wärq* or "gold" in the parlance of *qiné* hermeneutics), and gaining a different perspective that can lend fresh eyes for Americans when they are considering the areas where they lack flourishing wholeness as a society. Then the ideas that allow for flourishing in Ethiopia can be transformed by inspiring new, related (not identical) ideas that will allow for flourishing in America as well.

impoverished herself by insisting that she needed nothing and could learn nothing from her Non-Western brothers and sisters.

In the following pages I will suggest several ways that the American Church can remedy this situation by intentionally learning (in the spirit of 1 Cor 11:1) from the beliefs and practices of Ethiopian believers in the areas of spiritually informed and hospitable living and community cultivation, and then transforming that learning into new ideas for addressing the loneliness epidemic in the American context. These suggestions include recognizing loneliness as a form of poverty and prioritizing its alleviation accordingly while avoiding taking the short-cut of (self)-development or buying into the commodification of connection. Instead, this chapter includes a call to focus on the relational resources inherent in recognizing the interconnected interdependence of human identity, and will consider how hospitable actions naturally flow from that identity through creating liturgies of connection with God and others which go beyond programming and cultivate a culture of belonging to one another.

Frame Loneliness in Terms of Relational Poverty

Mother Theresa was often asked why she traveled to materially wealthy countries like America to speak when her calling was to the poor. She explained: "The poverty of loneliness and alienation is just as bad as the poverty of hunger and illness and disease, and in fact in some ways it is even worse. So we have to heal that need for love."[25]

Framing loneliness in wealthy countries in terms of poverty[26] is so counter-intuitive that the most common response may be to shrug and move on, since it is too deep to easily metabolize mentally, and we are trained to over-rely on our minds, which Jacobsen believes short-circuits true lifestyle change.[27] Instead, he says that even having an entire Sunday

---

25. Butterfield, "Stories of Mother Theresa."

26. Haddis, *Just Mission*, 123, observes that in Ethiopia "we talk about poverty mainly from a spiritual perspective. Parents pray over their children blessings such as, 'May the Lord keep you from an impoverished heart' to signify their desire for our communal culture and legacy to live on in their family tree. The prayer was also directed against a life that lacks community, living in isolation and only with those who reflect our values, which presents the dangerous territory of self-worship."

27. Jacobsen, *Three Pieces of Glass*, 190, interacting with Smith, *Desiring the Kingdom*, asserts that there are serious "limitations of cognitive solutions to problems," because "Descartes [of 'I think, therefore I am' fame] doesn't account nearly enough for

school class focused on mentally convincing attendees on an issue such as the importance of hospitality lacks power to create sustainable behavior change in the long run, helpfully pointing out that habits, not thoughts, are actually the major driver in determining our future behavior. While I will devote space to discussing habits in later recommendations, I am starting here with the heart-level idea of relational poverty, because, while I agree with and whole-heartedly support Jacobsen's idea that the West over-relies on Cartesian persuasion when seeking to initiate change, I do think that affective and values-level shifts are also necessary in order to be motivated to persevere when working for habitual, systemic and neighborhood-level change in lifestyle, when, as Jacobsen acknowledges, "trying to build something with local significance can feel like David taking on Goliath."[28] Rather than choosing any one method which will produce lifestyle change, I find it more advisable to use a multi-faceted approach which leaves no part of the person out, in keeping with a more Ethiopian—or perhaps broadly Non-Western—perspective. Perhaps Jacobsen's insights are actually pointing to the weakness of the thinking mind when separated from the affective aspect of people and from their habits; perhaps it is in the arbitrary separation of the mind from other aspects of a person that makes ideas inconsequential in creating change. In an attempt to live in the tension of seeking to bring unity to the inner being of Americans while also using the existing separated verbiage, I am starting with heart-level (that is, an idea that creates affective resonance, not simply cognitive assent) realization of our relational poverty. Only through this humbling, grief-inducing process can our pride of place as people living in the "greatest nation on earth" (as our politicians are fond of saying) be replaced with an understanding that while we may be materially secure—at least in a relative sense when compared with the majority of people living in the world—we are not in a good place when it comes to social capital, and that this may be the form of currency that matters most when it comes to mental, emotional, and

---

the way our bodies and our habits influence our behavior and even shape our thinking," connecting this assertion to his main argument about the negative impact of screens on belonging with an example: "We cognitively know that too much smartphone use is not good for us individually or societally, but we continue it almost unconsciously or out of force of habit." Mennasemay, *Qiné Hermeneutics*, 418, also lampoons Descartes by observing that "One of the manifestations of the Cartesian conception of the individual is the American understanding of civil society as an aggregation of individuals around single issues that each participant considers to be in his or her interest or conforms to the values he or she holds."

28. Jacobsen, *Three Pieces of Glass*, 226.

spiritual health and overall well-being. This realization of poverty will create the discomfort necessary to seek solutions, rather than shrugging off the problem with a cognitive-assent comment starting with "Yes, but," and ending with life being "crazy-busy" and a vague commitment to implement the ideas suggested by people like Jacobsen "when things calm down," which they unfortunately never do without intentional efforts to calm them down, as the Amharic saying goes, by our *eje* (our own hands).

To continue with the imagery of material and metaphorical poverty, we can consider that if a person is in true financial crisis or is an alcoholic and is roused from a state of denial to grasp at a gut-level the magnitude of her problem and the ruinous trajectory she is on, she will do whatever it takes to change her circumstances. This heart-level grasp of the problem is the linchpin which will enable spectacular changes: admitting problems, getting advice from trusted advisors—those such as Ethiopians which resource righteousness might have unconsciously blocked us from seeking out before—joining groups of people with similar issues who are committed to changing their habits, and spending significant time and energy in learning and growing in this area will follow. Conversely, everyone has experienced or heard of a person who was a gambler or an alcoholic who was forced into rehab or who began making superficial changes in order to appease another person, assuage guilt, or avoid consequences. While this person might be able to change their behavior temporarily, if the changes are not accompanied by the affective, denial-busting realizations mentioned above, these changes will only be short-lived and will ultimately prove unsustainable.

It is the same in our struggle against the loneliness epidemic. As the Ethiopian proverb ominously warns: "One who hides his illness has no medicine."[29] Before we are able to receive treatment and to heal, we must admit we are sick—not only sick but slowly dying as individuals and as a society due to disconnection and social isolation. Our growing anxiety and depression are only symptoms of the deeper problems, accurate messages signaling to us that all is not well. Small changes such as joining a programmatically oriented small group or inviting another family over for dinner a few times will not in and of themselves solve such a pervasive problem just as a band-aid or a single dose of medicine will not cure a complex disease. This is a difficult message to digest in the American culture which itches for a quick-fix, silver-bullet solution to any problem it encounters. That

29. Demoze and Armstrong, *Ethiopian Amharic Proverbs*, 42.

tendency to want easy, instant solutions, along with an avoidance of the reality of death and our own human limitations, often leads to a frenetic busyness[30] with accompanying shallowness of relationships which creates a vicious cycle that is actually hastening the very mortality we fear.[31]

Resist (Self)-Development as a Short-Cut

Americans tend to love self-development. There is a real desire to pull oneself up by one's bootstraps, learn new hacks and short-cuts to improve one's performance at work, at the gym, or in life in general, to learn the secret that will turbo-charge one's productivity, sex appeal, health, youth, or memory, to find a system that will perfect one's diet, pet training, home organization, or daily to-do list. Self-help book sales are enjoying a meteoric rise in the USA,[32] and, revealingly, the majority of the advice and tips contained in these books tends to be individually focused. While it is not wrong to work on one's personal goals, habits, or schedule, doing so is insufficient to solve problems that are systemic or communal in nature, such as the loneliness epidemic. More to the point, getting to inbox zero, curating a capsule wardrobe, and doing monthly juice fasts will not alleviate the problem of loneliness, because loneliness cannot be "hacked" on an instant, individual level. In fact, it could be possible that these very hacks are an attempt to reduce our feeling of powerlessness when facing the enormous, entrenched, and multi-faceted problem of loneliness by pivoting to make it simpler, creating a straw-man of self-development, the mastering of which will create the life we want, saying, for example: "I know what my problem is: I need to declutter my house and office/lose weight/learn to speed read/edit my resumé/download the newest productivity app, etc.

30. Jacobsen, *Three Pieces of Glass*, 164, suggests that American's denial of mortality and "unspoken fear of death" can lead to constant busyness in order to stave off facing the feelings surrounding that fear.

31. Mettes, *Loneliness Epidemic*, 25, states that "chronic loneliness . . . has destructive effects on human life and creativity. . . . Such loneliness pushes people toward death, senility, heart trouble, and poor responses to disease."

32. NPD Group, "Self Help Book Sales Are Rising Fast in the US," reports: "The self-help books category has experienced continued and solid growth in recent years. In fact, it has nearly doubled in size since 2013. Unit sales of self-help books have grown at a compound annual growth rate (CAGR) of 11 percent since 2013, reaching 18.6 million in 2019" (para. 1). Additionally, "the number of unique international standard book numbers (ISBNs) [has risen] nearly three-fold from 30,897 in 2013 to 85,253 in 2019" (para. 2).

That will fix everything." Deep down, we know this is not true, but admitting this is a challenge for Americans because we like to fix things, preferably quickly, and on our own.[33] This impatient individualism is an example of adaptive preferences. Impatience adapts as things get quicker—many Americans can remember patiently waiting for their dial-up internet to go through all its discordant gyrations to get them online but now feel frustration when a web page takes more than a few seconds to load. Likewise, individualism adapts as isolation grows—many Americans can feel an atrophy in their social muscles after enduring the enforced isolation of the COVID-19 pandemic, with some extroverts now behaving like introverts and many introverts now feeling nearly immobilized by any social activity. What changed between 2020 and 2022 was not people's fundamental capacity for interacting with one another; instead, our preferences adapted based on our daily lived reality of isolation, and even though it was an undesired shift, many of us gradually began to prefer isolation because it began to feel like the new normal. What happened in an extreme, relatively short period of time during the pandemic has actually been happening in a subtle, decades-long drift towards increased isolation which has been hard to detect or feel, much less make efforts to mitigate, without the benefit of hindsight. Thankfully, there are still modern day cultures, such as Ethiopia, who have managed to retain a prioritization of connection with God, connection with others and sharing space: if resource righteousness can be avoided, much can be learned from Ethiopia's example.

Even with the benefit of hindsight, however, addressing what has now been identified as a creeping loneliness epidemic—which was endemic before most people could articulate the problem—is not something simple that can be quickly fixed.[34] Just as the problem is complex, so will the solu-

---

33. As EI 42 pointed out, Americans tend to be reticent to ask for help, but perhaps it is in admitting that we are not sufficient unto ourselves that we will find what we truly long for: connection with others.

34. Jacobsen, *Three Pieces of Glass*, 100–101, observes that "as consciousness of the loneliness epidemic rises among academics and social-service providers, we see some attempts to address the problem," such as a helpline which is advertised as a number that people (particularly seniors) can call with specific questions (about the weather, cooking, etc.) but whose deeper purpose is to try to alleviate loneliness in the lives of the callers by pairing them with a volunteer who would be available not just to find an answer to their question but to have a conversation along the way. While not a bad idea, Jacobsen—referencing Jane Jacobs' system for understanding problems—questions the efficacy of this approach because it treats the problem of loneliness as a "problem of simplicity" when it is in reality a "problem of organized complexity." A problem of simplicity, says Jacobsen,

tion be. It is helpful at the outset to acknowledge that individuals did not create the problem and so individuals on their own cannot fix it, either. This is counter-intuitive to a Western worldview, where problems are personalized and solutions are expected to be found on one's own, but this only isolates each person to deal with a problem that has been primarily created by societal slippage, not individual culpability. How can one person fix a society's problems alone? Yet because of an atomized worldview, Americans feel the weight of doing exactly that. No wonder this burden quickly gets diverted through denial into side issues and micro-problems that can be fixed through individual effort. The weight of the world feels less painful that way. The example of many Ethiopians show a different way, however—dealing with societal struggles that leave individuals feeling disempowered and helpless by living in a way that is interconnected with others—whether in daily life or in organizations like *däbo, iddir, and iqqub*—because of their presupposition that interdependence is ontological and *säw le säw mädhanitu* ("Humanity is the cure for humanity").

Ethiopians are no strangers to "development," though in the Ethiopian context it usually has to do with addressing material poverty through a plan created by—or in partnership with—a foreign NGO. I respect many foreign (often Western) NGO workers and count several as my friends in my current Addis Ababa, Ethiopia, context, but I also have significant reservations about the top-down, outside-led nature of many NGOs because I think the system itself may lead to the disenfranchisement of the very people an NGO sets out to help. In considering Mennasemay's critique of NGOs in Ethiopia,[35] my mind was continually drawn to the parallels between the ultimately unhelpful short-cut of foreign-led development projects in Ethiopia and the ultimately unhelpful short-cut of self-development led by self-help gurus of all kinds in America.

5, only considers "two variables, and the solution involves adjusting one variable to positively influence another," whereas problems of organized complexity acknowledge the fact that the "crisis of belonging" is "a complex but ultimately coherent phenomenon essential to human thriving." Another way of saying this is that the problem of addressing the loneliness epidemic with a call center is that it is a "programmatic [read: simple] solution to a relational [read: organized but complex] problem" (102). This will be further discussed in subsequent recommendations.

35. Mennasemay, *Qiné Hermeneutics*, 417–37.

Unhelpful Personalization

Mennasemay observes that in the financial system which is propagated by those with individualistic Western mindsets—of which foreign NGOs focused on poverty-alleviation are generally a part—"*personalize[s] the causes* of the social sufferings that [Ethiopians] encounter in their lives and consider[s] such social sufferings as *individual problems* that are to be *self-managed*."[36] Such a system is "devoid of the ideas of shared needs, social bonds, and co-obligation,"[37] thus putting a burden on each NGO participant that they were not meant to bear while leaving on the table the power of community to initiate social change that goes beyond an individual level, but that benefits each individual as well.

In the American self-development world, a similar worldview personalizes the problem of isolation and social disconnection that Americans face—and the declining mental and physical health that go along with them—thereby putting an undue burden on American individuals to figure out how to be happy and calm when "the world is on fire"[38] and they are afraid they will die alone. It should be categorically emphasized that it is not pathological to feel anxious when one feels disconnected from one's community; it is primal. It is not abnormal to feel depressed when one is isolated; this is a sign that the mind and body are accurately *signaling* a real problem, not necessarily that they themselves *are* the problem. While I would never argue that anxiety and depression medications have no place in society, I do have serious concern that Americans are overmedicating because they have personalized the societal problem of loneliness and social isolation, assuming that the problem is within themselves and so suppressing true and right feelings that atomized hyperindividualism is slowly killing us, blaming their own brains for being perceptive enough to be bothered by an increasingly unnatural and dystopian existence.

---

36. Mennasemay, *Qiné Hermeneutics*, 399, emphasis mine.

37. Mennasemay, *Qiné Hermeneutics*, 399.

38. This phrase, "the world is on fire," seems to be used with increasing frequency in recent years to encapsulate the dystopian nature of life during the pandemic and the overwhelming sense of doom brought on by increasing exposure to world events via ubiquitous screens and internet connectivity, along with the many conflicts and terrible occurrences that many feel have happened with such frequency that the world cannot catch its breath before, to mix metaphors in an appropriately apocalyptic way, another "wave" of bad news breaks.

Instead of blaming the canaries in the coal mine for feeling faint, we should take humble note of the spreading and spiking anxiety and depression among Americans and ask the question if there is a better way that is more in line with the reality of ontological interdependence. By learning from the essence of the Ethiopian example, those who are reacting to the discordance of hyperindividualism can be empowered to catalyze autopoietic change to address relational poverty, just as Ethiopians have historically banded together to create autopoeietic change in the area of financial poverty. When those who are bowed low by loneliness realize that they are not at fault for feeling this way but actually are primed to be part of the solution in the context of community, the game is changed.

Commodification

Unfortunately, however, it is hard to hear the voice of sensitive souls suffering from loneliness who have inklings of community-building ideas because self-help gurus have proliferated who claim to have already figured out all the answers to our problems if we will just join their "communities" for a fee. In the United States, corporations and coaches have recognized Americans' legitimate loneliness and longing for belonging and have engaged in the "commodification of life and nature,"[39] creating synthetic versions of connection and community that center around things that can be bought and sold. These products can take many forms, including coffee in a setting primed for connection, sessions with a therapist (in person, or increasingly online), all manner of things sold by multi-level marketing businesses which tout joining a community as a reason to become a buyer and a seller oneself, and more. This commodification of connection is an obstacle that must be overcome through awareness that diagnosing the problem correctly—i.e. that Americans are lonely— does not necessarily mean that the corporations or coaches who sell a packaged version of community have a fully-orbed or sufficient solution to the problem of loneliness.

For example, Starbucks Coffee Company realized that when America "abandoned cafés, salons, city plazas, main streets, and front porches," a gaping hole was left in terms of a "third place" where people could casually meet up in a setting that was "both private and public"[40] and that

39. Mennasemay, *Qiné Hermeneutics*, 458.
40. Sweet, *Gospel according to Starbucks*,134.

"encourage[d] lingering and lounging"[41] In setting up this kind of third place, "Starbucks is less about coffee and more about community,"[42] and it has enjoyed wild success selling "not coffee but connection."[43] Starbucks seeks to differentiate themselves by emphasizing belonging, but Jacobsen observes that more and more, "'belonging' is supplanting 'branding' as a way to secure a loyal customer base" in many modern business strategies. Leading with belonging works because it purports to meet a felt need, and to be sure, Starbucks *could* theoretically help meet the need for connection in the same way that a store selling plastic drawers and bins and label makers could theoretically help a person get their house organized. Both provide some of the raw materials needed for a positive outcome, but they must be combined with a people's time, interest, and use to actually make the sustainable difference in society which they purport to sell.

The fact that a café like Starbucks is a for-profit company should not make us assume its CEO (or the CEO of an online therapy company or multi-level marketing business, for that matter) is intentionally concocting sinister schemes to take advantage of our longings in order to make millions, but it should give us pause. The goal of companies as companies is to sell something, and what they sell is usually a simple potential or partial solution to a problem, for example: "You are a victim of the loneliness epidemic? Come have a cup of coffee!" Meeting a friend at Starbucks and enjoying a drink together might indeed be part of a holistic, habitual lifestyle that prioritizes relationships and builds community not only at home or church but in third spaces as well. But as a single action, drinking a latte on a Starbucks couch with another person is not going to quickly fix a life that is mired in presuppositions and practices that keep a person stuck in disconnection and social isolation.[44] Particularly as Americans, we must be wary of our cultural tendency to want a solution that involves

---

41. Sweet, *Gospel according to Starbucks*, 133.
42. Liebmann, quoted in Sweet, *Gospel according to Starbucks*, 140.
43. Sweet, *Gospel according to Starbucks*, 138.
44. Jacobsen, *Three Pieces of Glass*, 176, helpfully mentions the idea taken from moral philosophy that ad hoc and fundamental choices are different. An ad hoc choice "involve[s] a single decision that is relatively self contained"—having a cup of coffee with another person at Starbucks one time would be an example of an ad hoc choice. A fundamental choice, conversely, is "a single decision that will significantly influence one's subsequent choices"—choosing to prioritize connection over busyness is an example of this kind of decision, which would naturally lead to subsequent decisions to regularly have coffee with a friend at Starbucks.

buying a product in order to fix what is wrong in our lives, especially coupled with the fact that if we are in denial about the larger societal disconnection that is collectively trending toward dystopia, nearly any product can be shoehorned into a plausible fix for the inchoate unease we feel. The problem is not ultimately with the businesses listed above, which are simply doing what businesses do, but with our assumption that buying what they are selling (or in the case of multi-level marketing businesses, selling what they are selling) will somehow impart health to our souls. Instead, we must realize that dealing with the loneliness epidemic is not something we can outsource to a company—connection is a DIY project, in which the Y stands not for "yourself" alone but "yourselves" as a community of people who recognize that interdependence is ontological and that in the very action of moving toward one another to address the loneliness epidemic, we are beginning to heal.

Consumption

Mennasemay continues his critique of NGOs in Ethiopia by observing that NGO workers are considered to be the experts possessing the *wärq* [gold] of "the secrets of 'development,'" whereas the local people become passive consumers of those secrets and are

> reduced to *säm* [wax] and thus considered to be malleable. . . . [They] are seen as embodiments of lacks of knowledge, skills and resources judged to be necessary for "development." The recipients believe in the belief of the development experts that 'development' could be reached through the acquisition of the knowledge, skills, and resources the experts consider necessary and provide. In the context of interpassive participation, however active the participants appear to be, participation is founded in the "belief in the belief of the other" (the expert) and is basically a process of *mäsmat* [hearing without reflection] and the consumption of and acting according to the pre-packaged knowledge that the "subject supposed to know" provides.[45]

In the same way, Americans are bombarded from bookshelves, billboards, commercials and social media feeds with pitches from gurus that claim to hold "secrets" of self-development. Through preternaturally clever algorithms that sometimes know us better than we know ourselves

---

45. Mennasemay, *Qiné Hermeneutics*, 421.

as well as advertisements that target universal insecurities and felt needs, our sense of lack is intensified, and we are presented with a way to regain equilibrium through the click of a button or the swipe of a credit card. The experts will tell us what we need to know. In this process, repeated every time another guru does not live up to our inflated expectations and we are still no closer to the elusive sense of well-being and belonging we are looking for, we give up our power and declare ourselves to be lumps of clay ready to be individually molded into something better, always *better*. The experts will know what to do.

What if a desire to become better—the goal of self-development efforts—is not accomplished in seclusion, but in solidarity with others who are equal and unpaid to be near us? What if we were made to develop in the give-and-take, push-and-pull of life in community with other imperfect people who all have something to teach us, not in a pseudo-relationship with an expert (whether accredited or self-declared) whose insights are shared as part of a transaction? True relationship is the context of true self-development, because the self is honed when sharpened by others, "as iron sharpens iron" (Prov 27:17).

Professionalization

Mennasemay continues:

> Thus, the structures and operations of NGOs rest on a "knowledge/power" hierarchy between those who are external and superior . . . and those who are mired in their problems . . . and are reduced to believing what the experts believe about "development" and what it takes to achieve it. The *säm ena wärq* [wax and gold] nature of the recipients is occluded; they are treated as subjects without a "surplus self" [that is, the potential to become more than they are currently through their own insights and efforts] who could be developed only through the force of expertise applied to the recipients externally.

Instead of affirming in Ethiopians their potential and ability to generate autopoietic solutions in partnership with others in their community, NGOs all too often deprive participants of this empowering experience because all the solutions have already been worked out and just need to be applied, preferably following a given handbook.[46] This leads to a dependence

---

46. NGOs are not the only entities guilty of this heavy-handed power dynamic.

upon the NGO—mentally if not financially—to solve all problems going forward, since no confidence has been expressed in the Ethiopian people's ability to come up with solutions to their own problems: they are only *säm* to be molded, there is no *wärq* (gold) to be found within.

In the same way, self-development gurus in America create cultures of dependency around themselves as they reinforce the idea that their followers are lost without them, and they hold the keys to achieving the desired outcome, whatever it is. When such a guru says to jump, their followers ask how high, when the guru asks for a fee, their followers ask how much, because their followers have not been given the confidence to face problems knowing that they can figure out real solutions with the help of their own communities, perhaps because they suffer from relational poverty to the point that their community is truly *not* strong enough to do so. If this is the case, however, engaging in self-development in a vacuum of community without seeking to strengthen interdependence with others (even if it means building a community from scratch), is like buying a gas mask and wearing it a few days a week in a city that is choked by smog and thinking one will be healthy and the pollution problem will be solved.[47]

This lack of strength of community support means that the ability of the average American individual to find and implement solutions to the loneliness epidemic that go beyond self-improvement is a real problem that must be addressed. Because of a lack of a sense of others "having one's back," Americans who have the means to do so have employed the same strategy which they do at Starbucks but at a larger scale and with higher stakes: they buy community. When hectic work schedules make time at home hard to find, housekeepers and nannies play the role that a grandmother or aunt might in another time and place. When a child needs help in a school subject, a tutoring agency provides a person to provide a service that might have been provided by a fellow church member or a neighbor's son not too long ago. When the cares of the world become heavy, an appointment

---

Recently, an Ethiopian friend told me of having a meeting with the leaders of a ministry organization of American origin with chapters all over the world which wanted her help to expand their ministry in Ethiopia. They gave her a handbook, and as she looked through it, she told the leader, "I'd be happy to translate and adapt this for you to be contextual for an Ethiopian environment," and the leader emphatically explained that my friend's services were only required for translation, because the handbook was followed in exactly the same form in every country where the organization operated.

47. The gas mask example is used by Hari, *Stolen Focus*.

RECOMMENDATIONS

is made to see a therapist rather than to have coffee with a close friend[48] or relative.[49] Hiring help is certainly an acceptable way of dealing with life's challenges, but the automatic impulse toward professionalizing—and paying for[50]—this help rather than relying on our existing communities for it is telling. Perhaps when we come to a place where we need help, we can take a moment to acknowledge that needing others is a true part of the human condition—we were not meant to handle everything ourselves—and we can consider community resources first before jumping immediately to more professionalized services.[51] In this way, our confidence to find autopoietic

---

48. In the course of my research, I have tried to listen to a wide variety of podcasts to get a sense of the cultural state of the union, as it were. Over the past few years, I have noticed literally dozens of podcast episodes about how to make friends as an adult after college dropping into my podcast feed, to the point that the sheer frequency of episodes has led me to conclude that lack of meaningful adult friendships is a common pain point for Americans.

49. In the same way that I would never argue that medications should not be taken to cope with anxiety and depression, I would never argue that people should categorically avoid seeing therapists simply because they are trying to value their communities, but perhaps there could often be a middle ground between bootstraps individualism ("I will figure it out on my own") and seeing a therapist ("I need professional help"). Strong friendships are that middle ground that provides the safety net of a cultivated community. There are situations where a trained professional is needed. However, I do think that in lonely America, therapy is over-used, and that therapists are over-relied on to give the benefits of friendship to their clients, when the relationship is at most a pseudo-friendship (in which the power-dynamics are skewed) and more likely a purely transactional relationship (which is not to say anything negative about therapists but simply to emphasize the fact that good listening skills, empathy and giving advice is the way they earn their living). Unfortunately, I have personally seen people I know experience the partial satisfaction of pseudo-friendship with their therapist and then lose the motivation to intentionally cultivate friendships with others in non-transactional settings with balanced power dynamics. I am concerned that the therapist effect may be unintentionally sabotaging the hunger of Americans to find the true connection of community in the same way that eating heavy snacks—even healthy ones—de-motivates people to do the work of cooking a nourishing meal.

50. If community is professionalized and must be paid for, it is out of reach of the lower classes, see Brooks, "Nuclear Family." This may be part of the reason that loneliness and social disconnection is felt more keenly by the American poor: there are no paid people to act as pseudo-friends or to have one's back (for a fee), so the full weight of lack of community is felt unless alternative means of mutual support—perhaps hearkening back to an earlier time by necessity or, in the case of some immigrants, re-creating a version of what existed in the home country—are found.

51. How the need for help is dealt with is different in Ethiopia as compared to America. In a Western worldview, it is expected that, says Mennasemay, *Qiné Hermeneutics*, 399, "social sufferings [are] individual problems that are to be self-managed," or

solutions can incrementally grow as we give and take in relationships with others, being helped and helping, facing life together with the confidence and comfort to be found in knowing we are not alone.

Identify Hyperindividualism as Unhealthy

Hyperindividualism should be identified as unhealthy, something that is slowly killing Americans by leading them toward loneliness.[52] Going down the path of increasing individualism eventually leads to the dead-end of isolation. In order to address the loneliness epidemic, Christian leaders should emphasize connection within community as essential (while of course not dismissing the inherent value of each individual). Especially in the wake of the coronavirus pandemic, people's social muscles have atrophied and it will feel even more unnatural to connect with others than it has in the past. However, this weakening of connection should be viewed by Christian leaders as a long-term need to address—helping those they shepherd to do the things that will lead to long-term flourishing rather than catering to short-term comfort.[53]

In my experience, American Christians often speak of beginning to grow in hospitality in the same way they would speak of beginning to go to the gym: "I know I need to show hospitality (or start exercising at the gym)—I just need to be more disciplined, make time for it, keep myself accountable, etc." While this is not a wrong way to speak about hospitality, I tend to want to nuance the comparison by taking it even further. Rather than focusing only on the painful first stages of engaging in the exercise of hospitality, it would be helpful to consider what happens after one has faithfully gone to the gym and endured the pain of new beginnings and gotten to the other side. Suddenly, as a result of doing what did not come easily, now the exercise feels natural and life-giving and even becomes a

---

else individuals should privately pay professionals to fix the problem. By contrast, the strength of the non-professional Ethiopian financial savings group *iqqub*, for example, says Mennasemay, *Qiné Hermeneutics*, 402, "is its recognition of powerlessness—the experience of the member who is in need—not only as an individual harm but also as a collective harm that must be overcome collectively."

52. For a recently published strong critique of hyperindividualism and its related issues from an American perspective, see Bethke, *Take Back Your Family*.

53. For a recently published work that deals with the loneliness epidemic from an excellently researched Christian perspective with helpful insights for Christian leaders from studies done before and then during the pandemic, see Mettes, *Loneliness Epidemic*.

healthy craving—the day or the week does not feel right until one has exercised in this way. It is the same with hospitality. Though it may not come naturally at first, intentionally making time to connect with others in a way that makes room for them in one's personal space (whether of home or of heart) becomes a way of life through practice. And those who can persevere through the initial soreness of shifting values find that living in a way that values relationships above tasks brings life to life as it were, enlivened with divine appointments and meaningful encounters, undergirded with a rooted network of deepening friendships. In this process, loneliness ebbs away, crowded out by a life-giving closeness with others.

While people may agree that they should go to the gym, the amount of gym memberships used twice in January and never again speaks loudly to the fact that knowing one should do something is not enough to motivate one to do that thing sustainably if there is any kind of resistance in the way. I suggest that bandwidth overload, attachment to control, and an over-identification with introversion may be blocking American Christians from recognizing and running away from hyperindividualism and in order to run toward one another in community.

Bandwidth Overload

Busyness is often cited as the trump card which puts community in its customary place in the American values hierarchy, under productivity. Bandwidth overload is the result, which leads to a feeling of being constantly overwhelmed, to the point that warnings about loneliness may go in one ear and out the other, because few people have time or margin to deeply consider the issue, much less to do anything about changing the status quo. Productivity is a value of many Americans,[54] but why is this frenzied action-orientation such a hard thing to let go of, even when we increasingly have an awareness that it is not good for us?[55] Jacobsen suggests that Americans' preoccupation with getting things done may be a symptom of "the unspoken fear of death" since "it has long been noted that Western civilization in general, and American culture in particular, is characterized by a strong impulse to deny our own mortality" which can lead to

---

54. This is attested by the proliferation of self-help books regarding time management hacks for doing more in less time.

55. This is attested by the proliferation of self-help books regarding burnout and stress management.

a coping mechanism of "keeping ourselves so busy that we don't need to think about such morbid topics."[56] This denial-fueled coping mechanism could be dealt with two ways: some Americans may want to consider the tradition of *memento mori* (considering one's own death) as a practice that has given clarity and guidance to many both historically and globally, where death has tended to be closer at hand and harder to deny. Doing so may help to avoid what is often confessed as a death-bed regret in the West: wishing one had spent less time working and more time with loved ones. If considering one's own mortality is too painful, other Americans may want to work with the denial and focus on the increased longevity of people with high degrees of social connection compared with the morbidity rates of those who are chronically lonely:[57] increasing one's social connections could be more significant for one's length of life than losing weight or quitting smoking.[58] Ironically, ignoring the problem of loneliness and social disconnection because of death-denying manic productivity is literally hastening the very thing that is feared the most.

Media consumption is also a silent contributor to the bandwidth overload experienced by many Americans today. Just as a phone will not function well or have the capability to download new apps when it is bloated with too many gigabytes of information, so a human will not function well or have the ability to take on new things like building community through hospitality if their minds and free time are already clogged with an overabundance of information. Information takes up mental and emotional space even if it is invisible—we have to metabolize each news story and Instagram reel and Netflix episode we imbibe, and it can leave us feeling drunk on information and unable to think clearly or walk wisely. Since a 24/7 news cycle, infinite scroll, and binge-able content at the click of a button are literally in our back pockets in formats that are designed to be addictive, there is little hope of regaining our bandwidth by going with the flow. Radical, intentional, even sacrificial actions are needed to free up both external (time) and internal (mental and emotional) bandwidth for moving away from hyperindividualism—vividly expressed in solo overconsumption of media—and to recover from an addiction to just one more drink from the seductive, destructive well of "a little bit of everything, all

---

56. Jacobsen, *Three Pieces of Glass*, 164.
57. Mettes, *Loneliness Epidemic*, 329.
58. Jacobsen, *Three Pieces of Glass*, 97.

of the time."[59] Interestingly, Barna research has also found "an imbalance of knowledge" which contributes to loneliness—people know possibly *too* much about many, many things happening all over the world, but they say, "There's all this weighty stuff out there, but I don't have the emotional safety net that I need to navigate that."[60] This becomes a vicious cycle when, due to being worn down by information overload, people withdraw from the social engagement necessary to form and maintain networks of belonging and its attendant emotional security, and then consume more media which further overwhelms them in the absence of community support.

Attachment to Control

In a materially wealthy country like America which excels in efficiency and innovative answers to life's inconveniences, it is easy to be lulled into an illusion of control. Relatively speaking, individual isolation plus the ability to curate one's environment with anything that one can imagine and money can buy—likely with free shipping included—means that there is a grain of truth to this sense of control. Yet getting used to this sense of control simultaneously gives us the wrong assumption that we should be in control of everything—the future, our image, other people—and also the fear that if people get closer to us in true community, we will not be able to maintain this sense of control. This fear is actually quite accurate, as people are unpredictable and hard to manage according to our wills for their lives. People are also not efficient and their relational needs can take up time we wish we had for something else. When people are in proximity to us with enough regularity to build true community through hospitality, we also cannot keep up the curated image that we present to the public: instead, our real self, the good and the bad, shines through. Perhaps this is why when Americans think of hospitality, they often jump to the idea

---

59. Burnam, "Welcome to the Internet." In unofficial research for my book about how young to middle-aged Americans feel about the current state and future of the USA and in seeking to follow the example of Paul is Acts 17:28 ("as even some of your own poets have said"), I found Bo Burnham's lyrics helpfully captured the zeitgeist in both tone and gist, poetically rendering the same despairing restlessness expressed by those with whom I spoke. Themes include deep distrust of corporations and existing power structures, ambivalence toward the ubiquity of technology, recognition of hyperindividualism and growing awareness that it is an adaptive preference, and dark humor that stems from a sense of powerlessness to change what seems like a freefall into dystopia.

60. Mettes, *Loneliness Epidemic*, 153.

of "entertaining," which can be practiced simultaneously with hospitality but is not necessarily equated with it. Entertaining has the connotation of putting on a show, and these shows can be tremendously life-giving and morale-boosting to put on or to attend, but the focus is primarily on the event, not on the people. Hospitality, by contrast, does not have to include anything special—it simply means valuing another person enough to make room for them in one's everyday life. Hospitality is also a letting go of control: the shedding of public image, the sharing of private space that may or may not be tidy,[61] the acknowledgement of mutual hunger around the table—hunger for food, deeper hunger for conversation. Only in the letting go of control can we let ourselves know and be known, thereby letting go of hyperindividualism and partaking in the most healing aspect of hospitality: recognition of our interconnected interdependence, that we are all in this together. Around this kind of table, loneliness cannot last long.

Over-Identification with Introversion

Introversion as a tendency can be observed worldwide—some people tend to be more energized by being in social situations, where others tend to be more energized by being alone—but in recent years, the idea of being an introvert has become an unhealthy trump card in the hands of some Americans who use it to deny their need for community while their capacity for interpersonal interaction atrophies, creating an adaptive preference which is also a self-fulfilling prophecy. While the Holy Spirit does not require every Christian to attend daily large-group social functions in order to mature, the fruit of the Spirit is assumed to grow in the soil of the cultivated community of "one another." We cannot opt out of other people. According to all the African sources I consulted as well as the Bible, there is no such thing as being a "people person." There is only being a person who simply by virtue of being human acknowledges that "I am because we are" (*ubuntu*). If Christians want to avoid succumbing to the loneliness epidemic and to create communities that foster a sense of belonging for both extroverts and introverts, they must move away from

---

61. Mettes, *Loneliness Epidemic*, 207, says: "Americans are more likely to hold off on inviting people over, waiting for . . . a chance to do a thorough cleaning. While I applaud clean bathrooms, they are not a biblical virtue, while hospitality emphatically is." Butterfield, *Gospel Comes with a Housekey*, 111, agrees, saying pithily: "Hospitality is necessary whether you have cat hair on the couch or not. People will die of chronic loneliness sooner than they will cat hair in the soup."

an over-focus on introversion as an identity and instead embrace a far more life-giving identity of one part of an interconnected, interdependent universe and one member of the body of Christ, whose gifts may be expressed in different ways in accord with the level of social energy that God has given them, but all for the upbuilding of the community, not for the isolated enrichment or entrenchment of the individual self.

For the exploration of spiritual giftings to avoid becoming an individual, self-focused exercise, the goal should not be primarily for a person to find out what they are "good at," but rather to live out the idea that "to each is given the manifestation of the Spirit for the *common good*" (1 Cor 12:7, emphasis mine). Helping others and being helped, in the spirit of interdependence, initiates healing connection and creates proximity as an environment for building community through hospitality.

Recognize That Identity Shifts Behavior

If behavior change is to happen, there must often be a shift in identity[62] with regard to hospitality for people to be able to form new habits and sustain the practice of these habits, for "by linking identity to hospitality, hospitable acts or words are not just additional actions one performs. Rather, they reveal as well as provide a worldview; one that is at its core a web of encounters."[63] When speaking about hospitality, all of my Ethiopian interviewees and several of my intentionally hospitable American interviewees mentioned hospitality as being primarily related to who they *were*, not

---

62. Gretchen Rubin, a researcher on habits and human nature, formulated a framework she calls the Four Tendencies to help people personalize their efforts to improve their habits. She observed that the group she called Rebels had the hardest time changing their habits because they tended to resist all attempts—their own and those of others—to force them to change. However, Rubin discovered that when working with Rebels, she could appeal to their identity, whether current or an identity they wanted to live into in the future, and that was enough to motivate even significant habit change. The reason for this is that the Rebels focused on who they were or wanted to be rather than the thing they were supposed to do. By focusing on their desired identity, they naturally began to act as someone with that identity would. While there are four tendencies and Rebels are the least common statistically, I believe it is instructive to see how effective the method of appealing to identity is even in the group that is the most resistant to change based on reasons involving "ought" and "should" alone. For more on Rubin's Four Tendencies framework, see Rubin, *Four Tendencies*.

63. Aihiokhai, "African Ethic of Hospitality," 30.

what they did.[64] And hospitableness at its core is the generosity of spirit that comes from the valuing of others as image bearers necessary to our own full humanity (in the spirit of *ubuntu/koinonia*) and the resultant prioritizing of relational proximity, as discussed in chapter 4.

When one's identity is imagined as one part of an interconnected, interdependent whole, cultivating community is prioritized, and hospitable actions flow from that identity naturally. Conversely, if one's identity is primarily individualistic, then one will see others not as indispensable but actually as impediments to one's own comfort, success, and/or safety, and one will actually avoid relational proximity, since closeness tends to upend these things. Any hospitable actions will be incongruous flowing from an individualistic identity, because the actions are not fueled by the identity but are produced out of guilt or from a gritted-teeth attempt to obey a command of Scripture despite not feeling any desire to do it. In one sense this kind of iron-willed obedience is admirable, and I have seen many American Christians attempting to do this very thing, but it is also unnecessarily difficult when there is a "more excellent way" (1 Cor 12:31) motivated by divine love and welcome and lived out through adjusting priorities to align with "ancient paths" where it is possible to "find rest for [their] souls" (Jer 6:16) walking alongside a welcoming savior whose "load is easy" and whose "burden is light" (Matt 11:28–30).

As with any discipleship area, it is certainly easier for Christian leaders to focus on outward results (which are generally temporary) and then to move on once a metric has been achieved rather than committing to the long, slow work in the agricultural way often employed by Scripture to describe spiritual growth. To grow in being *given* to hospitality (1 Tim 3:2) requires new growth at a heart level, with a seed that only God could plant there. Despite arid surroundings not favorable to easy growth, a commitment to cultivating community through hospitality is possible through the cultivation of an identity that acknowledges one's place in an interconnected, interdependent universe, drawing inspiration from the cloud of witnesses (Heb 12:1) in Scripture and from brothers and sisters from all around the world—including Ethiopia— for whom hospitality has come and does come more naturally and in more conducive surroundings.

---

64. The clearest example of this was from EI 31, who said: "Living in Ethiopia, I didn't mean to be hospitable, it's just how we do it, how we live life. It's more of the identity of the communal understanding of life."

RECOMMENDATIONS

I realized the necessity of an identity shift to organically motivate and consistently sustain hospitable living when Rosaria Butterfield's book *The Gospel Comes with a Housekey: Practicing Radically Ordinary Hospitality in Our Post-Christian World* came out in 2018 and was being talked about and studied in many groups with whom I was directly or tangentially connected. Hospitality became a common topic of conversation among American women in the seminary community where my family was living at the time, but the conversations had a heaviness that was tangible. The women I spoke with tended to feel burdened by the book, but not in the gently Spirit-led way that leads to joyful life-change. Rather, it seemed that they were being loaded with yet another to-do list while observing the practices of a radically hospitable person whose daily schedule involves "two to three hours a day chopping vegetables,"[65] feeling overwhelmed before they even got started.

I heartily recommend Butterfield's book and I have personally benefited from her practical advice about her daily schedule that supports a hospitable life. In puzzling on the burdening effect her book had on young American mothers in ministry training, however, I wonder whether the popularity of the book put the cart before the horse in a sense. Or to co-opt and tweak another metaphor, it seems that if the "big rocks" of identity-level values and the "little rocks" of practices were being put into the "jar" of life in the wrong order, such that they could not possibly fit. In trying to apply her book, the burdened people I was talking to were working hard to put small rocks of practical tasks like dinner invitations into their jar of life, when their big rocks were still unconsciously at odds with the practices they were seeking to add and so there was a sense that adding hospitable to-dos would be short-lived because it was not possible to then fit the big rock of an individualistic identity alongside them. A life characterized by individualism (even unintentionally, simply because of growing up in an individualistic society) cannot accommodate hospitable practices for long—the two are not compatible, and the bigger rock (identity-level individualism) will win out. If one's identity shifts, however, to a realization of the interconnectedness of reality and of ontological interdependence—perhaps gleaning from Ethiopians as examples who tend to hold such a worldview—then that identity can be added first to the jar, and then small rocks of tasks and practices related to hospitality will be able to fit alongside them.[66]

---

65. Butterfield, "Rosaria Butterfield."

66. For an explanation of the "big rocks" illustration popularized by time management expert Stephen R. Covey, see Nevins, "What Are Your Big Rocks?"

Perhaps for the ideas in Butterfield's and others' books on hospitality to be more widely and sustainably applied, yet more books are needed as prerequisite reading of sorts, examining the underpinnings of American society which cause us to undervalue hospitality and offering counsel for how to shift our individualistic identities towards ones that are more resonant with Scripture. These much-needed books might not be popular at all, due to the fact that many aspects of American culture as-such are often unconsciously equated with biblical teaching and thus are not examined critically.[67] Modern examples from other cultures—such as this book's exploration of building community through hospitality in Ethiopia—could be helpful to those Americans who suspect that loneliness is not a normal or necessary state either historically or globally and who are longing for another more biblically resonant way to live that also contributes to much higher levels of daily well-being. Practically speaking, immigrant believers (including but not limited to those from Ethiopia) could be the American Church's greatest allies in becoming characterized by hearts of hospitality.[68] As one of my Ethiopian interviewees suggested, intentionally becoming a minority by attending an immigrant church as a guest could be enormously helpful to American believers, and they could literally take notes on how they in all likelihood will be warmly welcomed and taken care of. Visits like this could perhaps lead to ongoing relationships with immigrant Christians with potential for mutual learning and growth, including in the area of cultivating community through hospitality.[69]

Focus on People over Programs

Americans tend to be excellent at creating well-organized programs that address problems, and this is admirable and sometimes extremely

---

67. This is due to the American tendency toward theological monopoly, reinforced by resource righteousness.

68. For more on the idea of immigrant believers as American Christians' greatest allies in addressing the loneliness epidemic as well as in addressing other issues in American churches, see Udall, "Ethiopian Immigrants as Cross-Cultural Missionaries."

69. To learn more about understanding welcome as an identity and cultivating belonging through true hospitality (with particular reference to welcoming immigrants but with much broader application), see Opstal, "Beyond Welcoming." Opstal explains that Christians "have to go beyond an action or task to a shift in our state of being or identity" (69) when it comes to welcoming, since "welcome isn't just a word we speak but a way we live" (70).

effective—depending on what kind of issue the program seeks to address. "Human relationships," however, observes Jacobsen, "are notoriously difficult to program," and because of this, "churches . . . should be wary of relying too much on church programs to build community," instead "focus[ing] on developing environments where relationships can develop and grow organically."[70] Thus, programs should be kept in their place: they are relational springboards, not ends in themselves.[71]

Elsewhere, I have written on the "vital importance of non-programmatic hospitality" both within the church and among the wider community. Church small groups, then, while a good idea, should not be the litmus test of whether a church is functioning well relationally as a community with regard to hospitality because:

> Viewing programmatic small groups as the single definition of community essentially vaccinates congregations against being characterized by hospitality, because it leaves people [except the hosts] in a passive mode, stunted in their capacity to connect with others and create community themselves in a consistent and holistic way.[72]

While there is nothing wrong with small groups, they are not an end in themselves. Their mere existence does not indicate that people in them have a sense of belonging within community. Instead:

> Small groups should certainly be a focus of the church, but they should be viewed for what they actually are: a helpful program that can be a springboard for hospitality and community beyond a weekly meeting and beyond the bounds of the small group. Lives characterized by hospitality and fellowship should be the goal, and small groups are one expression of that, but not the only expression or even the most important one. Church leaders should encourage their congregations not only to join a small group but to cultivate community in their lives in a variety of ways.[73]

---

70. Jacobsen, *Three Pieces of Glass*, 102.

71. Mettes, *Loneliness Epidemic*, 204, says: "Programs to help lonely people are not generally reliable for ending loneliness." While giving people an opportunity to meet up can be helpful, "It's important that a program's agenda not crowd out relationship building."

72. Udall, "Lives That Welcome," 2.

73. Udall, "Lives That Welcome," 2.

The activities of small groups should also be evaluated to ensure they make time for relationship building. Mettes explains that

> our traditions have tagged some non-prayer, non-worship group activities as holy and others as time wasters. It can be easy to confuse intellectual activities or discussions with spiritual development, when the Bible prescribes hospitality and encouraging each other, among other things. Leaders protect against loneliness when they make group quality time a priority and treat it as a biblically sound use of time.[74]

The American knack for programmatic ministry has a dark side: the satisfaction of checking tasks off of a list is so addictive that it can lead Christian leaders to treat others as objects or projects and to over-value control, which instigates an allergy among congregants to relational ministry. This allergy only gets worse as programs become better and better engineered (or, more to the point, better and better controlled), and there is no time and no place to delve into the messy reality of human experiences and emotions because there are tasks to be accomplished and programs to be run.

American Christians can learn from Ethiopian Christians that true, mutual relationships—whole people interacting with whole people, refusing to objectify or projectify them for the sake of personal gain—form the container within which true belonging and growth occurs. Since "we live in a culture that is experiencing a profound crisis of belonging, . . . [w]e desperately need something or someone to break through these elements of our self-imposed exile and draw us in to the belonging that we most desperately want."[75] In order to fully heal from the loneliness epidemic[76]— knowing healing is possible because history and global cultures attest that loneliness is not normal and does not have to be a given—belonging must be "address[ed] . . . in the realm of the built environment, of institutions, and of individual and communal practices"[77] since it is currently conspicuously lacking in all of these dimensions of life in America. Jacobsen brings to light the idea that earthly experiences of belonging—whether in church or in daily life—can lead a person towards ultimate belonging

---

74. Mettes, *Loneliness Epidemic*, 206.

75. Jacobsen, *Three Pieces of Glass*, 251.

76. Mettes, *Loneliness Epidemic*, 187, asserts that "belongingness is what addresses loneliness in the long run."

77. Jacobsen, *Three Pieces of Glass*, xv.

in Christ: "Incremental belonging builds off of the notion that ultimately we all need to belong to God by receiving forgiveness for our sins and being adopted into his family. Any other experience of belonging can be understood as a step toward that ultimate belonging, a step away from it, or perhaps a distraction from it."[78]

While Ethiopians love a good program, they also prioritize time spent with others that does not have a particular agenda but simply reinforces the beautiful and human reality of interdependence—that people need one another in order to experience the full extent of God's gifts by celebrating and stewarding his blessings together. Mennasemay notes that through autopoietic groups like *däbo*, *iddir*, and *iqqub*, members "gain a 'secondary identification' which includes a sense of belonging."[79] Though a copied-and-pasted imitation of these groups within an American context might not be effective, they are helpful examples of programs which creatively address contextual needs while reserving the relational right to resist institutionalization and instead to function from their shared humanity above all. Groups like these are means to an end—strong community—and thus are nimble and can flex and adapt to liminal circumstances and cultural changes, so there is no particular handbook of exactly what rules must be followed or rigid historical precedent of what has always been done. Instead, the groups are based on the concept of shared human needs which bring people together season after season (*däbo*), crisis after crisis (*iddir*), month after month (*iqqub*), and at times in between as well, as shared experiences and bonds of mutual trust grow and strengthen community cohesion naturally, creating enhanced well-being and a sense of belonging for all involved. At times, the group can make choices that seemingly "break the rules" of the normal functioning of the program, instead showing themselves to be governed not by programmatic rules but by a presupposition of ontological interdependence in the spirit of *yäne bite* ("He is like me, I am like him"), *eném inko säw näñ* ("I also am a human being"), and *säw le säw mädhanitu* ("Humanity is the cure for humanity"). The group's relational override of regularly scheduled programming allows *däbo* group members to work on a sick or disabled farmer's land without expecting any return, help an *iddir* member with something that goes beyond the death of a relative, or decide to give the money from the common pot to the group

---

78. Jacobsen, *Three Pieces of Glass*, 26.
79. Mennasemay, *Qiné Hermeneutics*, 393.

member with a dire need instead of conducting the monthly lottery.[80] All three types of groups show helpful examples of acknowledging the limits of the individual by banding together in community to dealing with precarious, liminal circumstances of social change by creating programs that prioritize people rather than vice versa.

This prioritization of people over programs tends to come so naturally to Ethiopians that they would not feel the need to discuss it when planning their groups, but it does not come so naturally to Americans because of our cultural predispositions toward transactional and programmatic thinking. Practically speaking, Americans can learn from Non-Westerners —including but not limited to Ethiopians—what, to coin a redundant but helpful term, truly *relational* relationships look like.[81] This kind of closeness may go beyond the limits that Americans are used to and may feel uncomfortable at first, but it can be helpful to realize that as freedom increases, so does isolation and loneliness.[82] And with increasing obligations or responsibilities comes an increased sense of belonging, safety, and well-being. Indeed, when freedom is mentioned most resoundingly in the Epistles, it is immediately coupled with concern for the common good, as if Paul wanted to make absolutely sure that his call to freedom was not taken individualistically: "For you were called to freedom, brothers. Only do not use your freedom as an opportunity for the flesh, but through love serve one another" (Gal 5:13). Community is the context of freedom, and freedom is a means to love and serve others. In case Paul did not yet bring his point home, he continues: "For the entire law is fulfilled in keeping this one command: 'Love your neighbor as yourself'" (Gal 5:14).

Is it possible that in over-valuing freedom as a symbolic national virtue, Americans have not been aware that the myopic pursuit of personal freedom above all comes at a steep cost: the loss of the ability to love neighbors well and the endangerment of healthy connection with others? While freedom can and should still be valued, bringing it back into balance with equally important virtues of community and the common good—so highly valued

---

80. Mennasemay, *Qiné Hermeneutics*, 433.

81. Relational relationships can be differentiated from transactional or shallow relationships, Sauls, *Befriend*, 2. For a look at how biblical ideas about relationships—particularly family relationships—differ from Western norms, with an acknowledgement that other cultures have much to teach and model that is biblically resonant, see Pryor, *Family Revision*.

82. For a recently published application of Dietrich Bonhoeffer's ideas to the modern church with an eye toward addressing isolation, see Werntz, *From Isolation to Community*.

by Ethiopians, as seen in the foregoing research—could go a long way to address the loneliness epidemic plaguing the United States. Ethiopian culture and biblical truth cry out that there can be "individuality without individualism";[83] there can be healthy freedom without selfish isolation.

A longing for belonging may well be the entry point for modern Americans who are considering the call of Christ. Hospitality, says Butterfield, gives Christians "street credibility"[84] to spend time in proximity with those who are skeptical or skittish of organized religion. Jacobsen suggests that rather than insisting on the Christian message being allowed airtime in the public sphere—and thus often wasting time beating heads against proverbial brick walls—Christians should major on "focusing on belonging as one aspect of a holistic witness of the gospel,"[85] since "the relational process is vital in evangelism"[86] and "people want a community to belong to before they want something to believe in."[87] The good news of the gospel speaks to this innate human need for belonging:

> By inviting others to Jesus, we are inviting them to an embodied process of hospitality, solidarity, and mutuality with other members of his body. We are reminding them that when they say yes to Jesus, they are saying yes to his body as described in Romans 12:5: "so we, who are many, are one body in Christ, and individually we are members one of another."[88]

The need for and beauty of belonging to God and to one another does not fade after one's initial experience of the good news of God's welcome. Rather, "These acts of hospitality, solidarity, and mutuality provide not only salvation for the one coming into relationship with Jesus but also an ongoing transformation and freedom for those who are in Christ."[89] Communing with God and with one another—through hospitality that involves solidarity and mutuality—allows us to thrive in the state of belonging in community for which we were created.

---

83. Mennasemay, *Qiné Hermeneutics*, 393.
84. Butterfield, *Gospel Comes*, 40.
85. Jacobsen, *Three Pieces of Glass*, 20.
86. Opstal, "Beyond Welcoming," 81.
87. Opstal, "Beyond Welcoming," 82.
88. Opstal, "Beyond Welcoming," 82.
89. Opstal, "Beyond Welcoming," 82.

Create Communal Liturgies

Jacobsen, interacting with James K. A. Smith, observes that "secular liturgies are habitual cultural practices that shape our behavior and our thinking" and they influence us through our bodies; therefore, teaching our minds is "of limited use." Because of this, "The best way to oppose the false teaching of secular liturgies," Smith maintains, "is not just to teach truth to minds but also to employ Christian liturgies" which are "based on a picture of the good life (*shalom*) as portrayed in Scripture. Insofar as Christian liturgies shape our behavior and convictions, they will draw us toward this picture."

Rather than focusing on micro-problems and programmatic micro-fixes that miss the forest for the trees, it would be more helpful for American Christians to ask themselves the simple, sacred question, "What is the good life?" In the very act of moving toward one another to create habitual practices that answer these questions together in light of the loneliness epidemic, we begin to create the community about which we are conversing, because community happens as the spaces between us shrink and the shared ideas and intentions between us grow.

This question manages to be simultaneously simple and paradigm-shifting. Using the language of liturgy to describe our answers to it also frames the exercise in terms of practices rather than disembodied ideas. In doing so, answers to the question become as numerous as there are contexts where the question is asked. While it is tempting to attempt to construct a ten-step program based upon what I have discovered in this research, it would be inadvisable because it would reduce readers to passive recipients of information that has already been figured out rather than an active collectivity of experts about the particular assets and challenges of their specific contexts and the unique strengths, weaknesses, and needs of their own communities.

The insights of Ethiopian interviewees and several African writers have provided a glimpse of what the good life includes—several aspects of which Americans have largely forgotten due to the adaptive preferences which are a side effect of the creeping loneliness epidemic in the past decades. The interconnected reality of ontological interdependence provides a clue for what the good life means in terms of other people: we were made to need each other, and we find the greatest well-being both individually and as a group when we work toward the common good together. A deep hunger for communion with God and others is natural: feeling unmoored and unhappy when that communion is not happening is not pathological; it is primal. Shared space (community) and shared tables (hospitality) naturally flow from that resonance with an interconnected interdependent reality. Shared need is not shameful but is—in the context of mutuality—the very opening that is needed to practice solidarity and to strengthen our bonds. Shared intentions of kingdom living—how Christians often express the idea of pursuing Mennasemay's "utopianism without utopia"—provide grounds, hope, and fuel for the day-to-day messy work of building community through hospitality.[90] Ethiopian theologian Abeneazer Gezahegn Urga describes the prayer "your kingdom come" (Matt 6:10) in utopian language as "a reminder for the disciples that the rule of the kingdom should keep ruling them. The . . . principles [of the Kingdom] . . . should guide them as the king is transforming them. God's children should seek the full realization of his rule in their lives."[91] In discussing kingdom-oriented living and the habitual practices (Christian liturgies) that flow from it, Jacobsen makes the utopian remark that "while these liturgies aren't likely to replace [dominant cultural liturgies], some participation in them can begin to shift our imagination toward a world where community and belonging are more highly valued."[92] Where our imaginations are, our actions will follow in the same direction.

It is no surprise that immediately after praying for utopia—God's kingdom to come and his will to be done on earth as it is in heaven—God's children are guided to pray for daily sustenance: "Give us this day our daily bread" (Matt 6:11). The daily experience of living in the already-but-not-yet—that is, practicing utopianism without utopia—requires hope as an anchor for the soul (Heb 6:19), because "hope is like injera [Ethiopian bread and staple food], which satisfies."[93] This daily provision is not described in the abstract as a vague sense of being enabled to go on; instead, it is

---

90. Mennasemay, *Qiné Hermeneutics*, 399, says that practices like *iqqub* "[suggest] a social imaginary of the good society as a living together that is based on shared needs, shared decisions, shared rights, and shared obligations. This is a social imaginary, a social ontology one could even say, that provides both descriptive and prescriptive criteria of what a 'good' person is, what a 'good' society is, and what 'good' social relations are. Its surplus meanings point to the kind of society worthy of being called democratic: a society that recognizes shared needs, shared decisions, shared rights, and shared obligations as the foundations of its institutions and functionings." Regarding the utopian imagination, he remarks, 453, that "utopian desires, impulses, and the emancipatory aspirations they incubate awaken us from our self-forgetfulness."

91. Urga, *Lord's Prayer*, 42.

92. Jacobsen, *Three Pieces of Glass*, 194.

93. Demoze and Armstrong, *Ethiopian Amharic Proverbs*, 56.

concretized and communalized. Sustenance is bread, which would have been understood as something partaken of in community. Together, in their practices of kingdom living such as hospitality (which can be understood as simply partaking of God's daily provision together), Christians become a sign, instrument, and foretaste of the divine feast to come.[94]

Instead of starting with program building, Christians can evaluate the habitual practices of their own lives and the lives of their communities and imagine new ones together using the guiding question, "What picture of the good life is suggested by this liturgy?"[95] As all of life is evaluated in this way, our identities will be made clearer as humans who belong to God and one another, and our priorities will be brought into line with what God prioritizes. The story God tells begins with the dance of the Trinity whose three-in-one community was all-sufficient and yet somehow not sufficient to hold all the love that it generated. The story ends with an all-nations wedding feast that joyfully consummates that exponentially growing love. In between Genesis and Revelation, God is portrayed in relentless pursuit of community with his people. In light of this cover-to-cover emphasis on community, biblically-resonant Christian practices may involve many things, but pursuit of community which is cultivated through hospitality of home and heart—following the example of what has been prioritized historically as well as currently in many Non-Western cultures, including that of Ethiopia—should be the hallmark if we intend to "be imitators of God, as dearly beloved children" by "walk[ing] in love" (Eph 5:1–2).[96]

In summary, based on interviews as well as bibliographic research, I recommend that Christian discipleship in American Protestant churches be focused on identifying hyperindividualism as the sin that it is and exposing the fact that it leads to the dead-end of isolation. Instead, through focusing on the common good through the cultivation and use of spiritual gifts, churches can seek to live out the exhortations of 1 Peter 4:8–11, which connects hospitality and spiritual gifts:

> Above all, keep loving one another earnestly, since love covers a multitude of sins. Show hospitality to one another without

---

94. For more on the role of Christians as a sign, instrument, and foretaste of God's kingdom, see Jacobsen, *Three Pieces of Glass*, 19.

95. Jacobsen, *Three Pieces of Glass*, 193.

96. Another question that may be helpful to ask when creating communal liturgies is from Pathak and Runyon, *Art of Neighboring*, 170: "'What could we do together that we could never do alone?"

grumbling. As each has received a gift, use it to serve one another, as good stewards of God's varied grace: whoever speaks, as one who speaks oracles of God; whoever serves, as one who serves by the strength that God supplies—in order that in everything God may be glorified through Jesus Christ. To him belong glory and dominion forever and ever. Amen.

I also recommend that discipleship in American Protestant churches should focus on cultivating a hospitable identity from which hospitable actions will flow. Instead of putting the cart before the horse or stapling apples to a tree, how much better and more sustainable to allow God to grow love to the point that it overflows from a believer's heart in the form of hospitality, since hospitality can be described simply as love in action. Instead of burdening believers with the task of hospitality, time should be spent showing the importance of relationships and the reality of interdependence, preferably in humble partnership with immigrant believers, to whom this orientation toward life often comes more naturally and who likely do not have the same cultural blindspots. When believers recognize the image of God in others and the centrality of proximate love through hospitality throughout Scripture and in the lives of Non-Western Christians, this will allow the practice of hospitality to begin organically in response to identity-level paradigm shifts through exposure to alternatives to the spiritual and social isolation common in the West. Lastly, I caution that programmatic hospitality, such as church small groups, should not be viewed as ultimate solutions to the problem of loneliness in the American Church. Rather, they should be seen as springboards for relationships that will stretch deeper and wider than the group's set meeting time and place.

If the American Church is willing, there is a great cloud of witnesses—both past and present—that can be used by God to equip and disciple American Christians to serve as first-responders in the midst of the loneliness epidemic. Moving out of hyperindividualism into an understanding of the interconnected nature of reality, the importance of communion with God and others, and the necessity of proximity through the sharing of space and human needs will naturally lead believers into a lifestyle of spiritual (heart) and physical (home) hospitality. When participating in this ancient practice of "love made real,"[97] American churches can be instrumental in addressing the loneliness epidemic in America in partnership with brothers and sisters from Ethiopia and from around the world.

97. Quenum, "Hospitality of God," 4.

6

Conclusion

IMAGINE IF THE LAST Supper took place on Zoom. Everyone logs on—the boss has said that there are some very important things that need to be discussed. Peter tries to talk, not realizing he is on "Mute." Andrew tries to make the meeting more personal by commenting on the upper room Jesus is in—they all wish they were there. When Jesus starts mentioning betrayal, the direct messaging starts flying back and forth from disciple to disciple, trying to figure out what he could mean. Eventually, Peter tries to message John to ask Jesus about it but inadvertently ends up messaging the whole group. Nevertheless, John asks. When Jesus opens his mouth to give an answer, Judas quickly logs off.

The other elements of the Last Supper would be impossible on Zoom, which is significant. When Jesus knew his time with his disciples was running out, he prioritized in-person communion—literal (the institution of the Lord's Supper) and metaphysical (gathering his beloved disciples together in one place). The elements of the last supper narrative are viscerally connected with embodied hospitality. Jesus stoops to serve, touching each disciple, washing the stink of the day off of twenty-four feet, making each man feel at home in his presence. Bread is broken, wine is poured—hunger for sustenance of body and belonging is satisfied. Jesus knows how he wants to spend his last hours: together, around a table.

How do Americans want to spend their time? In 2022, at the time of this writing, American society is at an inflection point. The loneliness epidemic was in full swing even before the pandemic, but after two and a half years of social distancing, cancellations or significant changes in community gatherings, and concurrently handling more and more aspects of life through the mediation of "pieces of glass," to use Jacobsen's parlance, we have been given a fast-forwarded glimpse of the future, and many of us do not like what we see. Disconnection feels like dystopia, but our adaptive

CONCLUSION

preferences are quickly catching up, and we must make a choice to change or else let what is decidedly not normal become the "new normal."

Significant societal change cannot happen sustainably only at the individual level of self-development, but must instead be made in the context of community, since "when spider webs unite, they can tie up a lion."[1] In America, community ties have been eroding for decades, however, and even the built environment where Americans live has often not been built to cultivate community, so committing to build community through hospitality can seem like an impossible task without mentors we can look to for help. Indeed, there may not be mentors in our immediate vicinity, since Americans are all swimming in the same situation where it is hard to discern that the water is wet, but the aim of my book is to bring good news: historical and global voices can give insight and cast vision for a way forward toward healthy interdependent communion and sharing of space with God and others again.

In this book, I have combined interviews and bibliographic research to create a space—setting a table, as it were—for conversation between the biblical writers, people with an Ethiopian cultural background, and those suffering from the loneliness epidemic. In chapter one, the reality of the loneliness epidemic in American society at large as well as in American churches is explained, and the need for my research is established: first, though there is much writing on the subject of hospitality, it is still not well-integrated into the lifestyle of most American Christians, and instead feels like a burden and just one more thing they have to add to their already too-long to-do lists. Second, Ethiopian Christians (and those of other religions) generally understand the importance of and naturally practice lifestyles which build community through hospitality, but their voices are often not accessible or listened to by Americans. Through this book, I seek to address misunderstandings about hospitality by American Protestant Christians with the perspective-shifting insights from Ethiopian Protestant Christians, particularly on the nature of reality as interconnected and interdependent, and the rightness and beauty of living in harmony with reality by prioritizing proximity with people.

Chapter two surveyed existing literature on the topic of building community through hospitality in three categories: works by Western authors, works by African (Non-Ethiopian) authors, and works by Ethiopian authors. By starting broadly and gradually zooming in on the context which

1. Demoze and Armstrong, *Ethiopian Amharic Proverbs*, 76.

I focus on in the bulk of my research, this chapter provided a comprehensive overview and gist of what has already been said on the topic at hand. The Western authors wrote about the loneliness epidemic which has been gradually creeping into Western societies for years, the need for Christians to show hospitality, and the possibility of learning from Africans on this subject. The African authors from nations other than Ethiopia wrote on hospitality as a cultural virtue in African cultures all over the continent, about hospitableness being part of African identity and the Christian identity, about the concept of *ubuntu*—I am because we are—in contrast to the individualistic Cartesian mantra—I think, therefore I am. The Ethiopian authors made it clear that Ethiopian culture—like many other African cultures who call *ubuntu* by other names—emphasizes the interconnected interdependence of all of life, expressed in several proverbs as well as the Amharic word for "synergy"—*medemer*. Hospitable attitudes and actions flow from this interdependent presupposition which equips Ethiopians to address both the prosperity gospel epidemic they themselves are facing as well as the loneliness epidemic in the West (which is being spread to other countries as well). The Ethiopian intellectual tradition called *qiné* was also introduced as a framework for thinking through Ethiopian beliefs and practices regarding building community through hospitality as well as for providing a different perspective for thinking through aspects of American society. Together, the authors featured in the literature review provided a solid foundation for this book to build on while also demonstrating that my research topic is unique and fills a gap: providing an exploration of a culture which is known for building community through hospitality specifically for the purpose of helping those from a culture which is struggling with loneliness and social isolation.

 Chapter three synthesized and shared the data collected from forty-three interviews with Ethiopian immigrants to the United States on the topic of building community through hospitality. Interviewees shared about their experiences with this topic in Ethiopia and in America, how a typically Ethiopian and typically American understanding of hospitality differ, what the biblical basis of hospitality is, and their thoughts on how the loneliness epidemic could be addressed. Chapter three also included the results of a second round of interviews I conducted, this time with Americans who have a reputation for building community through hospitality, with the goal of figuring out what was different about them and how they managed to be characterized by hospitableness even having been born and raised in a

CONCLUSION

country which has for decades been gradually succumbing to a loneliness epidemic. A key take-away from these interviews was that both groups viewed hospitality primarily as an identity rather than a practice: "It's who I am," was a common statement. This focus on identity guided and was corroborated by bibliographic research further on in the book.

Chapter four began with an overview of the history of Christianity in Ethiopia, including both the Ethiopian Orthodox Tewahido Church (EOTC) and the Ethiopian Protestant Church and the relationship between them. The *qiné* process of identifying *säm* (wax) and *wärq* (gold) was explained and key Ethiopian proverbs translated in order to set the stage for demonstrating the biblical resonance of Ethiopian culture in the area of interdependent interconnectedness and its outworkings, including hospitality. This orientation towards life leads to the prioritization of communion with God, communion with others, and the sharing of space and needs. These prioritizations were demonstrated to also be highly prioritized in Scripture as well. The idea of *ubuntu*—and its Ethiopian equivalent, *medemer*—were found to comport with the biblical idea of *koinonia*. As outworkings of these ideas, generosity of spirit, proximity to others, and mutual aid initiatives like *däbo*, *iddir*, and *iqqub* were discussed. Ethiopian culture and biblical norms recognize the limits of individual humanity, prioritize building relational friendships, and encourage the enjoyment and stewarding of God's gifts in an open-handed way, together. As an addendum to this chapter, a section synthesizing and reporting on nine interviews with Ethiopians who had lived their whole lives in Ethiopia was included in order to describe and analyze recent cultural change in Ethiopia due to globalization and modernization, and to discern whether and to what extent Ethiopia is affected by early stages of the loneliness epidemic. What was uncovered was that communal orientation remains among Ethiopians but it is increasingly being crowded out by the pace and pressures of life, particularly in the capital city. There was strong concern for coming generations and a felt need to articulate and intentionally pass on the hospitable identity that has been part of *Ethiopiawinet* for so many centuries.

Chapter five returned to America in order to develop recommendations based on the interviews and bibliographic research conducted and reported on in the previous chapters with the goal of distilling down the insights that biblically-resonant Ethiopian cultural understandings and practices could bring to the table to help American churches address the loneliness epidemic. Before delving into the recommendations, the idea of resource righteousness—that is, believing that the person with the fattest wallet is also the most spiritually mature—was introduced and addressed as a potential barrier to growth. Recommendations were given not with the intention of turning America into Ethiopia, but for the purpose of mutual learning and growth, instead of the unhealthy one-way mentality that has historically been a problem for Americans when interacting with Non-Westerners, including Ethiopians. The recommendations include framing loneliness in terms of relational poverty, resisting (self)-development as a short-cut, identifying individualism as unhealthy, recognizing that identity shifts behavior, focusing on people over programs, and creating communal liturgies.

Suggestions for Further Research

No book could ever fully explore all the questions related to this topic of building community through hospitality to address the loneliness epidemic. After coming to the end of my own research, I would suggest that further research be done on the following topics: How can building community through hospitality be inculcated as an identity—especially for younger generations, whether American and Ethiopian—when society offers less and less support in this process? How can American Christian teaching address hyperindividualism in a way that raises heart-level awareness about the ontological importance of interdependence? How can the American interest in self development be broadened to include others so as to be transformed into interest in community development (with the understanding that the self develops most healthily when in community with others)? How can church programs be evaluated and edited as necessary to form them into springboards for relationships and growth as a community? How can immigrants in America be equipped and empowered to hold onto their hospitable identities which were nurtured in their home countries and learn how to build community through hospitality in a less conducive environment? How can resource righteousness be addressed in American churches to the point that American Christians are able to humbly learn from Christians from other cultures even if they have fewer material resources? How can Ethiopian community-generated organizations like *däbo*, *iddir*, and *iqqub* be contextualized for American contexts and needs, particularly if the Americans involved are struggling with relational rather than financial poverty? How can rural Americans

CONCLUSION

who do not live in neighborhoods be involved in building community with those in their local areas? What communal liturgies—that is, habits of a household of faith—can be implemented by American churches and Christian families which demonstrate that the good life is characterized by community built through hospitality?

Appendix A

Google Form for Collecting Data from Ethiopian Interviewees

HELLO! MY NAME IS Jessie Udall, and I am researching the problem of loneliness that many in the USA are facing. I'm hoping to learn from Ethiopian culture to help Americans to address the problem to help people experience more of a sense of belonging and hospitality instead of loneliness. My reason for looking to Ethiopians for advice on this issue is because of my own experience of living in Ethiopia for some years with my Ethiopian husband and being welcomed and shown such hospitality that I couldn't be lonely even though I was far from home.

I wish that everyone in the USA (both locals and immigrants) could experience that same sense of belonging. As a Christian, I also hope and pray that the American Church will lead the way in addressing the issue of loneliness in society with the Good News that God has welcomed us in Jesus.

I would appreciate any ideas and insights you can share! If you'd prefer to talk through your answers instead of writing them, or if you have any questions, feel free to contact me at jessie.udall@gmail.com or 919-389-7865.

Your identifying information will be kept anonymous in my writing, and you can ask to withdraw your answers at any time and for any reason. I will send you a copy of my dissertation before it is published as well.

Thank you for your time! Tebareku!

1. Do you have an Ethiopian background?
2. What is your religious affiliation?
3. How old were you when you moved to the USA?
4. Tell me about your experience back in Ethiopia in your family and community. Did you experience loneliness? Why or why not?

APPENDIX A: ETHIOPIAN GOOGLE FORM

5. Tell me about your experience of loneliness and hospitality/community in the United States. Did you feel welcomed? You can talk about when you first arrived and then as you adjusted over time.

6. Do you think an Ethiopian understanding of hospitality/community is different than an American understanding of hospitality/community? If so, how are they different?

7. What do you think it means that the Bible tells people to warmly welcome strangers?

8. What do you think needs to change for people to be less lonely in America?

Name (this is for my information—you will be anonymous in my research):

Where do you currently live?

What is your best email (I will send you a copy of my dissertation before it is published)?

Appendix B

Google Form for Collecting Data from American Interviewees

Hello! I'm working on my dissertation exploring how the Americans can learn from an Ethiopian understanding of community through hospitality in order to address what the US Surgeon General calls "the loneliness epidemic" in the West.

Ethiopian culture has remarkable similarities to ancient Jewish culture and is also deeply religious, meaning that hospitality is woven into the cultural fabric, but that culture is rapidly changing through globalization and modern technology (hello, smartphones!).

I interviewed forty-three Ethiopian immigrants now living in the United States about their experiences of community in both places. They had many helpful things to contribute regarding their warm memories of their hospitable home culture, but most were at a loss when it came to figuring out how to live hospitably in a culture that does not value or support hospitable living.

In other words, they are struggling to answer this question: if the structure upholding the value (of hospitality) shifts or crumbles (whether through cultural change or through moving to a new place), how can the value be preserved?

That's why I'm coming to you. By God's grace, you have a reputation for being hospitable even in a country where doing so is atypical! Thank you for living hospitably in the midst of a lonely culture.

I've got a few questions about why and how you do what you do—would you do me the great favor of sharing your thoughts through this Google form?

If you participate (thank you in advance!!) your answers will be anonymously incorporated into the final chapter of my dissertation, where I am exploring what valuing hospitality and living hospitably (not just checking off the task of "invite someone for dinner") could look like for believers in United States. (By sharing your answers you consent to this.)

Lastly, if you are willing to participate, will you do one more thing for me? Usually, hospitable people have hospitable friends. :) Would you be willing to send this link to two other individuals/families you know whose lives are characterized by hospitality? The more responses I get, the more helpful the chapter will be! Thank you so much for your time!

1. What's your "why"? In a culture that does not highly value the practice of hospitality, what makes you value it?
2. Who/what has influenced you in your practice of hospitality (you can name people, experiences, books, travel, church teaching, anything you can think of), and how did they influence you?
3. Practically speaking, what does hospitality (of home and/or heart) look like in your life?
4. If you'd like to receive a copy of my final dissertation (by the end of this year, Lord willing!), what's your best email?

Appendix C
Google Form for Collecting Data from Ethiopian Interviewees Living in Ethiopia

Hello!

For the past two years, I have been working on my dissertation, studying how the American Church can learn from an Ethiopian understanding of maintaining community through hospitality. As you know, every culture has certain sins that are more prevalent within them and different virtues that people tend to have that honor God within them too.

As I've studied Ethiopian hospitality, I see that it is biblically resonant in many ways, both in practice and mindset. Note: When I say "hospitality," I don't just mean inviting someone to your house for a meal (though it includes that)—I also mean a general approach to life that recognizes the limits of individualism and instead prioritizes people and relationships, creating a strong sense of belonging and community through mutual care.

I wanted to study this topic in order to create resources for American Christians to use in addressing what is being called the "loneliness epidemic" in the West. In the course of my research, I interviewed nearly fifty Ethiopian immigrants to the United States, asking them about their experiences of loneliness and/or belonging/community in Ethiopia and then in America, also asking them about differences between an Ethiopian understanding of hospitality versus an American understanding of the idea, and their ideas for addressing the loneliness epidemic.

Something that came up again and again was their concern that Ethiopia is not the same as it used to be even a few years ago. Many report returning to Ethiopia to visit and being shocked by the cultural shifts that are taking place. Several said some version of: "Addis Ababa is becoming like America in some ways!"

APPENDIX C: ETHIOPIANS LIVING IN ETHIOPIA GOOGLE FORM

Most interviewees expressed concern about cultural change but not full understanding of what life is like in Ethiopia in 2022, since almost all of them immigrated to the USA years ago and return to visit but not for extended periods of time. They felt worried but unsure of what could be done so that Ethiopia could continue on as a beacon of hospitality (which is a preventer of the spread of loneliness epidemic) in the future, especially in urban areas.

As an Ethiopian believer living in Ethiopia whom I greatly respect, would you do me the honor of participating in my research by helping me answer these questions that my immigrant interviewees helped raise for me?

[Note: Your responses will be included in my dissertation anonymously. You can also choose to withdraw your participation in my research at any time.]

1. Do you feel that the Ethiopian value of building community through hospitality has been less expressed in recent years? If so, why? If not, why not?

2. Do you think the loneliness epidemic that is currently affecting the West is beginning to affect Ethiopia? If so, in what ways? If not, why not?

3. What do you think can be done to preserve and pass on the Ethiopian cultural value of building community through hospitality (and thus resisting the loneliness epidemic) even in the modern, globalizing world?

4. If you'd like to receive a copy of my completed dissertation, what is your best email address?

Appendix D
Demographic Information on Interviewees

Ethiopian Immigrant Interviewees:

EI 1—Male, living in Maine, interviewed June 10, 2021

EI 2—Female, living in Missouri, interviewed June 10, 2022

EI 3—Female, living in Indiana, interviewed June 10, 2021

EI 4—Unknown, living in the USA (no state identified), interviewed June 10, 2021

EI 5—Female, living in Michigan, interviewed June 11, 2021

EI 6—Female, living in California, interviewed June 11, 2021

EI 7—Male, living in Illinois, interviewed June 11, 2021

EI 8—Female, living in Virginia, interviewed June 11, 2021

EI 9—Female, living in New Mexico, interviewed June 11, 2021

EI 10—Male, living in North Carolina, interviewed June 11, 2021

EI 11—Female, living in the USA (no state identified), interviewed June 11, 2021

EI 12—Female, living in Washington, interviewed June 11, 2021

EI 13—Unknown, living in California, interviewed June 11, 2021

EI 14—Female, living in Colorado, interviewed June 12, 2021

EI 15—Male, living in Texas, interviewed June 12, 2021

EI 16—Unknown, living in Ohio, interviewed June 12, 2021

EI 17—Female, living in Texas, interviewed June 14, 2021

EI 18—Female, living in Charlotte, interviewed June 16, 2021

APPENDIX D: DEMOGRAPHIC INFORMATION ON INTERVIEWEES

EI 19—Male, living in Minnesota, interviewed June 17, 2021

EI 20—Female, living in Kansas, interviewed June 22, 2021

EI 21—Male, living in the USA (no state identified), interviewed June 23, 2021

EI 22—Female, living in Maine, interviewed June 26, 2021

EI 23—Male, living in Massachusetts, interviewed June 28, 2021

EI 24—Female, living in New York, interviewed June 28, 2021

EI 25—Female, living in Georgia, interviewed June 30, 2021

EI 26—Male, living in Colorado, interviewed June 30, 2021

EI 27—Female, living in Washington, interviewed July 1, 2021

EI 28—Female, living in Ethiopia (returned after living in the USA), interviewed July 3, 2021

EI 29—Female, living in North Carolina, interviewed July 3, 2021

EI 30—Male, living in Texas, interviewed July 5, 2021

EI 31—Male, living in Illinois, interviewed July 5, 2021

EI 32—Male, living in South Carolina, interviewed July 6, 2021

EI 33—Female, living in Texas, interviewed July 10, 2021

EI 34—Male, living in Ethiopia (returned after living in the USA), interviewed July 6, 2021

EI 35—Female, living in the USA (no state identified), interviewed July 6, 2021

EI 36—Female, living in Texas, interviewed July 7, 2021

EI 37—Female, living in Maryland, interviewed July 7, 2021

EI 38—Male, living in Maryland, interviewed July 8, 2021

EI 39—Female, living in Indiana, interviewed July 8, 2021

EI 40—Female, living in South Carolina, interviewed January 22, 2021

EI 41—Male, living in Texas, interviewed July 9, 2021

EI 42—Male, living in Colorado, interviewed February 1, 2021

EI 43—Female, living in the USA (no state identified), interviewed July 7, 2021

APPENDIX D: DEMOGRAPHIC INFORMATION ON INTERVIEWEES

American Interviewees:

A 1—Female, living in South Carolina, interviewed March 11, 2022

A 2—Male, living in South Carolina, interviewed March 11, 2022

A 3—Female, living in South Carolina, interviewed March 11, 2022

A 4—Couple, living in Maine, interviewed together March 13, 2022

A 5—Female, living in South Carolina, interviewed March 13, 2022

A 6—Female, living in South Carolina, interviewed March 15, 2022

A 7—Male, living in South Carolina, interviewed March 16, 2022

A 8—Female, living in North Carolina, interviewed March 17, 2022

A 9—Female, living in Colorado, interviewed March 18, 2022

A 10—Female, living in South Carolina, interviewed March 24, 2022

Interviewees Who Are Ethiopians Living in Ethiopia:

EE 1—Male, interviewed May 16, 2022

EE 2—Female, interviewed May 17, 2022

EE 3—Female, interviewed May 17, 2022

EE 4—Female, interviewed May 17, 2022

EE 5—Male, interviewed May 17, 2022

EE 6—Female, interviewed May 17, 2022

EE 7—Female, interviewed May 25, 2022

EE 8—Male, interviewed May 27, 2022

EE 9—Female, interviewed, May 28, 2022

Bibliography

Adeyemo, Tokunbo, ed. *African Bible Commentary: A One-Volume Commentary Written by 70 African Scholars*. Grand Rapids: Zondervan, 2010.
Ahmed, Abiy. መደመር *(Medemer)*. Addis Ababa: Tsehai, 2019.
Aihiokhai, SimonMary Asese A. "An African Ethic of Hospitality for the Global Church: A Response to the Culture of Exploitation and Violence in Africa." *Filosofia Theoretica: Journal of African Philosophy, Culture and Religions* 6 (2017) 20–41. https://dx.doi.org/10.4314/ft.v6i2.2.
———. *Fostering Interreligious Encounters in Pluralist Societies: Hospitality and Friendship, Pathways for Ecumenical and Interreligious Dialogue*. Cham: Palgrave Macmillan, 2019.
Ali, Teshager, and Aweke Shishigu. "Implications of Ubuntu/Synergy for the Education System of Ethiopia." *Hindawi Education Research International* 2020 (2020) 1–11. https://doi.org/10.1155/2020/8838077.
An, Keon-Sang. *An Ethiopian Reading of the Bible: Biblical Interpretation of the Ethiopian Orthodox Tewahido Church*. Cambridge: Clarke & Co, 2016.
Andria, Solomon. "Titus." In *Africa Bible Commentary: A One-Volume Commentary Written by 70 African Scholars*, edited by Tokunboh Adeyamo, 1509–12. Grand Rapids: Zondervan, 2006.
Aredo, Dejene. "The Iddir: An Informal Insurance Arrangement in Ethiopia." *Savings and Development* 34 (2010) 53–72.
———. "The Iqqub: Towards the Quantification of the Economic Importance of an Ethiopian Savings and Credit Association (ROSCA)." *Ethiopian Journal of Development Research* 26 (2005) 33–76.
———. "Rotating Savings and Credit Associations: Characterization with Particular Reference to the Ethiopian Iqqub." *Savings and Development* 28 (2004) 179–200.
Assohoto, Barnabe, and Samuel Ngewa. "Genesis." In *Africa Bible Commentary: A One-Volume Commentary Written by 70 African Scholars*, edited by Tokunboh Adeyamo, 9–84. Grand Rapids: Zondervan, 2006.
Baloyi, M. E. "Sex as an Expression of Hospitality: Theological Investigation amongst Some Africans." *KOERS—Bulletin for Christian Scholarship* 81 (2016) 1–8.
Banda, C. "Ubuntu as Human Flourishing? An African Traditional Religious Analysis of Ubuntu and Its Challenge to Christian Anthropology." *Stellenbosch Theological Journal* 5 (2019) 203–28.
Bartels, Lambert. "Dabo: A Form of Cooperation between Farmers among the Macha Galla of Ethiopia. Social Aspects, Songs, and Ritual." *Anthropos* 70 (1975) 883–925.

BIBLIOGRAPHY

Bartolo, Samuel. "The Concept of 'Ubuntu'—Nelson Mandela." *YouTube*, December 6, 2013. https://m.youtube.com/watch?v=D2IWQ6XvVgY.

Bethke, Jefferson. *Take Back Your Family: From the Tyrants of Burnout, Busyness, Individualism, and the Nuclear Ideal.* Nashville: Nelson, 2021.

Bisrat, Agegnehu, et al. "Are There Financial Benefits to Join RoSCAs? Empirical Evidence from Equb in Ethiopia." *Precedia Economics and Finance* 1 (2012) 229–38.

Boff, Leonardo. *Holy Trinity, Perfect Community.* Maryknoll, NY: Orbis, 2000.

Brooks, David. "The Nuclear Family Was a Mistake." *The Atlantic*, March 15, 2020.

Burnam, Bo. "Welcome to the Internet." *YouTube*, June 4, 2021. https://www.youtube.com/watch?v=k1BneeJTDcU.

Butler, Carolyn. "Hospitality as Spiritual Direction." *The Way* 52 (2013) 65–75.

Butterfield, Rosaria. *The Gospel Comes with a Housekey: Practicing Radically Ordinary Hospitality in Our Post-Christian World.* Wheaton, IL: Crossway, 2018.

———. "Rosaria Butterfield: Christian Hospitality Radically Different from 'Southern Hospitality.'" *Christianity Today*, April 24, 2018. https://www.christianitytoday.com/ct/2018/april-web-only/rosaria-butterfield-gospel-comes-house-key.html.

———. "Stories of Mother Theresa: The Poverty of Loneliness." *YouTube*, July 19, 2016. https://youtu.be/6gC5wOyF88A.

Chinchen, Del. "The Art of Hospitality: African Style." *EMQ* 36 (2000) 472–81.

Choge, Emily J. *An Ethic of Hospitality: The Pilgrim Motif in Hebrews and the Refugee Problem in Kenya.* Contrapuntal Readings of the Bible in World Christianity 6. Eugene, OR: Pickwick, 2020.

———. "Hospitality in Africa." In *Africa Bible Commentary: A One-Volume Commentary Written by 70 African Scholars,* edited by Tokunboh Adeyemo, 390. Grand Rapids: Zondervan, 2006.

Cigna. "2018 U.S. Loneliness Index." https://www.cigna.com/assets/docs/newsroom/loneliness-survey-2018-updated-fact-sheet.pdf.

Cresswell, John W., and Cheryl N. Poth. *Qualitative Inquiry and Research Design: Choosing among Five Approaches.* 4th ed. Thousand Oaks, CA: SAGE, 2018.

Demoze, Fisseha G., and William H. Armstrong. *Ethiopian Amharic Proverbs.* Washington, DC: Tigray Development Association in North America, 2019.

Deressa, Samuel Yonas, ed., *Christian Theology in African Context: Essential Writings of Eshetu Abate.* Minneapolis: Lutheran University Press, 2015.

Dreher, Rod. *The Benedict Option: A Strategy for Christians in a Post-Christian Nation.* New York: Sentinel, 2017.

Eshete, Tibebe. *The Evangelical Movement in Ethiopia: Resistance and Resilience.* Waco, TX: Baylor University Press, 2009.

Esler, Philip. *Ethiopian Christianity: History, Theology, Practice.* Waco, TX: Baylor University Press, 2019.

Flemmen, Anne Britt, and Mulumebet Zenebe. "Religious Mahbär in Ethiopia: Ritual Elements, Dynamics, and Challenges." *Journal of Religion in Africa* 46 (2016) 3–31.

Fobanjong, John M. *State of the Continent: A Mid-Century Assessment of Political Performance in Africa.* Denver: Spears Media, 2018.

Gathogo, Julius M. "African Hospitality: Is It Compatible with the Ideal of Christ's Hospitality?" *Swedish Missiological Themes* 94 (2006) 23–53.

———. "African Philosophy as Expressed in the Concepts of Hospitality and Ubuntu." *Journal of Theology for Southern Africa* 130 (2008) 39–53.

———. *Christ's Hospitality from an African Theological Perspective: Lessons from Christ's Ideal Hospitality for Africa*. Saarbrüken: Lambert Academic, 2011.

———. "Some Expressions of African Hospitality Today." *Scriptura* 99 (2008) 275–87.

Gentile, Yvonne, and Debi Nixon. *The Art of Hospitality: A Practical Guide for a Ministry of Radical Welcome*. Nashville: Abingdon, 2020.

Gichuru, Grace Kathure. "Integrating African Christian Refugees into the American Churches as a Strategy for Mission." DMiss diss., Asbury Theological Seminary, 2019.

Guta, Megersa. "Between 'Dependence' and 'Self-Reliance': The Legacy of the Rev. Gudina Tumsa and the Challenge of Self-Reliance in the EECMY." In *Church and Society: Lectures and Responses Second Missiological Seminar 2003 on the Life and Ministry of Gudina Tumsa*, edited by Gudina Tumsa Foundation, 125–56. Addis Ababa: Gudina Tumsa Foundation, 2010.

Haddis, Mekdes Abebe. *A Just Mission: Laying Down Power and Embracing Mutuality*. Downers Grove, IL: InterVarsity, 2022.

Haile Mariam, Damen. "Ethiopia: Potential of Traditional Social Insurance for Supporting Health Care." *IK Notes* 48 (2002) 1–4.

Hall, Kevin Allen. "The Hidden Conversion: Divine Hospitality as a Framework for Christian Discipleship." DMin project report, Gordon-Conwell Theological Seminary, 2015.

Hari, Johann. *Stolen Focus: Why You Can't Pay Attention—and How to Think Deeply Again*. New York: Crown, 2022.

Hiebert, Paul G. "The Flaw of the Excluded Middle." *Missiology: An International Review* 10 (1982) 35–47.

Holland, Sarah. *Culture Smart! Ethiopia: The Essential Guide to Customs and Culture*. London: Kuperard, 2021.

Jacobsen, Eric O. *Three Pieces of Glass: Why We Feel Lonely in a World Mediated By Screens*. Grand Rapids: Brazos, 2020.

Jipp, Joshua W. *Saved by Faith and Hospitality*. Grand Rapids: Eerdmans, 2017.

Kaemingk, Matthew. *Christian Hospitality and Muslim Immigration in an Age of Fear*. Grand Rapids: Eerdmans, 2018.

Kamwangamalu, M. N. "Ubuntu in South Africa: A Sociolinguistic Perspective to a Pan-African Concept." *Critical Arts* 13 (1999) 24–41. https://doi.org/10.1080/02560049985310111.

Kek, Aloys Nkoua. "Hospitality and Solidarity as Mediations of the Kingdom of God." PhD diss., Duquesne University, 1989.

Koenane, Mojalefa L. J. "Ubuntu and Philoxenia: Ubuntu and Christian Worldviews as Responses to Xenophobia." *Hervormde Teologiese Studies* 74 (2018) 1–8.

Kunene, Musa Victor Mdabuleni. *Communal Holiness in the Gospel of John: The Vine Metaphor as a Test Case with Lessons from African Hospitality and Trinitarian Theology*. Carlisle: Langham Monographs, 2012.

Lacey, Carolyn. *Extraordinary Hospitality (for Ordinary People): Seven Ways to Welcome Like Jesus*. Epsom: Good Book Company, 2021.

Lewis, C. S. *The Weight of Glory*. New York: HarperCollins, 2009.

Libresco, Leah. *Building the Benedict Option: A Guide to Gathering Two of Three Together in His Name*. San Francisco: Ignatius, 2018.

Lingenfelter, Sherwood G., and Marvin K. Mayers. "Tensions about Time." In *Ministering Cross-Culturally: An Incarnational Model for Personal Relationships*, 37–50. 2nd ed. Grand Rapids: Baker Academic, 2003.

BIBLIOGRAPHY

Linneman, Jeremy. "How Your Church Can Respond to the Loneliness Epidemic." *The Gospel Coalition*, August 14, 2018. https://www.thegospelcoalition.org/article/church-respond-loneliness-epidemic/.

Mansor, Fatheth Alsenoussi. "Politeness and Offering in Libyan Arabic Hospitality." PhD diss., Sheffield Hallam University, 2018.

Mariam. "'Medemer' by Abiy Ahmed, PhD, an Interpretive Book Review." *Al Mariam's Commentaries*, October 20, 2019. https://almariam.com/2019/10/20/medemer-by-abiy-ahmed-ph-d-an-interpretive-book-review-in-two-parts/.

Mayfield, D. L. "The Architecture of Loneliness in Refugee Communities." *Comment*, June 7, 2018. https://www.cardus.ca/comment/article/the-architecture-of-loneliness-in-refugee-communities/.

Mbaya, Henry. "Social Capital and the Imperatives of the Concept and Life of Ubuntu in the South African Context." *Scriptura* 106 (2011) 367–76.

Mbiti, John S. "The Forest Has Ears." *Peace, Happiness, and Prosperity* 7 (1976) 17–26.

Mennasemay, Maimire. *Qiné Hermeneutics and Ethiopian Critical Theory*. Los Angeles: Tsehai, 2021.

Mettes, Susan. *The Loneliness Epidemic: Why So Many of Us Feel Alone—and How Leaders Can Respond*. Grand Rapids: Brazos, 2021.

Mnyaka, Mluleki, and Mokgethi Motlhabi. "The African Concept of *Ubuntu/Botho* and Its Socio-Moral Significance." *Black Theology: An International Journal* 3 (2005) 215–37.

Murthy, Vivek. *Together: The Healing Power of Human Connection in a Sometimes Lonely World*. New York: Harper Wave, 2020.

Nevins, Mark. "What Are Your Big Rocks?" *Forbes*, January 21, 2020. https://www.forbes.com/sites/hillennevins/2020/01/21/what-are-your-big-rocks/?sh=23692814fae3.

Nkwocha, Levi. "Eucharistic Hospitality: A Bi-directional Dynamic." *Vincentian Heritage Journal* 33 (2016) 185–202.

Nnamunga, G. "The Theological Anthropology Underlying Libermann's Understanding of the 'Evangelization of the Blacks' in Dialogue with the Theological Anthropologies of the East African Context: Implications for the Contemporary East African Catholic Church." PhD diss., Duquesne University, 2013. https://dsc.duq.edu/etd/984.

NDP Group. "Self Help Book Sales Are Rising Fast in the US, The NPD Group Says." *PRWeb*, January 13, 2020. https://www.prweb.com/releases/self-help-book-sales-are-rising-fast-in-the-us-the-npd-group-says-877763424.html.

Oduyoye, Mercy A. *Introducing African Women's Theology*. Sheffield: Sheffield Academic, 2001.

Opstal, Sandra Marie van. "Beyond Welcoming." In *No Longer Strangers: Transforming Evangelism with Immigrant Communities*, edited by Eugene Cho and Samira Izadi Page, 68–83. Grand Rapids: Eerdmans, 2021.

Pankhurst, Richard. *The Ethiopians: A History*. The Peoples of Africa Series. Malden, MA: Blackwell, 1998.

Pathak, Jay, and Dave Runyon. *The Art of Neighboring: Building Genuine Relationships Right Outside Your Door*. Grand Rapids: Baker, 2012.

Pohl, Christine. *Living into Community: Cultivating Practices That Sustain Us*. Grand Rapids: Eerdmans, 2011.

———. *Making Room: Recovering Hospitality as a Christian Tradition*. Grand Rapids: Eerdmans, 1999.

BIBLIOGRAPHY

Polak, Regina. "Migrants as Agents of Social and Religious Innovation." In *Religion and Migration: Negotiating Hospitality, Agency, and Vulnerability*, edited by Andrea Bieler et al., 61–77. Leipzig: Evangelische Verlagsanstalt GmbH, 2019.

"PM Launches Government's First Loneliness Strategy." *Gov.uk*, October 15, 2018. https://www.gov.uk/government/news/pm-launches-governments-first-loneliness-strategy.

Pryor, Jeremy. *Family Revision: How Ancient Wisdom Can Heal the Modern Family*. Fort Thomas, KY: Family Teams, 2019.

Putnam, Robert D. *Bowling Alone: The Collapse and Revival of American Community*. New York: Simon and Schuster, 2000.

Quenum, Jean-Marie Hyacinthe. "Hospitality of God in African Cultural Contexts." Unpublished paper. https://www.academia.edu/4605430/Hospitality_of_God_in_African_Cultural_Context.

Reiner, Andrew. "The Power of Touch, Especially for Men." *New York Times*, December 5, 2017. https://www.nytimes.com/2017/12/05/well/family/gender-men-touch.html.

Ross, Cathy. "Often, Often, Often Goes the Christ in the Stranger's Guise." *International Bulletin of Missionary Research* 52 (2017) 176–79.

Rubin, Gretchen. *The Four Tendencies: The Indispensable Personality Profiles That Reveal How to Make Your Life Better (and Other People's Lives Better, Too)*. New York: Harmony, 2017.

Sauls, Scott. *Befriend: Create Belonging in an Age of Judgment, Isolation, and Fear*. Cambridge: Tyndale House, 2016.

Schwartz, Anita. "'Viens a la Maison': Moroccan Hospitality, a Contemporary View." MA thesis, Florida Atlantic University, 2011.

Smith, James K. A. *Desiring the Kingdom: Worship, Worldview, and Cultural Formation*. Grand Rapids: Baker Academic, 2009.

Smither, Edward L. *Mission as Hospitality: Imitating the Hospitable God in Mission*. Eugene, OR: Cascade, 2021.

Smucker, Shawn. *Once We Were Strangers: What Friendship with a Syrian Refugee Taught Me about Loving My Neighbor*. Grand Rapids: Revell, 2018.

Sorokowska, Agnieszka, et al. "Preferred Interpersonal Distances: A Global Comparison." *Journal of Cross-Cultural Psychology* 48 (2017) 577–92.

Stuer, Francesca, et al. "From Burial Societies to Mutual Aid Organizations: The Role of Idirs—Traditional Burial Societies in Ethiopia—In Ensuring Community-Level Care and Protection of Vulnerable Children." *Journal of HIV/AIDS & Social Services* 11 (2012) 57–76.

Stuit, Hanneke. *Ubuntu Strategies: Constructing Spaces of Belonging in Contemporary South African Culture*. New York: Palgrave Macmillan, 2016.

Sweet, Leonard. *The Gospel according to Starbucks: Living with a Grande Passion*. Colorado Springs, CO: WaterBrook, 2007.

Teshome, Temesgen. "Role and Potential of 'Iqqub' in Ethiopia." MA thesis, Addis AbabaUniversity, 2008.

Tutu, Naomi. *The Words of Desmond Tutu*. London: Hodder and Stoughton, 1989.

Twenge, Jean M., et al. "Birth Cohort Increases in Psychopathology among Young Americans, 1938–2007: A Cross-Temporal Meta-Analysis of the MMPI." *Clinical Psychology Review* 30 (2010) 145–54.

BIBLIOGRAPHY

Udall, Jessica A. "Ethiopian Immigrants as Cross-Cultural Missionaries: Activating the Diaspora for Great Commission Impact." In *Diaspora Missiology: Reflections on Reaching the Scattered Peoples of the World*, edited by Enoch Wan and Michael Pocock, 183–95. Pasadena, CA: William Carey Library, 2015.

———. "Lives That Welcome: How a Nonwestern Understanding of Hospitality Can Revitalize the American Church's Fellowship and Outreach." Paper presented at Evangelical Missiological Society national conference, October 9, 2020.

———. "Preparing Ethiopians for Cross-Cultural Ministry: Maximizing Missionary Training for Great Commission Impact." MA thesis, Columbia International University, 2013.

Uhls, Yalda T., et al. "Five Days at Outdoor Education Camp without Screens Improves Preteen Skills with Nonverbal Emotional Cues on Empathy." *Computers in Human Behavior* 39 (2014) 387–92.

Urga, Abeneazer G. *The Lord's Prayer: Pursuing a Holistic Theology*. Addis Ababa: N.p., 2015.

———. "Possessions, Greed, and the Christian Community: Interrogating the Prosperity Gospel in Africa in Light of Hebrews 13:1–6." In *Healthy and Wealthy? A Biblical-Theological Response to the Prosperity Gospel*, edited by Robert L. Plummer, 121–34. Dallas: Fontes, 2022.

———. *A Reflection on Diaspora Cross-Cultural Evangelism: An African Perspective*. Clemson: N.p., 2015.

Verner, Leslie. *Invited: The Power of Hospitality in an Age of Loneliness*. Harrisonburg, VA: Herald, 2019.

Werntz, Myles. *From Isolation to Community: A Renewed Vision for Christian Life Together*. Grand Rapids: Baker, 2022.

Willis, Dustin, and Brandon Clement. *The Simplest Way to Change the World: Biblical Hospitality as a Way of Life*. Chicago: Moody, 2017.

Wrogemann, Henning. *Intercultural Theology*. Vol. 1, *Intercultural Hermeneutics*. Translated by Karl E. Böhmer. Missiological Engagements. Downers Grove, IL: IVP Academic, 2016.

Yong, Amos. *Hospitality and the Other: Pentecost, Christians Practices, and the Other*. Maryknoll, NY: Orbis, 2008.

Zewde, Bahru. *A History of Modern Ethiopia, 1855–1991*. East African Studies. Athens: Ohio University Press, 2001.